STUDIES IN BRITISH IMPERIAL HISTORY

A. P. Thornton
Photograph by Kenneth Quinn, 1983, courtesy of University College Archives, Toronto

STUDIES IN BRITISH IMPERIAL HISTORY

Essays in Honour of A. P. Thornton

Edited by Gordon Martel

MACMILLAN

First published 1986 by
THE MACMILLAN PRESS LTD
Houndmills, Basingstoke, Hampshire RG21 2XS
and London
Companies and representatives
throughout the world

Printed in Hong Kong

British Library Cataloguing in Publication Data
Studies in British imperial history: essays
in honour of A. P. Thornton.
1. Great Britain—Foreign relations—
1837–1901 2. Great Britain—Foreign
relations—20th century
I. Thornton, A. P. II. Martel, Gorden
325'.32'0941   DA16

ISBN 0–333–36198–9

Contents

Preface

My first sight of Archie Thornton was a great shock. I had read *The Imperial Idea and its Enemies* early on as an undergraduate and, like many others, had been impressed with the erudition, the grand perspective and the wit to be found there. That book, like each of those that followed, was teeming with ideas, rich in new possibilities for eager students to pursue. Without giving it much thought, therefore, when I showed up at the great professor's office in 1970, I expected a white-haired antique, a man heavily burdened by his years of scholarship and further weighed down by the responsibilities incurred in chairing a famous department of some eighty members. What I found instead was a young man, even younger than his years, a man as lively and as vivacious as his books.

To those of us who were his students 'A. P. Thornton' will always conjure up a vision of 'Archie' sitting in his office, lost in thought, staring out at the Toronto snow, his cigarette slowly burning its way towards his lips, until the ash suddenly drops and the smoker is roused into a frenzy of activity. It is hard for a professor to remain remote while he weekly sets himself on fire in front of his students. But Archie has never tried to elevate himself to that lofty plane of the god professor. He has always been as willing to share his ideas as he has his scotch. For thirty years undergraduates and graduates alike at the University of Toronto have been blessed by his presence, and this book of essays is partly intended to betoken their gratitude to him; a small thanks for leaving his Caribbean paradise to join them in the frozen north.

But these essays, contributed by admirers from Australia, Ireland, Great Britain, and the United States as well as Canada, attest to an influence far greater and more widespread than through teaching alone. Two things, I believe, explain this. First, Archie was in the vanguard of those who rescued imperial history from the ineffable boredom of the Whig interpretation upon which so many of us were reared. After the publication of *The Imperial Idea* it became impossible for any imaginative student of the subject to continue to adhere to that dull progression from representative to responsible government, from the Durham Report to the British Commonwealth. Instead, imperial history became a study of the ideas, the ambitions and the follies of real men; complexity and irony replaced simplicity. Secondly, in the books that followed, in *Doctrines of Imperialism*, *The Habit of Authority* and *Imperialism in the Twentieth Century*, in numerous essays and reviews (some of them reprinted in *For the File on Empire*) Archie has steadfastly maintained that there is a *subject* in imperial history. While many have succumbed to the understandably alluring temptation of writing national, regional and local histories set in the age of empire, he has consistently reminded us that there are themes and problems, ideologies and structures, that can be properly appreciated only when viewed from the larger perspective of the whole imperial phenomenon. He has allowed his mind to roam widely over the vast terrain involved imperialism, sometimes breaking new ground, more often throwing new light on ground we thought familiar until he showed us that we had never really looked at it before. Neither of these effects would have been so pronounced, however, had his thoughts not been expressed in some of the liveliest and most engaging prose written by an historian in this century.

These essays attempt to show some of the directions in which Archie's work has led us. Here are familiar favourites: the difficulties of relations between foreign cultures when one takes the role of master and compels the other to play the part of slave; the ambitions of colonials enamoured of the imperial connection; the role of cultural imperialist played by the historian who imagines himself to be objective; the fusion of fact and fiction and the utility of literature as a source for the historian; the rise of colonial nationalists who come to suspect everything connected with 'empire'; and finally, the legacies of imperialism – not all of them bad – in the contemporary world. I think it is unlikely that essays of this kind would have been written, or found a receptive audience, had it not been for the stimulus proved by A. P. Thornton.

My main regret in presenting these essays to him is that many who wished to contribute were prevented from doing so, mainly from lack of space: J. S. Galbraith, Keith Sinclair, John Cell,

Roger Louis and the late Eric Stokes should be numbered among those wishing to pay their respects; I withdrew my own essay to make room for others. But no testimonial could ever be entirely satisfactory, and we hope that this imperfect one will suffice in signifying the gratitude of the profession and the affection of his students.

GORDON MARTEL

Notes on the Contributors

Gordon Martel is Associate Professor of History at Royal Roads Military College in Victoria, British Columbia. Educated at Simon Fraser University and the Fletcher School of Law and Diplomacy, he received his Ph.D. from the University of Toronto under the supervision of A. P. Thornton. He is editor of *The International History Review* and author of *Imperial Diplomacy: Rosebery and the Failure of Foreign Policy*. His articles have appeared in the *Historical Journal*, *Middle Eastern Studies*, and the *Journal of Imperial and Commonwealth History*.

Nicholas Mansergh, O.B.E., was the first Smuts Professor of the History of the British Commonwealth, Cambridge from 1953 to 1970, and Master of St John's College, Cambridge from 1969 to 1979. He is an Honorary Fellow of Pembroke College, Oxford, and Trinity College, Dublin. He has worked in the Empire Division of the Ministry of Information between 1941 and 1946, and was Assistant Secretary of the Dominions Office from 1946 to 1947. He has been Visiting Professor at the Australian National University, the University of Toronto, Duke University, the Indian School of International Studies at New Delhi, and at Jawaharlal Nehru University. His published works include *The Irish Speeches on Commonwealth Affairs, 1931 – 62*; *The Commonwealth Experience*; and *Prelude to Partition*. Since 1967 he has been editor-in-chief of the India Office Records on *Constitutional Relations between Britain and India: the Transfer of Power, 1942 – 47*.

Robin W. Winks is the Randolph W. Townsend Jr. Professor of History at Yale University and Master of Berkeley College. He attended the University of Colorado, Victoria University (New Zealand), and received his Ph.D. from The Johns Hopkins University. He has taught at Yale since 1957, except for leaves of absence to serve as US Cultural Attaché to the American Embassy in London; as chairman of the National Parks Advisory

Board of the United States; and to be a Visiting Professor at the universities of Malaya, Sydney, Stellenbosch, the American University Beirut, and as Fellow of the Institute for Commonwealth Studies, University of London, and more recently as a Guggenheim Fellow. In 1985 he is a Fellow of the School for American Research. His published works include *Canada and the United States: the Civil War Years*; *British Imperialism* (ed.); *The Historiography of the British Empire – Commonwealth*; *The Age of Imperialism* (ed.); *Blacks in Canada*; *Canadian – West-Indian Union*; and *The Relevance of Canadian History. The Idea of American Imperialism* is in the press.

Ged Martin was educated at Cambridge, where he was President of the Union and became a Fellow of Magdalene College. From 1972 to 1977 he was a Research Fellow at the Australian National University, before moving to teach Modern History at University College, Cork. In 1983 he was appointed Director of the Centre of Canadian Studies at the University of Edinburgh. He is author of *The Durham Report and British Policy*; *Reappraisals in British Imperial History* (with R. Hyam); *Bunyip Aristocracy*; and *The Founding of Australia* (ed.). He has published in many journals, including the *Historical Journal*, the *Journal of Imperial & Commonwealth History*, *Acadiensis*, and *Ontario History*. In 1981 he was awarded the Ontario Historical Society's Riddell Prize.

D. M. Schreuder is Challis Professor of History at the University of Sydney. Born and educated in South Africa, he received his D.Phil. from Oxford. He has served as chairman of the department of history at Trent University in Peterborough, Ontario, and was a Research Fellow at the Australian National University. His published works include *Gladstone and Kruger* and *The Scramble for South Africa*.

Edward Ingram, who is Professor of History at Simon Fraser University and Senior Editor of *The International History Review*, was born in Calcutta. He attended Balliol College, Oxford, and Claremont Graduate School, and received his doctorate from the London School of Economics. He has published *The Beginning of the Great Game in Asia*, *Commitment to Empire*, *In Defence of British India*, *Two Views of British India*, (ed.) and writes regularly for *Middle Eastern Studies*.

John M. Carland graduated from the University of Arkansas at Little Rock with a B.A. in history and political science, and then attended the University of Madras as a Rotary International Fellow. He received his M.A. in political science from the City College of New York and a history Ph.D from the University of Toronto, where he studied with A. P. Thornton. His first book is *The Colonial Office and Nigeria, 1898–1914*. He is currently working on a monograph concerning William Lyon Mackenzie King's role in the British Empire's transformation into the Commonwealth. His articles on British imperial history have appeared in *Albion*, *The Historian*, and *The International History Review*.

D. A. Low is Smuts Professor of the History of the British Commonwealth and Fellow of Churchill College, Cambridge. Educated at Oxford, he has taught at University College of East Africa, worked as the Uganda correspondent of *The Times*, was the founding dean of the School of African and Asian Studies at the University of Sussex, and served as the Vice-Chancellor of the Australian National University. He is the author of *Buganda and British Overrule, 1900–55* (with R. C. Pratt), *Buganda in Modern History* and *Lion Rampant*; he edited Volume III of the *Oxford History of East Africa, Soundings in Modern South Asian History*, and *Congress and the Raj*.

Introduction:
A. P. Thornton:
Realism Tempered by Wit

NICHOLAS MANSERGH

When I was invited to write a commentary on Archie Thornton's work by way of introduction to this volume of essays in his honour, a title other than the one I have used came first to mind. It was_Imperial History: Retreat from Solemnity. Indicative though I think it is of one aspect of his work, which will have been altogether welcome to many besides myself, I discarded it as doing a good deal less than justice to the range and depth of his contribution to imperial history. Traditionally gravity of tone, associated with a sense of destiny, has characterised imperial historiography – as in Seeley's appraisal of the responsibilities inseparable from England's 'prodigious greatness' by contrast with countries like Holland and Sweden, whose history might be thought of as being in a manner 'wound up'; or in Salisbury's bland agnosticism, apt to be received as near revelation, about how vast tracts of Africa came to be added, or in Joseph Chamberlain's imagery of the 'Weary Titan' staggering under the 'too vast orb of her fate'. Nor is the historiography of succeeding Empire–Commonwealth transition years unen-cumbered with exalted concepts or grand designs, not to mention a newly found sense of the undesirability, as pointed out by Professor A. P. Newton, and alluded to by Archie Thornton, of giving foreigners a false impression about how the Empire was acquired by dwelling overmuch, as Seeley, alas, had done, on the wars of the 18th century. To all such expressions of presumption or pretension, Archie Thornton has provided a welcome antidote, puncturing the portentous with a well-directed shaft of scepticism

1

or ironic note of interrogation. He delights in deflating the solemnities – he himself has used the word in this context – for which imperial history at one time provided so rich a quarry. Indeed, if it does so no longer, it would, I believe be no exaggeration to say that Thornton more than any other single person has altered the tone of historical writing on Empire.

No mean achievement this, but lightness of touch may serve to mask the basic qualities Thornton has brought to the study of imperial history – the industry and the realism (albeit I suspect of a romantic) one may perhaps take almost for granted in one born in Glasgow, schooled at the Kelvinside Academy and the University. Then, the captain of the East Riding Yorkshire Imperial (how appropriate!) Yeomanry has not been useless to the historian of the British Empire. Unlike Gibbon, however, he did not find his time in Oxford 'the most idle and unprofitable of my whole life': on the contrary, there he engaged in his doctoral research on the West Indies which later was to influence his career. Two years as a Lecturer at Trinity College, Oxford, were followed by seven years (1950–7) as a Lecturer at Aberdeen, which were followed in turn by a Chair (with headship of the department) at the University of the West Indies, 1957–60. In the latter year he moved to Toronto, serving as Head of the department, 1967–72, when I benefited from his enterprise in inviting scholars from elsewhere. He had a sabbatical year, as many besides myself recall with much satisfaction, as Smuts Fellow in the University, and Commonwealth Fellow at St John's College, Cambridge.

Archie Thornton's natural ebullience of spirit has been little quenched by the responsibilities he has discharged. In the liveliness and range of his academic interests he remains the Archie Thornton of whom Dame Lillian Penson remarked to me on his election to the chair in the West Indies, 'The only problem I see here is how is he going to keep all his ideas under control.' My impression is that he has done so, because of a dominant preoccupation and a clear perception of the way in which he would pursue it. The preoccupation is with imperial power, the purposes it is intended to serve, the ideas behind it, the conditions of its successful exercise, the reasons for the almost universal hostility it has excited in our time and for its decline. The way in which Thornton has pursued this theme, certainly in his later work, is one in conformity with a precept of F. W. Maitland, still the most admired of Cambridge historians. Maitland maintained that the essential matter of history was not what happened but 'what people thought and said about it'. Thornton is fascinated by what was thought and said about imperialism, his works revolve around ideas and doctrines as propounded, debated and reformulated. 'Imperialism' he has written in a sentence close to Maitland, 'is less a fact than a thought. At its heart is the tinge of dominance, of power asserted: and power is neither used nor witnessed without emotion – imperialism is therefore more often the name of the emotion that reacts to a series of events than a definition of events themselves.'

Professor Thornton's doctoral research was later Stuart policy in the Caribbean, his dissertation being published in 1956 under the title of *West India Policy under the Restoration*. This was a period which witnessed the heyday of the West Indian economy and it was 'England's possession of the islands while the sun was still strong upon them that gave point and purpose to the construction of that close circle "sea power, commerce and colonies" defined by G. L. Beer as "The Old Colonial System".' For a future historian of Empire, what an enviably well-chosen subject, with its threefold strategic, commercial and governmental interest to illumine foundations and focus on problems that in different settings remained close to the heart of 18th and early 19th century empire! For that reason Professor Thornton's enquiry retains its interest for students of succeeding generations.

From the West Indies, Professor Thornton's interests moved on to the Central Asian question in the new and more formidable manifestation which it assumed in the second half of the 19th century, in the early decades of which Russia made bigger strides in her inexorable advance into Central Asia than at any other period. Afghanistan composed only a part of the Question; there was also Persia, where British interest was founded on the need to maintain her imperial position in India, and where Teheran was the capital in which Indian and European politics met. Thornton's articles (listed in the bibliography) on the place of Afghanistan and Persia in the Anglo-Russian diplomatic manoeuvres, that went by the name of the 'Great Game', provide a backcloth still relevant to exchanges and assessments made in 1946–7 in Delhi and Whitehall as the British prepared to pull out of the sub-continent and, even more immediately, 32 years later when for Kiplingesque rumour of 'a grey-coat guard on the

Helmund ford', there was substituted the reality of one at the top
of the Khyber Pass.

The depth as well as the range of Archie Thornton's interests
in time and space – and as I write this, I believe he is planning
to follow in the footsteps of two 19th century travellers (whose
notebooks he is editing) in 'the Himalayan Provinces' of Soviet
Asia – may look peripheral, but they are in fact an integral part
of the main corpus of his work. They add the span, the breadth
of experience, the range of reading and interests that alone can
give overall coherence with regional insights to a comparative
analysis of imperialism. At a time when the great continental
empires have achieved world ascendancy, the wider dimension
yields a rewarding dividend not least in relation to variations in
the concepts of empire and their presentation to subject peoples
and to the world at large, where some have been if not more
skilful, at any rate more successful than others in deflecting
the hostility which Professor Thornton has remarked upon as
inseparable from the exercise of imperial power.

Professor Thornton has explored the theme of Empire directly
in three major works – *The Imperial Idea and Its Enemies* (1959),
Doctrines of Imperialism (1965), *Imperialism in the Twentieth Century*
(1977) with a further work, *The Habit of Authority* (1966) which
looks at English history in terms 'of a certain tradition and
practice of governance', that of successful paternalism, as deeply
entrenched on the Left as on the Right at home and at the heart
of English government overseas. On reading what Thornton has
to say about the latter I remembered my own confirmatory
surprise at the paternalist approach of the Labour government
in 1945 to political progress and, even more, to economic
development, designed to be of equal or at any rate near equal,
benefit to African as to British interests.

The first of the quartet, *The Imperial Idea and Its Enemies* needs
no gloss from me. Title and content have alike become part of
the vocabulary of Empire. Ideas may move men but their history,
and even more their influence upon history is difficult to assess.
Yet in *The Imperial Idea*, Thornton essays more than that. He
seeks not only to analyse changing British attitudes to Empire,
but also to measure the impact of those changing attitudes upon
Britain's role in the world over the past 100 years, on the
assumption, if I follow him aright, that it was not what happened,
but what men thought and said about it that mattered the more.

In the late 19th century, when the imperial idea was at its zenith, the interaction between idea and action is brilliantly illuminated with telling quotations from likely and unlikely sources to convey the flavour of the anti-imperialist challenge and the sense of ebbing imperial confidence. Professor Thornton's approach is realistic. Disraeli, he writes, by contrast with the 'unimaginative' Gladstone 'knew what politics were about. What were they about? They were about power'. This is perceived not least in the unfolding Egyptian question, central to Thornton's view of empire, as it was to Robinson and Gallagher in *Africa and the Victorians*, though for rather different reasons. One quotation must suffice as reminder of treatment and style. In 1884, Cromer felt it was 'a cruel fate that drives me to be constantly making proposals which at all events at first sight, have a strong Jingo flavour'. Thornton proceeds: 'By 1887 he [Cromer] had reached the firm conviction that to give power to any of Wilfrid Blunt's nationalist friends in Cairo was "only a little less absurd than the nomination of some savage Red Indian chief to be Governor-General of Canada". By 1892 he was lecturing the new khedive, the young Abbas, in such round terms that he expected to have "no further trouble" with him – but in fact he made Abbas an enemy of the British for life. Power cannot corrupt the incorruptible, but it certainly grows on people and although anything written by Blunt about Cromer must always be read with caution, there is much point to his remark that the latter's annual reports on Egypt, presented to Parliament, were written "as usual, in his first-chapter-of-Genesis style".'

Yet Thornton accepts that Cromer in his conviction that good government was better than self-government, like Milner who thought it useless to bring European skills into Egypt without bringing in European authority to control their employment, was sincere. 'Imperialism', Thornton writes, 'in its best days, of its best type, was always equated with service.' It was in itself by no means jingoistic, but devotion to it even when little qualified by less exalted purposes ineluctably drew lesser men than Cromer along that road. In particular, the sense of imperial mission nourished and encouraged notions of racial superiority. Nehru noted in the British approach to India 'the calm assurance of always being in the right' resting upon faith in racial destiny. Any challenge to this assumption implicit as well as explicit touched on sensitive chords. Ripon was never forgiven for having

as Viceroy permitted the 'impropriety' of Indian judges trying
Europeans, his statue in Calcutta being financed by Indians
alone, no European, Thornton recalls, 'having contributed an
anna towards it'. There was another category of imperialist rarely
mentioned in academic works, men from the pages of Henty's
heroics. They, too, had a sense of mission, inspiring and inspired
by what was written in Henty's books. Thornton, a collector,
credits Henty with some 90 historical romances. The heroes may
not, he tells us in an early article, always have been 'successful
in a quest *For Name and Fame*', but they held themselves the
'straighter for having been *Through the Afghan Passes*'.

'History', remarks Thornton, in *The Doctrines of Imperialism*, 'is
usually content to record the successful imperialisms and that
history is written either by imperialists themselves or by those who
approve their achievement.' Hence he sees it as something handed
down from élite to élite using 'a spiritual and an intellectual
currency' they did not mint. Overtones from many imperialisms
have entered into doctrines which were fashioned and refashioned
to conform in some degree to the circumstances and opinions of
their own times. Thornton analyses the doctrine of Power, Profit
and Civilisation, in their historical settings and his study is at
once stimulating in itself and valuable as an introduction to
Imperialism in the Twentieth Century. This is a book, necessarily
provisional in its assessments but an example of near contemporary
historical writing preserving insights which, when official records
are open, are apt to be neglected or discarded. Yet how much of
the significance – and it was great – attached to insignia in the
governance of empire is conveyed in one terse comment on
Tagore's resignation from the rank of Knight Commander of the
Indian Empire – 'an unheard of impertinence'. Then there is Ho
Chi Minh distinguishing from without between types of imperial
behaviour with the remark that the Gandhis and de Valeras
would 'long since have entered Heaven, had they been born in
one of the French colonies'. Well de Valera, as number 17 on a
list of 16, might have felt overmuch was being made of that.

Professor Thornton has noted that nothing is filed under the
heading 'Imperialism' in the archives of any nation state that
owned an Empire, imperialism always being something listed in
someone else's index, never one's own. But 'imperialism' is in the
catalogue of libraries and under it students of that large and
elusive subject will find Archie Thornton's works duly listed

and will turn to them for perceptive and original comment,
illuminating anecdote and in order to find out what people at
different times have thought and said about it.

1 A System of Commands: the Infrastructure of Race Contact

ROBIN W. WINKS

Men do not allocate a secondary and subordinate place to other men without developing a contempt for them.
A. P. Thornton, *Doctrines of Imperialism* (1965) p. 158

In general, men govern other men badly. Most governments prove inefficient, inspire cynicism, and practice physical and psychological cruelty in dozens of small (and sometimes large) ways. To those inside an ideology, tireless energy must be spent convincing non-believers to accept the ideology as being in their interest. Non-democratic governments often use unprincipled power to achieve their ends; democracies often use the principled abuse of power, in order to persuade those who do not share the principle of democracy that they must. Certainly the imperialism of a democratic nation differs from that of a totalitarian one; less certainly, but frequently, native peoples could see that this was so, and on the whole preferred the empires of the democracies. This was a practical, not a moral, judgment based on the greater range of options open to native peoples when democratic governments worked through the mechanism of the collaborator, as for example the United States in the Philippines and the British in Nigeria did.

But the collaborator mechanism itself depended upon the nature of race relations as established between the encroaching power and the lesser-technology society, and those relations, while the product of evolutionary processes of cultural interchanges which were to some degree always in flux were set on their broad path in the early years of race contact. Initial contacts obviously differed between

8

white settler–indigenous groups; relations differed less where no permanent white settlers invaded the land of the native society; they differed even less where the white settlers sought (usually not successfully, of course) to avoid interfering with the indigenous economy, but merely to tap it. That is, the infrastructure of imperialism, as the game of the collaborators was played out, rested on the nature of race relations.

These relations broadly fell into three types, therefore, depending upon whether the imperial nation intended to implant white settlers on the lands of the native population, or intended to limit settlement to coastal enclaves from which the traditional indigenous trade could be modernised to meet high technology needs, or found the indigenous trade already congruent with such needs and thus sought only to tap that trade. Examples of the first type include relations experienced in 'fragment' or 'open space' or 'frontier societies' of which Louis Hartz, Walter Prescott Webb, and Frederick Jackson Turner wrote: the United States, Canada, Australia, New Zealand, South Africa, etc. Examples of the second type include those places where Europeans annexed and administered the lands of native peoples, the better to improve trade, communications, transportation, sanitation, and education: Nigeria, or the Philippines, or Indonesia. One might belatedly move from the second type of colonial relationship to the first, as when British settlers began to occupy the highlands of Kenya and Rhodesia, or the *haole* (or 'stranger') began to play in Hawaii a role similar to the *pakeha* (or 'white inhabitant') in New Zealand. Annexation was not inevitable, since modes of informal empire might well (as in the Middle East, first for the British in the Persian Gulf states, later for Americans in Iran) serve the same modernising ends by bringing an indigenous economy into congruence with the needs of the high technology nation. Examples of the third type of relationship include Singapore, built by the British as an *entrepôt*, in part to tap the tin trade of the Malay peninsula, or Hong Kong, or St. Louis, Seattle, and modern San Juan.

However, all three types of relationships have in common the 'double effect' of which the Spanish philosopher, José Ortega y Gassett, once wrote: 'someone is commanded, and he is commanded to do something. And in the long run what he is commanded to do is to take his share in an enterprise, in an historic destiny. Hence there is no empire without a programme of life; more precisely, without a programme of imperial life'. Empire is not mindless: it must be seen to have a purpose, a justification. This justification arises from a complex interaction between the encroaching high technology society and the indigenous lower technology society. Thus the infrastructure of imperialism is built into the nature of race relations. This is especially so where the races most impact upon each other: in the first type of relationship, where white settlers challenge native peoples for their lands. Where race relations develop in the context of such a confrontation, attitudes of mind are set which influence all future inter-racial encounters, whether between the same racial groups or not. A Heisenbergian principle comes into play: white settlers apply the 'lessons' they have learned from early contact to later contacts, so that once racial contact has begun, there is no way to return to the conditions prevailing before it began. This is so whether the contact is benign or brutal.

Our purpose here is to examine the context in which these early contacts are shaped. Such an examination can be done no other way than comparatively. A comparison among in particular, the United States, Canada, Australia, and New Zealand suggests that four factors above all others determine the nature of race relations; the following is an effort, then, to suggest how the system of commands within the imperial experience begins, grows, and differs, and to move a step toward an historical theory of differentials in race relations. In showing that race relations do differ, we may also show that the notion of 'victims' – that all native peoples suffered equally, had no recourse but to surrender, and were brutalised in common by rapacious capitalist powers – is racist nonsense from the left. We may also demonstrate that all such racial experiences have certain conditions in common, and that the United States shared these experiences and conditions. And we may also be able to explore, at least by nuance, the question of whether there is a moral and logical continuum between cause, responsibility, and guilt, three words with different intentions which are at times conflated into one by the rhetoric of those who construct History with an end in view. As one philosopher revealed recently in commenting on the work of another commentator of more historical bent, there will always be those who say 'it is surely deplorable to find practical issues of the moment treated with . . . moral disengagement'. Surely that is precisely the historian's goal.

THE PROBLEM OF FIRST ENCOUNTERS

To complain that Europeans affixed their names, their mental map, to the world is to miss a point: of course they did so, for they thought they were discovering the world. That American Indians did not 'need to be discovered' is a rejoinder that reveals the cultural bias inherent in Western language, but the bitter wit in the rejoinder does not, in itself, prove that the mental maps are themselves functionally wrong or imperialistic. Rather, it is the actions taken upon the basis of those maps that are imperialistic. Some think the world's time zones a symbol of the imperialism of the 'advanced societies'. In one sense this is true, for when, in 1884, the International Meridian Conference meeting in Washington, D.C., decided to establish Greenwich, in England, as the prime meridian for the world, the delegates were simply recognising that the measurement of time on a uniform scale was important to a high technology nation and that Britain still was the exemplar of technology. The clock motif in English and American literature, in Scrooge (Past, Present, and Yet to Come), in the White Rabbit ('if you knew *Time* as well as I do, you wouldn't talk about wasting *it*. It's *him*') was wed to the idea of Progress. J. S. Mill prattled on about Time, Hazlitt tried to capture it in *The Spirit of the Age*, the Germans invented a word for it (*Zeitgeist*), and Americans would tell you that time was money (Ben Franklin, actually). 'Africans had no history', for they did not regard Time as significant; indeed, having no visible and dramatic technological changes by which one could conveniently demark scientific, industrial, commercial, and other 'revolutions', they seemed changeless; so did the Navaho, the Zuni, the Acoma, dreaming in their hogans and on their mesas, such Time as they knew being thrust upon them from outside.

Guns, sails, ships and clocks are but symbols of technology, and each represents a particular preoccupation of a high technology society. These symbols (taken from Carlo Cipolla, a leading analyst of the history of technology) do not mean that the West was preoccupied with killing (guns) or technical improvements (sails); rather, the West was preoccupied with power (guns) and speed (sails). Expressed this way, non-Western societies had the same preoccupations, if such they were: power, war, speed, human achievement, mark the art many forms of non-Western societies. These are symbols of technological gaps, not of evil vs. innocence.

The symbolism of time, the mental map of the world as viewed from Greenwich, means that Europeans particularly had reason to care about perfecting and maintaining a predictive capacity over the movement of ships. In itself this concern is neither brutal nor benign. Such judgments enter only when actual relationships begin with actual peoples elsewhere who do not share these concerns, and whose desire for predictive capacity – for virtually every society has sought, through magic, to attain such a capacity – were for a different purpose. One may remark upon the Europeanisation of the world by measuring when an event occurred in terms of Greenwich Mean Time, but the aboriginal peoples of America or Australia were not victimised by this fact, for they knew – in the manner and to the extent they wished to know – that 'real' time was where they were. The division of the United States into time zones, engineered by the railway companies, was a white man's game which did not affect Indian life, or even the Indian's perception of his life.

That is to say, when discussing the interaction between aboriginal and settler groups, between two different conceptions of technology and two diverging urgencies, one must recognise that the words, the place names, we use are freighted with emotions, and that the parties to a confrontation did not relate to that confrontation in the same ways. Western man had, long before the age of exploration and discovery, developed concepts for assimilating the unknown. These concepts were unsophisticated and by definition ethnocentric – so too were those of the native peoples – and by inversion they emphasised that which was alien in another society. When people confront the unfamiliar, they translate it in terms of what they know – this is the function of language, and literally of translation – so that it does not frighten by its unfamiliarity.

Some anthropologists argue that Western man conquered because he had tools for classifying other peoples. Thus he could put people to use, being able to incorporate them into definitions of his needs. European languages, for example, were complex and systemized, with conjugations intended to deal with the future, with the unknown, with the distant and unassimilated. The tricks of the passive voice, the use of collective nouns, the development of complex modifiers all served to express a sense of contingencies.

So-called preliterate languages affirmed the known: the Eskimo had many separate ways of speaking of different types of snow and no single word for snow, since snow itself was so taken for granted as known and language needed only to make differentiation possible. To the European, description was more flexible, for it could absorb the Eskimo distinctions of technical significance while manipulating its own more generalising complexities. We do not know what the slave thought in Diderot's *Jaques the Fatalist and His Master*; we do not learn that Friday thought of Robinson Crusoe; and because preliterate societies did not have a means for relating, in ways we can grasp descriptively, to the higher technology society, the West concluded that their language was, in its lack of sophistication, indicative of an inferior people. Once students of language held that societies of tropical Africa, allegedly having no need to develop grammars to deal with seasonal changes, were inferior because 'the luminosity of language' did not force them to expand their minds. This was sheer racism, of course, but the more valid point lurking behind this notion should not be lost: in the structure of language and myth a people are revealed.

Western man found at least part of what he expected to find in the New World and in the Pacific: not riches, but new experiences. The most exciting land discovered by Renaissance man was a land of the mind. In one form, it was Utopia, and once Sir Thomas More had introduced his readers to Raphael Hythlodaeus, that noble seeker after human perfection who, More says, was 'more anxious for travel than about the grave', the New World often would be called upon as a rebuke to the Old. Those intent upon reform in the Old could always find innocence in the New; those convinced that the Old was decaying, corrupt, depraved, could find in metaphor and in true event a way to criticise the Old through the New. Europeans did not come to the New World plain, they came to it so that it might serve their needs, economically, socially, and philosophically. Since economic and philosophic needs are seldom compatible, as defined by the interest groups intent upon them, the New World would be a mirror to the Old, serving all the purposes thrust upon it: it could confirm racism, or confirm the evils of racism; it could contribute to an economic boom or contribute to economic decline; it could prove man innocent or prove original sin. Hythlodaeus arrived at one set of conclusions about where Utopia was to be found, and as a 16th century precursor to Wordsworth's Newton, 'a mind forever/Voyaging through strange seas of thought alone', he assimilated to Europe one set of expectations about the new imperial world.

Published in 1516, *Utopia* set the mold for the many works that would follow, up the chronological path and down the dialectical ladder, through the repeated European expectation that Utopia would be found in America, in the 'land of beginning again'. Innocences and ultimately perfection might be recreated at Brook Farm, or Fruitlands, or New Harmony, or the Gardens of Paradise of the Far West, on the shores of the Great Salt Lake and in the Elysium of health-restoring California. Islands, hidden mountain valleys, rivers of no return, all self-contained, unexplored, capable of sustaining unknown forms of animal life and unknown societies, these were the natural habitat for the science fiction (and science fiction's mirror image, moral philosophy) of the time, while the burnt out planets and other worlds to which we would come in time were still hopeful.

Utopia came to be invested with 'modernity'. Marx and Engels thought it 'modern', and it may be read as such, though More himself concluded that there were 'very many features in the Utopian Commonwealth which it is easier for me to wish for . . . than to have any hope of seeing realized'. Succeeding generations hoped to find More's wishes realized in the innocent societies they encountered abroad, and *Utopia* was subtly altered, and re-read again against next experiences, in ways that wrenched it away from the past More thought he was describing. Both Utopia and noble savages changed as Europe's need to change them grew, but both ideas persisted in colouring encounters between Europeans and native peoples, in part because *Utopia* was a very short book – always dangerous in the hands of those whose patience for *explication de texte* is limited – and the Noble Savage was both an aesthetically pleasing and a simple idea for the imagination.

The Great American Desert, even the Pacific Ocean itself, are intellectual figments of the imagination. Several of the cultures most associated with the latter in the popular mind are, more properly, cultures of the Indian Ocean. The North Pacific is utterly different from the South, and neither is particularly pacific. Human beings, historians among them, feel a need to visualise the past, and a place, in terms of their own conception of their present position in time and space. Thus: the Middle Ages, which stand, one must assume, somewhere on a dialectical plane between the beginning and the present, the middle of the span, yet a middle always receding. Thus: the 18th century, which as everyone knows lasted until 1815 – that is, those phenomena of human develoment which we choose to think of as peculiarly 18th century lasted, so that one must extend the time chart in order to mark a 'watershed', that odd biological and ecological term which historians borrow. Thus: the 19th century, which endured until the lights went out all over Europe, as Sir Edward Grey said, not to come on again in his generation's lifetime. Indeed, as the historian lazily leans upon his biological metaphors – settlements being plantations, colonies maturing, civilisations decaying – he accepts the bias of Progress. The bias of the Pacific remains even more to be examined, expecially as Americans reached their West coast. Image and reality, as so often, do not coincide in hindsight, but at the time there seemed to be few distinctions between them. This is not because men did not know that there was a difference between image and reality in the 18th century, for they knew there was a difference between faith and works; rather, it is because, in the slowness of time, technology and trade, few could be expected to draw the distinction fine.

As we have noted, the first achievement of the explorers was to make the world's terminology European. Not only were the Middle and Far East middle and far with respect only to Europe, but the many capes, bays, mounts, and rivers which testify to the saints of the Europeans' god in North and South America, Africa, and the Pacific showed who was in command of moulding knowledge. He who arrives first tells us what to expect, and who is there to doubt today that the moon is as Alan Shepard says it is? To implant Europe upon the globe was to implant oneself as well. As Richard Hakluyt noted of Martin Frobisher, whose Bay testifies to the truth of the observation, exploration and discovery were 'the only thing of the world that was left yet undone whereby a notable mind might be made famous and fortunate'. Accepting Christianity and their own superiority as one must accept a mathematical given, explorers were the Common Readers of their time.

Hakluyt's collection of accounts from the explorers' voyages, issued in 1600, was only the greatest of many – and a bit more

accurate than most. The printing of such accounts, like prison-
camp escape stories after World War II, provided a cycle of tales
no less impressive than those of Canterbury. Ludovico Varthema,
sailing from Venice in 1502, ultimately to reach Malacca on the
Malay coast, was 'determined to investigate some small portion
of this our terrestrial globe'; and Shakespeare, not alone of *The
Tempest* but of *Midsummer Night's Dream* as well, helped pass this
determination on to whose who stayed at home. The legends of
medieval travel became the facts of the moment. Fortunate Isles
abounded, fountains of youth sprang from the savannah of the
New World, Hindu temples showed unmistakable signs of early
Christian influence since it was known to all that saints had
passed that way, the Sargasso Sea reached up to claim its victims,
the Krakan awoke, Amazonian women anticipated the future
and the Anthropophagi reigned. One does not need Sir John
Mandeville, for even so clear-headed an observer as the good
Pigafetta, who returned from the Philippines after Magellan's
death there, remarked upon East Indians who stood not more
than eighteen inches high and who had ears so long that one was
used as a mattress and the other as a blanket when they slept.
From Aruchete to Fu Manchu, and even to Charlie Chan and
Doctor No, is not a long voyage.

Sentiments which today would undoubtedly be taken as racist
lay behind these visions of strangeness. Though savages were
noble, since innocent, they were ignoble as well, ignorant and
unclean. Today there is much new evidence on the old debate
concerning whose gift syphilis was to whom, and while it appears
that we need no longer accept that it was a 'white man's disease'
in origin, undoubtedly the white man did help carry the disease
to the innocent who, in having it, soon were the ignorant and
the unclean. Natives did not feel pain, explorers thought, and
tested this notion from time to time. Natives did not grasp the
relationship between intercourse and pregnancy, it was said – a
happy vision of innocence later taken up by some anthropologists.
Racially different, those of red, yellow, black, or brown skins who
once held romance in their loins for homesick men later became
the savage redskin, Yellow Peril, the black horde, that might
inundate American settlers or Australian innocence, the bastard
combinations of Chigroes who, Ian Fleming would tell us, were
bred to kill virtually without thought because virtually incapable
of thought. An Oddjob indeed.

Even those explorers who sought to hold to the hard bone of reality could not resist overpraising that which they saw. After all, one would wish to go voyaging again, and one's sponsors must be told of the attractions the future held, if not over this mountain, then over the next. (Travel books today in no wise differ, for all inns are quaint, all waters crystal, and all winds warm.) A rose was never a rose nor a rose, for it was always at the least an unconscious metaphor for something else, white herons the harbingers of the Fortunate Isles, birdsong the sounds of an approaching Heaven, a branch afloat in the sea advance notice of a continent over the horizon, a feather cloak proof of an Empire built upon gold. Ultimately Montezuma's feather cloak, seized by Cortez, would come to rest in Vienna as the proud display of a heartless pillage, but the priest-kings themselves would be less tangible and further into the hills. All was beautiful, all was savage, and because savage, beautiful. But let us not belabor these Marvellian green thoughts in a green shade. Familiarity bred more romance, not contempt, and the many reprinted editions of the explorers' tales came down little challenged to the 19th century.

Governments made the voyages, the explorations, and the profits possible. Noble leaders, enshrined in national dictionaries of biography, led the way. Common seamen provided the energy, the continuity, and perhaps most of the word-of-mouth knowledge of the voyages. What was more natural, when dangers were common enough in Gloucester harbor, than for those seamen to colour slightly, and more than slightly, that which they experienced, saw, or wished they had seen. The chances of returning were little more than even, and one might as well return with a good adventure under one's belt, a little more self-discovery, and a little more legend. Someone has said that self-knowledge is the ultimate form of aggression, and these were aggressive men. Martin Frobisher's crew undressed an Eskimo to see whether she (as the figure proved to be) was a witch. As anyone who had seen the Eskimo stone, bone, and wood carvings of Baffin Bay and above would know, devils were common enough to the Eskimo, and surely a people's self-image was to be trusted? If a dusty Indian told Coronado that there were cities of gold in Cibola, then there were cities of gold, whatever the drying remnants on the Kansas plains may say today to that unromantic dry salvager, the archaeologist.

The entire history of exploration is fraught with fabrication and invention, rather than being simply the scientific unrolling of a map. The latter was the case for those inclined to think scientifically, to be sure, and in time fewer and fewer blank spots appeared on the charts of the voyagers. But most people prefer a good story to a colourless fact. Many of the charts of the time intentionally omitted islands for fear that crews might mutiny on long water passages and force pilots to turn toward them if they discovered their existence. How many people later saw these deliberate falsifications and – ignorant of their purpose – read their knowledge of the seas from them? Most of the captains and crew were eternally tired, indeed 'tired of being always tired'; they were often ill and in a state of barely-controlled fear and nervous anticipation. How many of them could be expected to observe accurately whether the Maori who came down to the shore to greet Abel Tasman (who prudently drew no closer) were, as they reported, eight feet tall or not? One of the chief driving forces behind the men who voyaged into the unknown was personal glory, and virtually no one who has sought glory has ever been an astringently accurate reporter.

The result of these early encounters, largely with the indigenous cultures of the New World, profoundly influenced the nature of the encounters that followed long after with the cultures of the southwest Pacific or the interior of Africa. Canons of literary conceit were well established. Declaratory narratives – 'adventures of the eye alone' – may reveal to us the explorer's inadequacies, but not in the day of the explorer. Narratives of discovery, exploration, and settlement became the popular reading of Europe, and in time, the equally romantic literature of the American westward movement. Explorers' narratives invented time, for each presented the Western reader with an innovation in society, a moving zoo of new cultures through which the explorer moved as observer; whole Indian tribes came into existence for Western man simply because an explorer first 'created' them in the sense of giving them literary, concrete form in a context that related them to Western ways of life. They invariably were 'out there', distant, away or to be driven away if not already so. Even to the present time the British speak of going 'out to the colonies', and Bostonians think of going 'out' West. Californians who go '*back* East' have most obviously not freed themselves from cultural dependency, as New Zealanders who refer to Britain as Home have not, but neither have those Californians escaped provincialism by speaking of going 'out East' as many now do. To see any culture as outside one's own is to erect a barrier of distance and taste, and this the explorers did through the nature of their narratives. The stumps of a decaying literature still thrust from the ground.

The period of 'first encounters' with indigenous people, whether in North America or the South Pacific, were not truly 'first' occasions, therefore, since the initial confrontation already was, in some measure, shaped by both practical and philosophical expectations. In this way, the encounters were part of a continuum. Nations possessing a high and rapidly expanding technological capacity invariably forced a language of commands upon native peoples who, though not without their own technologies, appeared to be relatively unchanging, 'unhistorical', innocent, noble, and savage.

TOWARDS A THEORY OF RACIAL CONFLICT AND ACCOMMODATION

If four of the major fragment societies – those countries constituted, in modern terms, by the transplantation of Europeans – in which settler groups quickly became the majority of the population were put into a comparative scale with respect to the degree of racial accommodation struck with the indigenous peoples, we would find that the harshest race relations developed in Australia, the least harsh in New Zealand, and that the experiences with white-Indian contact in the United States fell more toward the Australian side, and the experience with white-Indian contact in Canada more toward the New Zealand side, of the scale. (I omit South Africa, where white settlers have always been in the minority, and the case of the American Blacks, who were not of the indigenous North American population.) Taking this as an hypothesis, as it were, one can then put the question, why should such differences in settler–indigenous relations have existed? In answering the question one also tests the hypothesis.

There were four major considerations at work which helped to determine the differential nature of relations between the encroaching white settler peoples and the indigenous populations in these four societies. Other considerations which may, at first, appear to be distinct can be subsumed under the four which are examined here. The four factors are, first, the nature of the white settler group itself, second, the nature of the indigenous culture, third, the nature of the landscape in which the confrontation is played out, and fourth, the nature and quality of the relationship between the white settler colony and the metropolitan power.

The first factor at work, obviously enough, is the nature of the white settlers. White settlers differed markedly from time to time and place to place, and their motivations differed for going to one colony or another. The skills and attitudes they took with them differed depending upon the point of technological change Britain had reached, their position in British society, and the unique skills they acquired in relation to the act of settlement. The attitudes carried into Canada during the period (roughly 1815–30) when Britain was 'shovelling out paupers', were quite different from the attitudes of the New Zealand settlers who paid their own way and who saw New Zealand as a positive goal rather than a negative escape, seeking to recreate what they thought was the best in British society. Having different conceptions of themselves and of their purposes, they would apply different attitudes toward those native populations they encountered. If one intended permanent settlement, one might attempt to cooperate with the aboriginal society, if only for the purpose of turning it into a reservoir of cheap labour. Equally, one might wish to remove the aboriginal society because it competed, or potentially could compete, for the land on which the settlers intended to live permanently. Nor might land be the primary issue, for depending upon the prevailing technology and the nature of the demands of world markets, other resources might be the primary targets of settler-indigene competition. Each high technology culture perceives of the role of technology differently, places different values upon specific aspects of technology, and conditions those who go overseas in the service of each technology differently. Within a managerial group the nature of interaction with the local culture will vary depending upon such matters as the generation, training, marital status, income, rank expectations, and goals of those sent out.

To contrast Australia and New Zealand: the settlers who went to Australia did so, for the most part against their will, being convicts who lived under coerced conditions. Often illiterate and brutalised, unread even in Biblical charity, and little given to accommodationist practices in personal relations, not to speak of interracial ones, they were ill-equipped to find any positive values in the aboriginal population. Most probably the early Australian settlers never heard of the beau sauvage, and they were not inclined to romanticise the native peoples with whom they made contact. The New Zealand settlers, on the other hand, were quite possibly among the best educated ever to go out to a colony as a group. Many had been Chartists who were determined to recreate an Arcadian garden in New Zealand, the England they had lost being, they hoped, capable of being transplanted. Others were merchants and farmers who were literate and reared to the Bible or, at the least, to read the secular Bible, newspapers. Yet others were fully familiar with the idea of the noble savage and were prepared to encounter him in the far reaches of the Pacific. Virtually all of the males, at least, were in New Zealand because they had chosen to be, and the coercive elements in their society were relatively few. Most had, after all, come in groups as an organised community, having paid either the whole or a major portion of their passage. While all Australian settlers were not drunken rapists, and all New Zealand *pakeha* were not Rousseaus, there was a very real distance between them as intellectual and social types.

A subsumed aspect of the question of the nature of the white settlers is, then, what images did they carry with them by which they prepared themselves for meeting the indigenous population? The answer in the Australian case is, virtually none. The answer in the New Zealand case is far more complex, and drew upon the positive stereotypes of both *Utopia* and the noble savage. The white settlers of New Zealand found what they expected, the white settlers of Australia also found what they expected, and what they had expected had differed remarkably.

Obviously, then, the second factor at work is the true rather than mythical nature of the indigenous population, and the extent to which it did or did not fulfill expectations. British settlers never assumed that all native people were alike culturally. Nor did Americans make any such assumption, counter-stereotyping to the contrary. Even the harsh aphorism attributed to General Philip H. Sheridan, that 'the only good Indian is a dead Indian' (a misquotation for 'the only good Indians I ever saw were dead'), did not mean that Sheridan was ignorant of the fact that Indian cultures differed enormously. Rather, he meant the obvious: from a professional soldier's point of view, he preferred to encounter the enemy dead than alive. Sheridan was a bigot but not a stupid bigot.

The aborigines of Australia, small, very black, unclothed, were the very image of what the prevailing aesthetic mythologies of race-thinking in Britain held to be ugly. They were an unattractive people. Furthermore, they had no apparent social organization, no apparent art, no cohesive religion, they were nomadic, they had nothing that the 19th century could seize upon to interpret as worthy of attention. In short, they could not command the respect of the settlers, and especially not of the particular settlers who were arriving – as in the United States – little inclined to think in terms of native societies as worthy of study but merely as worthy of removal.

On the other hand, New Zealand settlers encountered the Maori, the most complex indigenous society in the South Pacific. They lived behind fortified walls in settled villages or *pa*. They had a highly-developed religion that was visible in the western sense, in that they could be seen being 'at' their religion. The Maori had a highly-developed art which expressed itself in greenstone ornaments, handsome (if too phallically exact) wood carving, and well-developed dances accompanied by compelling chants. The Maori fought wars in the European manner, on occasion even to the point of declaring truces on the battlefield. They were the very image of the noble savage, coinciding for some with a positive set of biases. Am I perhaps being Turnerian when I pose the first two factors dialectically?: what was the cultural baggage the white settlers brought with them; what was the cultural reservoir from which the indigenous society drew its response?

The Maori were more difficult to ignore than the Australian aborigines because of their more complex, intrusive culture, but also because they were more numerous in relation to the settlers. Today Maoris form 9 per cent of the population of New Zealand, while aborigines form 1 per cent of the Australian population; soon after the time of settlement, while figures are guess work, the effective ratios within the areas of settlement most probably were much the same. While in Australia the aborigine appeared to be a dying race, in the language of the time, accommodationist practices meant that one could project a growth in the Maori population despite further white immigration (the estimate for

1990 is 11 per cent). Population growth, an effective Maori political organization, even the slow awareness on the part of the *pakeha* that the Maori and his arts comprised a tourist attaction, once his *maraes* were in reach of the white man's quest for the exotic, helped cushion the Maori. The aborigine, on the other hand, remained unattractive into the twentieth century. The result was that in New Zealand the Maori had their own representatives in Parliament from 1876 – when Sioux killed cavalrymen in Montana – while the Australian aborigine continued to be treated as a primitive ward of the state.

In Australia, white settlers never negotiated a treaty with the native peoples, and today no serious question of compensation for dispossession of land arises. In New Zealand, the imperial government, at the Treaty of Waitangi in 1840, assured the Maori of the full enjoyment of their rights (even while viewing these rights as 'in trust'), and when the Maori Wars broke out, even the settlers recognised that the war was one between Her Majesty's settlers and Her Majesty's native subjects. Maori land claims were, in part, reaffirmed in 1865. In Canada Indian reserves were owned by the Crown, held in perpetuity for the Indians – that is, they had possession though not ownership – through treaty arrangements. In the United States, most lands were, at least in theory, taken from the Indians by treaty, and in 1980 the Supreme Court acknowledged the validity of the treaties, and recognised that their provisions had not been followed, by awarding the Sioux $122 million for theft of their land, with interest. Though the two billion dollars to be paid out to the Sioux may be conscience money, the payment rests solidly on legal precedent. In New Zealand, the precedent was there, and since the treaties, though infringed upon, were not broken, conscience money has taken other forms, largely through welfare payments. Again, on any scale relating to racist outcomes, Australia would stand lowest in its harshness and continued racist assumptions, New Zealand would – despite very real racial prejudice in employment and housing – stand at the top of the scale, and Canada and the United States at a mid-point on which the ultimate relative location between them is still to be determined by other cases pending in the courts. These positions on a scale are statements about imperial relationships, and even if contained within the confines of a single nation, they cannot be dismissed as otherwise.

The third of the factors is the nature of the landscape in which the confrontation took place. Australia was a continent. On a continent one may make one of two decisions with respect to native peoples – to postpone any application of a final solution (I use the term deliberately) or to move as quickly as possible to an ultimate resolution. In Australia the decision by and large was to move to that final decision. In Tasmania, part of Australia though an island appendage, aborigines were tracked down with hunting dogs, and the Tasmanians were wiped out in a war of genocide, the last dying in her native land in 1876 – again the same fateful year that the Sioux annihilated George Armstrong Custer and his command at the Battle of the Little Big Horn. On the Australian mainland, the aborigine – now called the central Australian aborigine – was made truly central by being pressed into the interior of the continent or to its unproductive northern extremity.

In New Zealand, consisting of two smallish islands, one was faced with the same question and different voices posed the same solutions. Time was short, however, and one could not postpone for long, because white settlement was encroaching rapidly upon traditional Maori areas. A decision had to be reached much more consciously. The decision might have been different had the settlers been different, or had the indigenous group been different; it might have been for a war of genocide. But given the first two factors, and the nature of the landscape which forced an early decision, that decision ultimately was in favour of racial accommodation, and this despite a series of Maori wars.

The landscape forced the early decision (or, more accurately though negatively, made postponement and avoidance of a decision impossible) in several ways. Most Maori lived in the North Island, which was exceedingly rugged. The Maori quickly demonstrated that they knew how to use the terrain to their advantage in war, retreating into the hills and turning to guerrilla warfare. The arable land was rich, capable of producing perpetual forests so large that by the time one had cut the timber at one end the cut-over forest had grown to new maturity at the hither end. Britain saw that New Zealand might become the market garden of empire. In New Zealand all the pressures were for resolving conflict over land quickly so that it might be brought into production for settler and imperial purposes, while in Australia some time passed before technology made possible any variants on a pastoral, essentially sheep-bound, dry land economy. Still, whatever the imperatives of the land, the decision might well have been different had any of the other factors been transposed in the Australian–New Zealand comparison.

The fourth of my factors arises from a general question: what was the nature and degree of commitment to retention of the area on the part of the metropolitan (or federal) government? In a formal sense the commitment in New Zealand was not very great. In the midst of the most bitter of the Maori wars, the New Zealand settlers found the British government moving deeper into its Little England phase and withdrawing the imperial troops who were fighting the war. There is a great deal of difference between a war which is being fought for you by others, who are spending their wages in your shops, and discovering that you will have to take up your musket and fight the war for yourself. The New Zealand settlers quickly came to the conviction that they did not care to continue the war solely for themselves, given the nature of the enemy they were facing. In Australia the nature of the commitment on the part of the imperial government was different, making further postponement possible.

Viewed from the metropole, New Zealand required little coercion or formal commitment, for its pre-fabricated collaborators continued to think of themselves as an outpost of Britain. There was little agitation for independence, and the processes of preparation for independence pragmatically devised by the British fit New Zealand like a glove. While strategically important, New Zealand was less so than the harbours of Australia, and so long as the British Navy, and later British sea-borne commerce, dominated the harbours of Auckland, Wellington, and Port Lyttelton, there was little chance of another Western power preempting Britain's claims in New Zealand. Britain could remove its troops in the midst of a Maori war because, despite this withdrawal of support, white settlers in New Zealand were not likely to turn elsewhere for assistance. There were no turbulent frontiers, on the hither edge of which a rival power was working mischief. Thus the imperial commitment, while actually substantial, was subtle, flexible, and largely cooperative rather than coercive.

Again Australia offers a contrast. Britain could not count on the convicts, once freed, to have any love for the Mother Country. Heavy Irish immigration to Australia followed, creating a highly ambiguous sense of loyalty to the Crown. Fearing the Yellow Peril, the white settlers of Australia needed Britain for protection, but the need did not stem from affection or shared imperial goals, and there always were elements in white Australian society ready to go it alone. Continental in size, Australia was strategically important to many purposes, including the retention of New Zealand. Potentially turbulent frontiers lay nearby, across the water, in the Dutch-held colonies and in Asia. The British tended to view Australia less as a continent than as a series of harbours – indeed, since communication between the centers of settlement was largely by sea well into the nineteenth century, Australia is better seen as a string of islands, from Brisbane to Adelaide, followed by a great sea voyage to Perth, on the Indian Ocean. Control of these islands was sufficient, and the settlers might make of the interior what they could. British retention was assured, tight though distant, with an effective, class conscious, ruling elite, owing its continued dominance to the British connection, in the saddle.

Which of these four factors was most important in determining the nature of racial relations in Australia and New Zealand, and the considerable difference in those relations? To say definitively would be to play the game of counterfactual history – would there have been an American Civil War if slavery alone amongst the customary list of causes of the war had not existed? – but one can hazard a guess or two. To an extent, the nature of the white settlers was controlled by the metropolitan power – that is, Australia might not have been used for convict settlement, or New Zealand settlers might have been blocked in their desire to migrate. The latter was highly unlikely, since Britain wanted to settle those areas it controlled within the temperate zones, while the former decision was at least possible, since transportation might not have continued to be so common a form of punishment, or if continued, another site (such as South Africa) might have been used more generally. This would suggest that the quality of the relationship between the metropole and the colony might, though it did not, override the nature of the white settlers as the prime factor.

Again, the metropole might have decided for reasons of its own unrelated to the experiences of the settlers to wage a war of genocide on the indigenous populations. While the metropole decided just the contrary in both Australia and New Zealand, in the former it was unprepared to commit the resources necessary to keep the white settlers from waging such a war themselves, while in the latter, by the negative action of withdrawing imperial troops, it assured that the white settlers could not easily opt for such a choice. That the white settlers most likely would not have opted for genocide in New Zealand, given their nature, does not shift the focus in terms of the croupier: the metropole still dealt the cards and raked in the money.

The nature of the landscape contributed significantly, since it conditioned the nature of the confrontation, determining the arena in which it occurred. Neither white settler group itself had the technological capacity to conquer the landscape without continuing to collaborate with the metropolitan power, however, so that even the relatively small size of New Zealand, which made postponement of a solution to racial conflict difficult though not impossible, must be seen as less important than the nature of the settler's perception of their dependency on metropolitan technology. Britain controlled this technology, and thus one may argue that the most important of the factors, though not so important as to override the others, was the fourth, that of the imperial commitment to retention of an area in a relationship defined by its own needs.

Clearly the manner in which the four variables interacted is important too, for in practice they did not separate themselves self-consciously, as presented here, and no accountant of empire or student of command weighed the variables as suggested in this summary. Rather, to the man on the spot, other variables must have seemed more pressing, though such other variables as one can imagine may be subsumed under those mentioned. Sex ratios were important, of course, as was mobility, the land–man ratio, and the prevailing technology as it related to that ratio and the intended use white settlers had for the land. But these are sub-questions within the larger question of the nature of the white settlers taken as a group. Clearly the perception of distance from the metropole by the settlers, and of distance from the native threat, both as perceived and as actual, are important, but these relate to the nature of the societies in conflict and their perceptions of the landscape. Clearly a class variable may be at work, for the New Zealand settlers were from the middle and lower middle class, while the coerced settlers of Australia were, by the definitions of the time, of the lower class because criminals. But this too simply restates the nature of the settlers themselves.

Most important as an independent variable is the time-frame: perceptions of technology differed because the technology itself actually differed. While one may see the settlements of the 1790s and of the 1840s in a continuum, the technology of transportation and communication, as well as ideas about colonial government, education, trusteeship and responsibility, and the value of life in general, had changed somewhat. That new arrivals in Australia, never convicts, continued to cast the aborigine aside, suggests that the nature of the time-frame is not the most important issue, but one must remember that an extension of the attitudes first struck upon contact in each colony – that is, the experiences of the first encounter, embedded in the first two factors – continued to run through time, so that the old time-frame extended into the new, and in itself this is a comment upon the notion of 'different' time-frames. If natural laws know no pity, neither does historical experience.

What of North America? Where do Canada and the United States fall on the scale of repression? In Canada, as in the United States, the nature of the settlers, the nature of the indigenous peoples, the nature of the landscape, and the nature of the imperial commitment, led to a different conclusion than in either Australia or New Zealand. The conclusion Canadians know for themselves from the Indian Act of 1876 – that interesting comparative year once again – to the British Columbia Evidence Act of 1964, for it remains in their laws. The latter act attempted to define an Indian as 'Any Aboriginal native or native of mixed blood of the continent of North America or its adjacent islands, *being an uncivilized person*, destitute of the knowledge of God, and of any fixed and clear belief in religion or in a future state of reward or punishment . . .' [italics added]. How many of us would be embraced by such a definition, destitute of the knowledge of God, of any fixed and clear belief in religion, or in a future state of reward or punishment? How many could function under a law containing, in the italicised portion, the fulfillment of its own prophecy? This kind of classificatory legislation comes so late to Canada because it, too, had the option to postpone any ultimate decision. In a continental-sized nation the Indian could be pressed, as in the United States, ever westward or on to reserves, so that it was not necessary to pose the question of survival in the brutal terms of genocide. Canada thereby postponed what for others was a 19th century decision deep into the 20th century and is only now truly at the point of decision making – at a time when, given public sensitivities, the decision has a good chance of being made very differently than it would have been a century earlier.

Not only could Canada postpone its decision; it could, to an extent, export it. In the Indian question, the Canadian relationship to the United States also was important. The international border worked like a sieve, the Sioux, for example, grazing their animals on both sides of the border while, with minor exceptions, fighting only in the United States. Indeed, from the Indian point of view there was no 'Canadian Indian' and 'American Indian', even though a long history of loose treaties dating back to the so-called French and Indian War showed that Indians were quite capable of entering into collaborator relationships with identifiable nationalities. The effect of postponement and export together was, in a sense, to soften the Canadian story so that the Indian wars, atrocities on both sides, massacres and consequent hatreds, took place largely in the context of that which we label 'American history'.

The function of this brief comparison, which so far has touched only lightly on the United States, has been to demonstrate both that comparison in itself is helpful in leading us to an understanding of *degree* – that is to say, of the ways in which we must qualify assumptions of generality or assumptions of uniqueness – and to saying something of value about discrete experiences. This comparison is also meant to suggest that historians who have not looked elsewhere when examining the white settler–indigine question, such as American Indian historians who have not looked outside North America, have placed themselves in so limiting a context of enquiry as to cut the historiographies to which they contribute off from the broad contact on which all historiography must grow. Put succinctly and in a cliché, he who only his own country knows, knows not his country.

As one contrasts the New Zealand with the Australian experience, or the woodlands Indian with the plains Indian experience in the United States, one sees that the indigenous population played different roles within the needs of the encroaching society, roles that changed in relation to those societies' rank order of culture imperatives. If the society saw 'fair play' and organised warfare as a symbol of maturity and sophistication within itself, it respected those qualities when found elsewhere, just as Canadians respect other hockey players, the British may evaluate the maturity of a culture on the quality of its use of language (especially in the theatre), and Americans respect ambition, efficiency, and hospitality. Or so it is said. As a culture considers what it most takes pride in within itself, it reads other cultures in relation to the ranking of those cultural morés and practices it most values. The aborigine showed no characteristics the Australian culture *could* admire even had it wished to; the Maori showed many characteristics that were deemed admirable in the context of the times and the culture making contact with them. The Indian was 'useful' at first, and thereby in some measure admirable in an Eastern woodlands environment, but as the American character changed (and the Indian seemed not to), the Indian was seen to be without regenerative means, while the advancing frontier culture steadily regenerated itself through change. Whites admired the way they became new men or they would not have called the West the land of beginning again; the Indian seemed entirely too consistent.

Consistency meant an unchanging nature. Whites could, of course, see that Indian culture changed, and dramatically, dysgenically, in the face of Western encroachment. Indians lacked 'the will to survive,' *élan vital*, they suffered a failure of nerve; the clash between two moralities in the American forest, in which the Indian was viewed as more sensitive to nature, higher, and paradoxically therefore doomed to destruction as the garden gave way before the machine – all these literary notions, even those friendly to the Indian as a group, suggested that his survival was unlikely.

EMPIRE AND THE AMERICAN INDIAN

In the United States, forms of native resistance to metropolitan dominance were markedly similar to the ways in which indigenous societies in Africa and the Pacific sought to resist British and French imperial administrators. In examining the typologies of resistance, we can again discover how closely a major theme in American history follows a theme in imperial history viewed broadly. Further, in examining the views held by the high technology society with respect to how best to deal with resistance, we can also see whether the encroaching societies generally shared reactions in common. There are, when examined in this way, close parallels between American settler–Native American interaction with respect to resistance, and American administrator–Native American responses with respect to 'reform,' on the one hand, and Afro–Asian modes of resistance and British approaches to the social engineering deemed essential to effect reform, on the other hand.

In American (and in British imperial) history, resistance movements traditionally have been seen in the light of military exploits, and the history of the indigenous resistance movements in the United States was, until recently, written by military historians, sometimes sympathetic to the Indians, even nostalgically so, but usually from the perspective of the white society. Resistance in subtler forms became the back-drop for tales of moral uplift from missionary or settler who led or forced the native American along the path from barbarism to civilisation. Thus it was the end of the account that determined the story: despite an apparent focus on the Indian, studies of resistance generally were contributions to an understanding of colonial achievements, of the westward movement, and of the triumph of American democracy.

Unlike British imperial experience, however, in which it was possible for commentators to believe that resistance on any large scale had never really taken place in many colonies, Americans emphasised the opposite: a steady white conquest of a continent in the face of a wily, tenacious and often brave, Indian opposition. Because independent nations grew from the British empire after World War II, nationalist historians were able to reinterpret the past in terms of resistance movements, those movements being seen (as in the Sepoy Mutiny of 1857) as the beginnings of an emerging nationalism. The American Indian never succeeded in establishing a separate nation, so the usual canons of nationalistic historiography were not applied; further, Americans were confident that they had given independence to the Philippines, while in Kenya, for example, indigenous historians were confident that their countrymen had won independence from the British. These perceptions meant that while a school of resistance studies grew in British imperial history, resistance was taken over as a concept in the United States largely by those historians concerned with civil rights, slavery, and Black history. As a result, comparisons were inexact, since the body of European thought concerning resistance had been developed to explain the reactions of an indigenous people.

Third World nationalist history formed two camps. One school held that resistance came from élite groups within the native society, the other that it had a populist base. The latter needed to show continuity between modern political activities and earlier resistance movements, while the former could show that élite groups had changed, often by using the collaborator matrix to their own advantage, ultimately to the ruination of European hopes. While these two views appeared to be opposed to each other, and certainly their principal exponents were opposed, the two views were in fact compatible, further proof that most problems either have many answers or no answer. Both views argued that resistance passed through several stages, and while the populist argument tended to see these stages unfolding in temporal succession, they obviously did not truly do so in practice.

Resistance tended to pass through four fundamentally different phases. For convenience these may be called the initial contact (or 'primary'), the fragmented (or 'secondary'), the 'modern' (or 'tertiary'), and the 'urban' stages of resistance. These stages may overlap, or more than one may occur simultaneously, so that they do not represent a precise temporal progression, though there is a clear tendency for them to do so. One élite group may be pursuing one course of action, a second group another. Since the impact of Western technology has differed from region to region and ethnic group to group, primary resistance may work in tandem with secondary resistance occurring elsewhere; when that tandem is self-conscious and contrived, one has moved well toward the third stage. Nor is any stage fully abandoned, for it becomes part of the following stage.

The first stage of resistance begins at the moment of initial contact. This 'moment' may, in fact, last for scores of years. It is the period when the indigenous population is puzzled by the invader, when the native may respond with apparent friendship or with hostility, but when the responses are largely isolated, individual, and dependent upon the circumstances of the actual contact. The Indians encountered by the Pilgrims helped them learn how to plant and nurture corn: the Maori waved their spears at Abel Tasman; the *strandlopers* at the Cape of Good Hope watched the Western sails with curiosity; the Caribs attacked. In general resistance at initial contact was unformed, ineffective, and cautious. This first contact conditions the often lengthy period of primary resistance.

Many factors shaped the nature of this first period of resistance. Since cooperation was more common than hostility, 'initial contact' went on until cooperation broke down. During this initial period of contact, the indigenous élite and the encroaching power usually created a mutually beneficial collaborator mechanism; it was when this phase of collaboration failed that a 'local crisis' occurred, bringing to an end the period of 'initial contact'. On the whole native groups sought co-existence; few were either wholly negative or wholly irrational (in the sense that they sought to stand in the face of a technology they could recognise as superior, or more magical). Competition between the generations within the élite leadership was created by those Europeans who sought to bring improved sanitation and transportation, or changed methods of education and communication, for a younger group of collaborators with access to modernising education would in time be at odds with the older occupants of chiefly offices. Some commentators believe that Westerners intended this conflict to occur; others believe that the conflict would have occurred whatever the West intended once contact had begun; yet others argue that the West was unprepared for and disturbed by the conflict. The middle path is surely the most rational judgment since it does not exclude the others.

The expanding settler society, or the expanding nation of merchants, would bring administrative and economic changes to the native society as well. Cash-crop agriculture, the introduction of price mechanisms, changes in the nature of land tenure (even when the indigenous population was left in possession of its lands, which was not usual in settler societies, though customary in Africa), the creation of a white-dominated bureaucracy that changed hunting grounds or agricultural practices, said to be (and on rare occasions actually so), for the benefit of the native peoples though certainly to the benefit of those who hated to see waste lands unused; and the eventual creation of marketing arrangements over which the Europeans possessed the only predictive capacity – all these changes brought the European or American settler into an active political role in native affairs. As the indigenous groups became more aware of what was happening to them, élite group began to cooperate with élite group, and this visible cooperation in turn helped create a groundswell of populist response. These groups, whether ready to accept modernisation or striving to protect traditional values, became power brokers who, when having attracted sufficient followers, became collaborating classes. Thus their resistance took place in a context increasingly determined by the West.

The metropolitian power invariably strove for economy of effort. If white settlement was involved, money and energy were best spent on settlement itself; the Indian could be pressed away once again at relatively little expense. At times the collaborators used the imperialists to their own ends, for often the speed of encroachment was such that settlers did not fully understand the native culture and could be drawn into taking sides in an inter-tribal war. But such equality of service to each other did not last long, for the West soon realised that dealing with a single group was inefficient and limiting.

The moment that customarily ended the period of 'primary resistance' or initial contact came when the traditional society saw, through the eyes of its élite groups, that it had lost all initiative. The American Indian was relatively slow to see this, partially because of the sieve-like nature of the frontier; the Filipino recognized it almost immediately, and Emilio Aquinaldo's rebellion became a classic example of primary resistance to American empire. The imperial power then crushes resistance, fragmenting the traditional élite. Thereafter members of the élite retreat into other forms of resistance or, more likely, collaborate once again, awaiting displacement by a more modernizing élite. A period of diplomacy, when the European played at the game of dealing with the native rulers as though they were political equals, had passed and a period of Victorian, or American, progressivist 'improvement' and reform had begun. To improve a native people one must administer them, and new treaties were struck, old treaties broken, reservations created, enclaves defined.

Fragmented resistance followed. This secondary stage is marked by various modes of adapting to the high technology society: millenarian movements, as in the Ghost Dance religion amongst the Sioux, when Wavoka sought to return his people to traditional sources of pride; collective welfare groups aimed at ameliorating conditions within the tribe; trade unions which work across narrow intra-tribal conflicts so as to unite the Iroquois or Navajo; and independent churches which seek to combine Western religion with traditional thought, as in the Native American Church, the Hau Hau movement amongst the Maori, or John Chilembwe's church in Rhodesia. All these movements tend toward displacement of traditional élites, with new groups rising to show how best to resist the European on his own terms. Each form of resistance seeks mass commitment, and when such commitment is given, the white settler group is more likely to be frightened by evidence that the native society has, apparently, united. The trade unions may be outlawed, missionaries will work more vigorously to combat the syncretic religious movements, legislators will declare the religions illegal.

In response to reactive harassment, the indigenous society – heretofore fragmented amongst various leaders who propose diverse solutions to the growing sense of native bewilderment – will begin to unite behind a leader who is, in Western terms, essentially using political means to a political end. At this point resistance enters its modern (or 'tertiary') stage, when political unity is the goal, new leaders knowledgable in Western ways of thought emerge, and the games of collaboration and resistance are played on a field defined in Western terms. In entering the phase of modern resistance, traditionalists will grieve that the battle already has been lost, while the modernising élite will insist that it seeks old goals in new ways, turning the white man's weapons against him. Amongst these weapons will be his technology, not in the simple sense, as when the Zulu used British rifles against British troops at Isandhlwana or Apaches attacked Black cavalrymen along the Santa Cruz Valley, but in the complex sense of using the information networks represented by science to carry the attack through the voting booth and into the courts.

In the continental United States, the indigenous population resisted in these three ways, fulfilling the expectations of both hindsight and theory. Thus resistance was, in broad outline, much as it had been to the British and French in West Africa. In the Philippines, on the other hand, the third stage of resistance was made more complex by the underlay of Spanish colonial heritage, by the presence nearby of competing empires, by price inflation, by the countervailing attractions of another world ideology, Islam, and ultimately by embroilment in Cold War politics.

The Philippines became an independent nation in the context, though not because of, Cold War politics. And it is with the moment of disillusionment with independence that resistance enters its fourth phase. For in many former colonial dependencies, including those of the United States, the people – already loosely aligned through the generally mass movements associated with the second and particularly third phase of resistance – believe they have discovered that a ruling élite has been fastened on them from outside. Either the Young Turks must throw off the fathers of independence precisely because, as the fathers, they were 'moderates' who accepted independence on the imperialists' terms (the dilemma facing the political leadership of Puerto Rico today), or they must wait out the fathers of nationhood and take control in the next generation. To forestall this, the fathers of independence often turn to one-party rule, to military dictatorship, or to massive manipulation and 'modernisation' of the economy. Whether this hastens the day of their fall (as in Iran) is a moot point, but an urban resistance movement invariably begins, arising from frustration that little has changed though the colour of the flag is different. Marxist argument seems best to explain why all has changed and yet nothing has changed, and the Young Turks flock to that ideology as unthinkingly as earlier collaborators flocked to the high technology of the Western democracies. One form of collaboration replaces another.

Whether from within a group of new collaborators, or from within yet another group, in despair that one form of dominance appears to be replacing another, the fourth stage of resistance thus begins, usually in urban revolt though often by groups from rural bases who recognise that high technology societies are most vulnerable in their urban centers. The rural satellites strike back and urban terrorism replaces systematic political organisation as the mode of resistance. The fathers of independence, once the new élite, determined to maintain stability and their new predictive capacity, 'temporarily' set aside the democratic principles to which they gave lip service, or true commitment, to combat the anarchy of terrorism, fulfilling the prophecy of the terrorists. A new doctrine of trusteeship is put into action, the rights of the people once again being placed 'in trust' by a presumably benevolent power, to be given back when the people prove themselves worthy of the exercise of those rights again. The colonialism of the imperial powers replicates itself in the policies of the new nations.

The terrorists then conclude that they can be effective only if they strike at the heart of something they call 'world imperialism': the highest technology powers. Urban terrorism thus comes to the United States, Germany, Great Britain, and Japan, each democratic enough not to be able to forestall it. Urban terrorism does not come to the Soviet Union. Viewed from the perspective of the high technology nations of the West, the urban phase of resistance therefore appears to be (and indeed may be) inspired by the Soviet Union, and the problem of resistance is hurled onto the international arena where the stakes are highest and the game is no longer to be described by that mathematically helpful though morally useless term, a zero sum game.

Since independence was the object of the first three stages of resistance, and since resistance did not end when that object was achieved, one cannot predict what the next, or fifth, stage of resistance may be, and in that inability to retain predictive capacity, the once imperial nation discovers that it is no longer imperial, the powers of the weak having turned it into a 'pitiful, helpless giant.' The United States, in particular, would take up the responsibilities of other imperial powers no longer able to carry the burden, entering into new collaborator relationships, creating new resistance responses and counter-responses. This is not the inevitability of capitalism, it is the inevitability of life. 'The United States is a Pacific power. Europe has been withdrawing the remnants of empire, but the United States, with its coast reaching in an arc from Mexico to the Bering Straits, is one anchor of a vast Pacific community. Both our interests and our ideals propel us westward across the Pacific, not as conquerors but as partners...' Both quotations come from the works of a one-time member of the American Historical Association, Richard M. Nixon.

The typology fits. Perhaps this proves nothing except that American history is more congruent with other histories than we have thought. There is one more typology that promotes the same awareness.

SOCIAL ENGINEERING AND AN AMERICAN EMPIRE

The study of colonialism has moved away from its essential but narrow focus on political and economic questions into the arena once called intellectual and social history. The impact of the imperial experience was at least as much a matter of the mind as the pocketbook. In part, all situations that arise from the dominance created by a society that holds one individual superior to another partake of the nature of colonialism. Such situations are present in all societies. Such a sense of potential dominance is present wherever a formal structure of education has been created: when a colonial power uses the teacher-student relationship to inculcate a set of values which are contrary to those of the traditional, indigenous society. This is not to say that such education is either 'harmful' or 'beneficial' in any meaningful sense, for harm and benefit are not absolutes but must be read against a perceived goal. Rather, it is to acknowledge that, by its nature, education both relies upon and creates patterns of dependency. Any imperialism which seeks to 'educate the natives' is engaging in a form of social engineering.

Social engineering can take many forms, of course, just as 'educating the natives' – in the classroom, at the counting table, or at the mouth of a Krag – takes many forms. The customary British trinity of education, sanitation, and transportation, which in turn led to new forms of trade, and under which might be subsumed communications, represent areas in which social engineering might take place. Often the engineering was done to meet or forestall resistance; quite often social engineering began in earnest only after the 'crisis of displacement', or the collapse of the collaborator relationship inherent in the early contact between societies. The exact form of social engineering depended in good measure on how the imperial power read the four factors already adduced to explain differences in race relations: what he thought the indigenous population capable of 'learning', what the colonial population was capable of 'teaching', within what environment would the lessons be taught and learned and to what purpose, and to what extent would the metropolitan power commit itself to pay for, and in the end deal with the consequences of, these processes of formal learning, conscious cultural diffusion, or simple pacification. Whether teaching was seen to fall from the mouth of a gun, the pages of a Bible, or the discs of a plow, one must be prepared to consider the consequences. Any form of social engineering represented a risk, for social change would impair the predictive capacity so dear to industrial hearts; not to carry out some social engineering would be to deny the principle of trusteeship, the belief in mission, the expectation of bringing progress to the heathen. Almost anything is easier to get into than out of: instinctively any good imperialist knew this lesson well. Still, in responding to resistance movements, the high technology nation unvaryingly turned to social engineering, so that change and the further entanglement it brought was irresistable.

Broadly, imperial opinion concerning social engineering fell into two camps, both in turn divided into warring bodies, so that viewed from a distance there appear to be four fundamental positions on the issue. All these positions were taken at one time or another by all imperial powers, the United States included. Despite fragmentation within the two major camps, they could at times work together, so that policy with respect to social responsibility in the colonies tended to swing between two arcs of a pendulum. All four schools of thought shared the misperception that the decision to apply or not to apply social reforms rested almost solely with the Western power because it possessed the technology to effect change. This was a misapprehension on two counts: it could effect change only with the active cooperation of the indigenous society, and it did not, in any event, possess sufficient technological power to achieve the kinds of changes envisioned by the more ambitious and progressive imperial nations. The United States was especially ambitious and progressive; it was destined to be especially disappointed.

Social engineering relates to prevailing notions of 'good government' or, more broadly, of the 'good life'. Americans shared with Western Europeans the conviction that both were attainable. Americans also felt that the effete and monarchical nations of Europe were incapable of good government, and almost from the beginning of the Republic, extending the area of freedom, applying American definitions of good government (which included the elimination of corruption), and helping a people to live a good life, were high on the nation's priorities. To secure the good life for non-Americans while maintaining the good life already achieved for white Americans did not seem an incompatible set of goals in the period of American formal empire.

Definitions of corruption (which must be stamped out) are invariably ethnocentric, since they speak to a society's moral values. Americans were somewhat more relaxed on this subject than the British were, for a nation of immigrants was bound to believe that protecting the family unit, helping one's brother find a job through the influence one had gained by virtue of the opportunities America offered, was legitimate. Family ties were even closer in the South, which changed less rapidly than other sections of the country, and the sense of kin, together with high tolerance for the 'good 'ole boy', meant that Southern politics tended, by British or New England standards, to be more corrupt than elsewhere in the nation. Since Southerners predominated in the military overseas, they may have been more tolerant of the need to resort to forms of bribery in the Philippines or Vietnam, in order to attain the higher ends of social reform.

This broad and unprovable generalisation notwithstanding, Americans shared the British disinclination to allow a colonial people to remain 'corrupt'. Baksheesh, the pourbois, dash, hush money, the tip were all part of the system somewhere in the world, for 'services rendered' or about to be rendered. But 'good government' operated either on military command, in which there was no baksheesh (other than promotion) for services rendered, or to rather academic and Brahmin concepts of civic virtue which would have surprised many a civil servant in Washington or Tammany Hall. To show themselves better administrators than the British or the Spanish, Americans in the Philippines and elsewhere had to make demands of themselves and of their wards more stringent than they made at home. Tinkering with the structure of government might best achieve the social reform necessary to good government, itself preliminary to any effective social engineering. That Filipinos thought it more corrupt not to award one's family members with jobs when in a position to do so, the family having higher moral priority than the state, than to make family members compete as equals as though family and *compraedor* had no meaning, did not alter the taciturn, unblinking demands of an administrator like William Howard Taft.

Before social engineering could truly begin, therefore, there tended to open a gap between the local élite, who thought they detected hypocrisy in a conqueror who worked through collaborators while declaring an intent to root out corruption, and the imperial administrators, who took the need to use collaborators for granted. Indians had been bought off on the crimson prairies, after all, and both Malay and Tagalog contained words for graft. Spanish always had.

A second preconception interfered with plans for social engineering. By whatever language, by the time the United States acquired formal colonies economists were arguing that mounting inflation (which invariably followed war and occupation) and stagnation of real incomes required an outside injection of capital into a unified nation, so that economic growth could broaden the base of prosperity. This idea, simple and circular, presupposed the need to give a people a sense of being unified, so that a colonial power committed to bringing the good life to another people had also to think of generating unity without generating nationalist resistance. The British, having long experience, were relatively (though not really very) good at this. The Americans were not, despite producing by the 1950s the language for what was wanted: economic take-offs, modernisation, foreign aid, development, under-developed, lesser-developed, a conjugation of conditions as read from the vantage point of high technology and an expanding economy. Again, developmental goals and custodial goals were not always compatible.

The four conflicting schools of thought thus developed, conditioned in part by these concerns. For the British in India, each view held sway for a substantial time and each could be said to have been tested by experience. For the Americans in the Philippines, the views overlapped, remained in contention, and none was 'proved' right or wrong. All four views could be found crystalline in the debate over the annexation of the Philippines – a debate so closely examined by other writers, and so frequently, as to require no detailed rehearsal here – and all four could be heard again 70 years later, though in more careful language, over the question of Vietnam.

Simply expressed the views were simple. The two broad positions may be called 'interventionist' and 'non-interventionist'. One view was that the imperial power had a moral obligation to uplift the heathen and bring him from the bondage of his loved Egyptian night. This would require massive interference with the traditional mores of native society. Such massive interference would require close administration. Britain or the United States would also benefit, though incidentally. The second view held that the traditional society should be changed as little as possible, that to change it would involve the imperial power in more cost and grief than it could sustain, and that the idea of trusteeship held that native rights would be returned unimpaired. Any substantial intervention would make it impossible to protect the native in the full enjoyment of his rights.

The first view, in turn, represented an alliance – some would find it unholy – between two points of view. The first was that native peoples were essentially innocent, capable of great improvement if led upward to the light, and that intervention, though massive, might also be relatively brief (in 1900 Americans spoke of 50 years in the Philippines, as the British spoke of needing only three hundred more in India, the base from which the 'more' sprang being the 1930s). The second was that native peoples were degraded, evil, incapable of self-regeneration, rotten almost beyond redemption, and only the most radical surgery, the most massive intervention, might rescue some few of them. Thus those who would have insisted they harbored not a racist thought, and those who would have posited their entire policy on an open racism, could unite on the question of intervention. As Theodore Roosevelt, then Police Commissioner for the City of New York, wrote when reviewing Benjamin Kidd's *Social Evolution*, 'A perfectly stupid race can never rise to a very high plane; the negro, for instance, has been kept down as much by lack of intellectual development as by anything else; but the prime factor in the preservation of a race is its power to attain a high degree of social efficiency.' The 'sum of social efficiency' was made up of 'love of order, ability to fight well and breed well, capacity to subordinate the interests of the individual to the interests of the community . . .'. If the West were to help other races, it would be through the social engineering that produced social efficiency.

In the same way, as mirror images, non-interventionists were an alliance of different views. Some felt that the West had nothing it could teach so noble a people as the Hindu, or the Moslem, or the Nez Perce, and that altering their lives as little as possible was the only prudent policy. Others felt that because such people were savages, degraded beyond redemption, British or American lives ought not to be lost on such waste lands of the soul. Americans should not die for gooks. As Henry Labouchere wrote in satirical reply to Rudyard Kipling, 'Reserve for home consumption/The Sacred 'rights of man'!' Henry Adams, with the long view of the historian, thought Filipinos were 'the usual worthless Malay type' and he grieved (more precisely, turned 'green in bed at midnight') over slaughtering 'a million or two of foolish Malays' so that they might be given 'the comforts of flannel petticoats and electric railways . . .'.

Of course both the debate over imperialism, and the subsequent discussion of appropriate policy in the Philippines, was more subtle than all this. When the question was put, 'what ought' rather than 'what can' we do with the Philippines, for its good and our good, different answers were given. To 'what can', there was reasonable evidence that the best policy was to interfere with local customs as little as possible, correcting only the most scandalous abuses; but Americans at the turn of the century were full of confidence, and 'what ought' was never an abstract philosopher's question. The issue of wealth – what was its true source, how best to increase it, how to share it and in what proportions – always obtruded. Congress had no economic policy for the Philippines, so the question fell to the private sector and to the Philippine Commission. The Commission sought to prepare Filipinos for self-government, to educate the masses, and to stimulate economic development. In the end the United States failed at all three.

The Philippine Commission did set in train changes in a number of areas. They gave rather more opportunities for experience in self-government to their subjects than most colonial powers did. They emphasised primary education on a broader base than other colonial powers did, and they insisted upon instruction in the language of the ruler more than Britain or Germany (though not more than France). They did not develop the colony for economic exploitation nearly so much as most other imperial nations did, in part because they were unable to agree upon a policy and in part because many of the annexationists had seen the Philippines as significant largely in relation to the China market and not for any economic benefits the islands might bring of themselves. The Commission did introduce reforms in public health and the law, create a constabulary it hoped might be free of corruption, and modify the land holding system. It did not need to Christianize the natives, for ninety per cent of the Filipinos already had been Christianised by the Spanish, although to Roman Catholicism rather than the preferred Protestantism. (Where the indigenous people had not been 'pacified', as with the Muslims of the southern islands and the animists of the interior uplands, the Commission established different methods of administration.) The policies were those of conservative Americans who often sought, with courtesy, to hide their racist feelings; they were not progressive policies. When one member of the Commission, Bernard Moses, a professor of history and political science from the University of California, called Filipinos 'one of the less advanced races', he probably spoke for all the members of the Commission, though all save one of the others had the wisdom to keep their mouths shut. The key Commissioner, Dean C. Worcester, a professor of zoology from the University of Michigan, thought Filipinos 'big children who must be treated like little ones'.

The Commission did not favor too much regulation, however, for it knew that the United States lacked the interest, and perhaps the resources, for wholesale intervention. Though indolent, many of the natives were clever, and they ought in many respects to be left to their own devices. Left they were, since the Americans put little stock, as the British had in India, in the notion of 'the improving peasant' who, like 'the improving landlord', might if gently helped along, bring change from within the structure of indigenous society. Poverty was not the Commission's primary concern, except in the sense that mass primary education in English might attach the Philippines to the engine of American free trade and slowly eliminate the indolence on which the poverty of the peasant was based. The Philippine nationalist writer Jose Rizal had admitted to the indolence of the Filipinos and attributed it to the Spanish and to their Christianity, which had taken the pagan, active Filipino away from his accustomed trade, fishing, and warlike enterprises, and exploited him through *encomenderos*. While the Americans were inclined to agree, they were unlikely to encourage the Filipinos to return to paganism and war.

It may have been fortunate for Filipino traditional society, to the extent that it survived after the long period of Spanish rule, that the Philippine Commission was essentially conservative and only mildly interventionist. For had it been filled with evangelicals, utilitarians, and liberals, social engineering would not have been limited in the ways it was. While Protestant missionaries were admitted to the islands, the Commission made no attempt to subvert the Catholic faith (itself strong in the United States), and when the Commission learned that Filipinos might not attend the new public schools if there were no religious instruction, they decided that while teachers could not discuss religion during classes, priests or ministers could give religious instruction in the schools outside class hours. As Taft said, 'the Commission did not come here to change the religion of anybody . . .'. Even so, *ilustrados* thought the decision that instruction would be in English might subtly militate against Catholicism, and many members of the élite continued to send their children to private, Catholic, schools where the medium of instruction was Spanish.

The problem of intervention and non-intervention was further complicated in the Philippines by the fact that the Americans followed upon nearly three hundred years of Spanish occupation, and while the Spanish had not been actively interventionist save in matters of religion, in three hundred years they had eroded traditional Filipino practices to the point that the Americans could not tell when they were dealing with a Spanish (or *ilustrado*) custom or with an indigenous custom. Indeed, 'indigenous' had little meaning in this context. In most places where one colonial empire has inherited the colony of another – the British from the Germans in Tanganyika, for example – the time-frame was contracted. In the Philippines, the principle of intervention had long been established, complex collaborator mechanisms were inherited from the Spanish rather than created, and debates concerning social improvement turned as much on the feasibility of introducing railways, or electric telegraph lines, or an improved steamer service to remote islands, as it did on the more abstract issues of bringing the greatest good to the greatest number.

Americans wanted efficiency. In this they were much as the British had been in India. But efficiency to what end? Less clear than the British as to their colonial responsibilities and goals, the Philippine Commission, and the American governors-general, were less vigorous in their pursuit of social engineering. The promise of eventual independence hung in the air; so too did the strategic argument, and increasingly so as tensions with Japan grew; and in the end the Americans passed through the various stages of what, in the British Empire, later was known as 'the Great Debate' concerning colonial administration without having arrived at any clear decisions. Drift *was* mastery after all.

Americans did not escape one phase of the Great Debate, however. In India the British had begun a serious discussion of economic theory. Allocation rather than development preoccupied them. By the 1870s, so did Social Darwinism and a growing commitment to cultural relativism in administration. *Laissez-faire* principles – setting free the energies of individuals through an even-handed administration of justice – had not worked in India because of the inherent native corruption, the British had decided, and from 1879 they began actively to interfere in native political and economic practices, especially to achieve agricultural reform. The British had begun to carry reform into the village, or so they thought, and they were beginning to apply the lessons they felt they had learned in India to Africa. By 1900 the British empire was an actively interventionist one in many quarters – indeed, it had not been so sweepingly activist since 1833, when it had intervened overwhelmingly against the sacred concept of property in freeing the slaves throughout the British Empire – and the Americans had, at the least, to give thought to being as effective colonial masters as their former masters were being. The British were now thinking of white settlement in Cecil Rhodes's pink-tinted Africa in order to create a money economy and to transform native society, while Americans – still with vast empty lands of their continent to fill – gave little consideration to white settlement on a permanent basis. Outside Hawaii, the American empire did not create a laboring proletariat which was to serve a white-dominated society fastened upon the proletariat's own homeland, as the British did in Kenya, Rhodesia, and at the Cape. Though the British chose 'indirect rule' outside white settlement areas, this never meant quite what Americans thought it meant, and the United States, though thinking it was using indirect rule in Puerto Rico or American Samoa, really was not. As the British remarked, there was some difference between indirect rule and ruling indirectly.

By the inter-war years, the British were learning from the Americans as well. Development plans included technical institutions that would not put the burden of a useless European-style education on the native, but would – as at Achimota College, in the Gold Coast, modelled upon the Tuskegee Institute in Alabama – train a native people to 'do a job of work' within the labour needs of the colonial authority. Americans, being a pragmatic people, had always emphasised practical education, and they had used the schools they opened in the Philippines to generate a clerkly élite. As development fever began to mount, the need for a class of managers became more apparent. For the British, the fever was high by the early 1930s; for the Americans in the Philippines, it was postponed by the approaching conflict with Japan, and then briefly by independence, so that wide-spread social engineering came to the Philippines only in the context of informal empire, after the United States had met its obligation to grant the Philippines political independence and economic aid. The late arrival of this phase of social engineering within the American empire was made far more complex by the concerns of post-World War II thought: the Keynesian argument for a managed economy, which justified social engineering far more broadly than in underdeveloped colonies; world-wide anti-imperialism, which led the United States to use development as a means of proving its good intentions; the Cold War, in which those good intentions had to be seen in competition against alleged Soviet good intentions of an apparently similar nature; a rising tolerance for the idea of welfare states; and competition with the British as they began what was meant to be a long process (and was, of course, an exceptionally short process) of decolonisation.

Resistance to social engineering was not great in the formal American colonies. Effective collaborator mechanisms, and a relatively modest commitment to interventionist policies by the Americans, kept Young Turks from displacing traditional élites too quickly. The casual American approach to imperial administration, reflected in the belief that there was no empire to administer, kept the bonds of colonialism relatively light. Most of the American empire was informal in nature in any event, and after decolonization of those portions which were formal, far greater problems presented themselves than the British ever faced, though these problems were seldom seen as colonial in nature. Two great empires, neither benign as no empire can be, yet at least one genuinely seeking to benefit its subjects (though not to a degree equal to the masters), caught up in a struggle for ideological authority, represented conflicting systems of commands. One, having long studied the rhetoric of imperialism, was tough minded enough to know that it was dealing with commands; the other, never really clear that the possession of colonies involved commands, continued to speak of its 'moral commitment to humanity' in terms at once global, ennobling, and impossibly vague.

*   *   *

This essay is written somewhat to the style of A. Thornton, whom it is meant to honour. Documentation has been omitted, in part because the author assumes that readers will recognize the source of most literary allusions – and the burden of their message – and the origins of most of the theoretical arguments. The idea of 'the collaborator', for example, derives from Ronald Robinson, Jack Gallagher, and Alice Denny; the prefabricated collaborator from Robinson; the forms of resistance from Eric Stokes and Terence Ranger; the turbulent frontier from John S. Galbraith. Elsewhere readers will readily recognize that I have argued from Richard Hale, Marshall Sahlins, Keith Basso, Anthony Lowe, and A. P. Thornton himself. This essay will form part of a larger book, *The Idea of an American Imperialism* (forthcoming), where full documentation is supplied.

2 An Imperial Idea and Its Friends: Canadian Confederation and the British

GED MARTIN

If an idea is sufficiently grand to inspire general support within a society, it will be 'strong enough to force circumstance itself to obey its dictation'.[1] A. P. Thornton's great contribution to the writing of imperial history has been to remind us that ideas may themselves be numbered among the causes of events, and are not merely reflexive patterns deduced from them. If this be true of the overarching 'imperial idea', it is equally the case with its component elements. Canadian Confederation is one such example. Although James A. Gibson, Bruce Knox and L. F. S. Upton have demonstrated that the idea of British North American union had long been discussed on both sides of the Atlantic, most historians have concentrated on explaining British support for the initiative of 1864 in the purely contemporary terms of a reaction to the crisis of the American Civil War.[2] Although this interpretation is correct in perceiving American events as the crucial context of Confederation policy, the deductions do not necessarily follow. In the face of a victorious and vengeful North, already angry at the French adventure in Mexico, it might well have seemed best to leave well alone among the British provinces. With the Reform issue dominating the British agenda in the mid-1860s, it might have seemed better to sidestep the issue of parliamentary engineering in autonomous colonies with their broad franchises. Moreover, as Thornton himself noted, there was a 'desperate optimism' about the launching of a superficially

49

federal ship of state in the aftermath of the explosion in the United States.[3] It is possible to imagine reasons why the British might not have welcomed the provincial initiative in 1864, and easy to see that if London had been as lukewarm in 1865–6 as it had been in 1858–9, a regional union would have emerged, if at all, in a different form, certainly delayed and probably tempestuous. We cannot explain the achievement of Confederation without accounting for the vital element of British support, and only the easy wisdom of hindsight will explain that support as the necessary deduction from circumstance. The perspective which Thornton has indicated is the key to understanding the problem. Between 1837 and 1867 British opinion was steadily captured by the idea of an eventual regional union in British North America. This particular imperial idea had become so entrenched in British collective assumptions in 1864 that it did not have to impose itself upon circumstance, for circumstance could only be understood as indicating that the time had arrived for the idea to come into its own. Thus the idea of Canadian Confederation became itself a cause of Canadian Confederation. In embracing this idea the British were probably ahead of their provincial cousins, who could be forgiven a sharper appreciation of the problems involved. Yet they were more than armchair observers, and their view was not confined to the windows of the Colonial Office in Downing Street. But their idea of regional union for British North America requires clarification. Who exactly constituted 'the British'? What kind of regional union did they contemplate? Why did they embrace the idea? When did they expect it to come about? And these questions in turn require the discussion of the context of Anglo-Canadian relations and attitudes.

Yet that context defies clarification. The historian must abandon his usual task of producing ordered explanation from the raw muddle of the past, accept that vagueness and misunderstanding characterised British attitudes – and then proclaim that these miasmic perceptions were in fact favourable to the embracing of the Confederation ideal. There was certainly widespread ignorance about the North American provinces. Canada was far away – 'beyond London a good bit I reckon; and quite in foreign parts' as that stout Mancunian Mrs Wilson declared in *Mary Barton*, and in an age of slow communications colonies appeared 'to be shadowy and almost fabulous possessions, distance producing, in some respects, the effects of time'.[4] Governors complained that the British press was 'horribly ignorant' of Canadian affairs, and *The Times* regretted 'we only hear of these provinces as we do of Mount Etna, that is, when there is an eruption'. But ignorance too can have its context, and the less the British actually knew of their North American provinces, the more they were likely to think of them as overshadowed by the United States, an imbalance of information, although not perhaps of understanding, which the Civil War increased. 'We listen with open ears to the faintest rumour of a cabal that threatens to cripple or depose one of Lincoln's Generals', remarked *The Times* in 1863, '. . . but who is Minister, if any, at Quebec or any other seat of British Government in America, we none of us know'.[5] Travellers' accounts – 'the wretched gossip of tourists' as one eminent American dismissed them – underlined the relationship. The *genre* was sufficiently popular to lure such writers as Marryat, Dickens and Trollope across the Atlantic, and in each case a visit to the provinces was an appendage to a tour in the States. It was probably these exhaustive travelogues which led the British to discount the sheer scale of British North America. The Colonial Secretary thought 'the N. American provinces and their capitals to be as near each other as Downing Street to the Parks', one Governor-General grumbled when it was suggested that he should run down to Halifax to solve a Nova Scotian problem.[6] Indeed, very little was known about the Atlantic provinces. 'If an Englishman thinks of North America at all, he divides it between Canada and the United States. Except in some sets and circles, chiefly commercial and mercantile, you rarely hear of Nova Scotia, New Brunswick, Prince Edward Island or Newfoundland.' Those Englishmen who did know their names frequently thought they were parts of the United States.[7]

Inability to grasp the scale and diversity of the provinces encouraged the British to think of them in stereotypes. Russell once complained that people generalised about Canadians 'as if a million & a half of people were like one man, who wished for British rule, or were against it'.[8] French Canadians were especially perceived in these terms. Until the late eighteen forties, they were generally regarded with pessimism, as summarised by James Stephen of the Colonial Office in his reference to 'the French and Roman Catholic Population, distinguished chiefly by their bigotry in Religion, their ignorance in Politics, and their antipathy to the English Race'. By the end of the decade, a more optimistic view was being fostered by the apparent success of the responsible government partnership. French Canadians were seem more as a sleepy peasant people, as untouched by the disturbing currents of 1789 as they had been unstirred by those of 1848. Analogies with Ireland – itself moving into a period of quiescence betwixt Famine and Fenians – were less frequent, and indeed the French fact dropped remarkably from sight altogether.

This combination of factual ignorance with general incomprehension might seem to vitiate any serious consideration of British notions about the future of the provinces. Yet, in fact, almost every element in British misunderstanding helped foster support for some form of British North American union. Overall ignorance of Canadian reality made the provinces a *tabula rasa* on which distant mental utopias might be projected. The automatic footnoting of British North America to the United States ensured that the British always thought of their future within the context of the States, and made it natural to transfer American federal ideas, suitably laundered, to the provinces. Failure to grasp the problem of internal distance obviously did nothing to cast doubt on the practicability of union, while a public mind which was barely aware of the existence of the Maritimes was hardly likely to appreciate that local particularism might stand in the way. Most notably the stereotypes of French Canada interposed no obstacle to the building of federal castles in the colonial air. If the French were hostile, they should be outvoted by the largest possible English-speaking majority; if quiescent, they might be happily caged in their own provincial unit and left alone. Either way, it never seriously occurred to British opinion that the French might have to be consulted and won. It was their good fortune that from 1864 the almost comical vagueness of their perceptions apparently coincided with British North American reality. Provincial leaders embraced Confederation as a means of overcoming the problem of internal distance through railway construction. French Canada did behave as if it were an acquiescent bloc, and complaints of the Maritimes could be brushed aside. And however wayward British notions were in other respects, they had perceived the basic element in the future of British North America: the proximity of the United States.[9]

The vagueness of British perceptions of British North American reality was parallelled by a more deliberate imprecision about the nature of Anglo-Canadian relations. Responsible government, as it emerged in the late 1840s, managed in practice to reconcile the incompatibility of British supremacy with colonial autonomy, but only by carefully avoiding definition of spheres. This grey area did not inhibit the vision of eventual British North American union, but it did leave in doubt the means by which it might be achieved. Constitutional change was tacitly accepted to be the ultimate prerogative of the Westminster parliament, but did this mean that only the British could initiate discussion of constitutional change? Here the experience of the Canadian Union intruded two further complications in the British mind. First, it had been virtually imposed by act of parliament in 1840, although Francis Hincks was to warn in 1853 that even then legislators had been reluctant to act 'without the appearance at least of an appeal to the people of the Colonies themselves'.[10] Some enthusiasts, however, assumed that the British alone could carry through the larger exercise in constitutional engineering involved in uniting the whole of British North America. In this, the experience of the creation of the Union of the Canadas in fact dogged the possibility of launching a movement for wider union at least until 1858. But in another respect, the Canadian Union developed a more benign ambiguity. Designed as a unitary system and intended to anglicise and control the French, it rapidly developed into a quasi-federal communal partnership.[11] Even more ironically, that model federation, the United States, seemed to be moving in the opposite direction, towards a national rather than a federal system, swollen by the conquests of the Mexican War, in which men fought for control of the increasingly dominant central government. 'The Union is no longer a cluster of independent states,' declared *The Times* in 1849, 'it is now an empire dominating over a continent and giving laws to a world.'[12] Faced with two transatlantic systems, a union which behaved like a federation and a federation forging itself into a nation, it is hardly surprising that British opinion tended to blur the distinction between unitary and federal government. The imposition of the Canadian Union created unhelpful misunderstandings about the means through which a wider union might be brought about; the operation of the Canadian Union fostered a much more constructive vagueness about the nature of that larger polity.

*   *   *

Who were 'the British' whose opinion favoured the eventual creation of a regional union in British North America? Traditionally, historians have used the all-purpose phrase 'the Colonial Office' as the origin and vehicle for all British contributions to colonial history, and in recent decades this 'great house at the bottom of Downing-Street' has become the geographical location of an odd concept called 'the official mind', a super-brain which carried ministers and officials down the tides of history despite their individual doubts.[13] These unhelpful devices are especially alluring because 'that fabulous monster, the Colonial-office' was so freely abused by contemporaries that it is tempting to conclude that there is 'historical proof' that the beast really existed. More instructive is the irritated riposte of one Colonial Secretary to a governor-general who had criticised 'the Colonial Office (in which phrase I understand you to be comprehended)'.[14] It is certainly misleading to project into the Colonial Office our modern idea of a 'policy-making body'. William Baillie-Hamilton, a recruit of the 1860s, was soon disappointed in his hopes of becoming 'a participator in some of the most important and delicate ideas of State'. Instead he was engaged principally in entering up despatches, which he thought 'a singularly elaborate waste of time' and which an earlier permanent under-secretary had called 'office fiddle fiddle'. On the eve of Confederation, Carnarvon complained:

> The staff is in its lower departments ineffective and needs reorganisation, whilst in its higher branches it is so overtaxed as to be quite unequal to its work.[15]

We should not seek here for the driving forces behind British support for regional union. In fact, officials were rarely involved in the subject and exercised little influence in either speeding or slowing its progress. An instructive exception was Stephen's attempt in 1836–7 to produce a 'forecasting Policy' to prepare the way for British North American union. Howick, the later Earl Grey, warmly embraced Stephen's federal solution, only to be brusquely warned by his prime minister, Lord Melbourne, not to 'fall in love with the beautiful erection of Mr Stephen's fancy'.[16] Two officials who had actually visited Canada commented on British North American union in later years. T. W. C. Murdoch, former secretary to Sir Charles Bagot, prepared a memorandum on the subject in 1849, probably for the Commons debate on Roebuck's federal scheme. Despite a self-denying ordinance that it was 'beyond our province to offer any opinions upon it' since 'such a measure must be discussed and decided on purely political grounds', Murdoch nonetheless damned federation in praise so faint as to be inaudible. Ministers, however, acted on his principle rather than his prejudice, and declined to condemn all prospect of regional union.[17] T. F. Elliot in 1858 had freer rein in expressing a hostility to the Canadian federal initiative which probably owed its origin to his memories of service with the Gosford commission a quarter of a century before, but he was influential only because his political master, Sir Edward Bulwer-Lytton, was already terrified by the political implications of such a major change.[18] Thereafter the officials took little part in the moves to Confederation. Arthur Blackwood, chief clerk at the North American desk, a man of wooden rectitude inherently suspicious of colonial initiatives, had no impact on government policies, while the permanent under-secretary of the eighteen-sixties, Sir Frederic Rogers, hardly bothered with Canadian matters. ('I have been a good deal interested by the proposed American union', he casually commented in December 1864 after meeting George Brown, who he thought was prime minister of Canada.)[19]

The idea of Confederation was significant, then, not in capturing a small group of influential policy-making officials, for such a group never existed, but through its general acceptance among a group which is best described in the eighteenth-century expression, 'the political nation'. In the years between the Reform acts of 1832 and 1867, the governing group was still narrow. Ministers feared attack in the House of Commons – as did Lytton in 1858 and Cardwell over Canadian defence in 1865 – but the Commons itself was likely to respond to a very restricted choir of voices in the press. If shared assumptions can be traced within the mid-Victorian political nation – and there were probably more issues on which it was united than it was divided – those assumptions may functionally be equated with the term 'British opinion'. Contemporaries certainly perceived this narrow range of influence and – if, like the *North British Review* in 1852, felt excluded from it – protested that politicians drew 'their information from the same set of organs', such as the *Edinburgh* and *Quarterly Reviews*, 'they all listen anxiously to the language of The Times, and are not wholly without concern about the articles in the Morning Chronicle, the Morning Post, and the Daily News. But beyond these they seldom go'. Even in 1852 the magic circle might have been defined a little more broadly, and later arrivals like the

Saturday and *Fortnightly* modified it in the 1860s. But the pattern is clear enough, especially in stressing the influence of *The Times*. The 'misleading journal of Europe', a rival bitterly called it but, as Lord Clarendon declared, '*The Times* forms or guides or reflects – no matter which – the public opinion of England.'[20] A critic complained that Canadians had been taught to look upon it 'as an exponent of the feelings of the British people' and care was taken to keep its support after 1864. Indeed, two of the key elements in British 'pressure' on New Brunswick came from non-ministerial sources. *The Times* parted company with Robert Lowe, who had written its colonial leaders for a decade, because he sympathised with the objections of a small colony being swept unwillingly into union, and Lord Derby, the opposition leader, made it clear to the Anti-Confederates that a future Conservative government would not support them.[21] Bereft of support both from the organised opposition and from the journal most capable of stirring up independent parliamentary attack, the New Brunswick Antis found themselves facing a pressure which – within the confines of the system – can be genuinely labelled 'British' and not merely 'ministerial' or least of all 'Colonial Office.'

*   *   *

Is it possible to trace a shared assumption in favour of British American union among these sources which constitute the opinion which counted? Most discussion of the subject before 1837 had come from colonists, but in the late 1830s the first signs of a sympathetic consensus in British circles can be traced. In January 1837 the cabinet adopted a scheme, drawn up by Stephen, for annual meetings of representatives of the four mainland colonies, a plan which its author accepted 'points towards a new Congress on the North American Continent.'[22] It was swept aside by the developing crisis in Lower Canada, although J. A. Roebuck, agent for the Lower Canadian Assembly, also preached a federal solution.[23] Not surprisingly, the outbreak of rebellion switched the bulk of public discussion towards union of the Canadas pure and simple, but several journals on the fringe of the political nation thought it 'better to unite federally all the provinces'.[24] Although Howick was defeated in cabinet debate when he championed general federation in the early months of 1838, he did succeed in converting Durham to the idea. 'On my first arrival in Canada, I was strongly inclined to the project of a

federal union.'[25] The idea was adopted with a bizarre measure
of stealth, in sharp contrast to the flamboyance of the mission
generally: when Thomas Turton reported to Edward Ellice that
they were at work on a general federal union, he lightly deleted
the word 'federal' adding '(I beg pardon that word is not to
appear so I have run my pen through)'.[26] Ellice, however, for
obscure reasons of his own, decided to attack the plan, although
a few months later he was appealing to ministers to shape their
Canadian Union scheme in order to make it easy to extend to
the rest of the colonies.[27] Federation was attacked by the arch-
Conservative *Morning Herald*, but the fashionable *Morning Post*
was more cautious, identifying federation as 'clearly of
Washington origin' but declining to dismiss it for that reason.[28]
Durham's intercolonial meeting coincided with his resignation,
and although he continued to believe in a general union of British
North America, it could be claimed in June 1839 that the scheme
'has been at present abandoned by its proposers'. Yet not only
had the idea been sown, but identification with well-known
radicals like Roebuck and Durham had not prevented it from
receiving a wide measure of support. The leader of the opposition,
Sir Robert Peel, stated in 1840 that he would have preferred that
'the government of our entire North American colonies might be
under one supreme control'.[29]

The early 1840s were unpromising years for constitutional
engineering, but no sooner had Earl Grey, the former Lord
Howick, returned to the Colonial Office in 1846 to inaugurate
the more harmonious era of free trade and self-government, than
he began to plan for some form of British American union. Self-
government gave the colonies a wider area of autonomous action,
and in December 1846 Grey urged them to delegate some of their
new freedom to a central body.[30] He and Elgin discussed the
possibility several times in correspondence during the following
year, but the governor-general, a practical man with a distrust
for political science, was more concerned to achieve his immediate
aim of partnership with the French. Despite discouragement,
Grey was the first British minister to behave as if he were
expressing a long-term political consensus:

> Short as the tenure of office generally is while one holds it one
> ought to act as if it were to be permanent or as if ones successor
> was likely to carry forward the policy one has begun.[31]

Grey's assumption was increasingly valid. Roebuck's federation scheme, although part of a plan for colonial reform resisted by the ministers, received some support in the House of Commons, and general acceptance in the press – from the Protectionist *Morning Herald* to the liberal *Daily News*.[32] Even *The Times*, which had grumbled in 1847 about the prospect of 'a hostile republic or a rebellious federation', now turned to welcome the idea. The most notable convert was Lord John Russell, previously wedded to the Canadian Union as a sacred principle. Concerned at the growing agitation among Canadian Tories against alleged French domination under responsible government, he espoused what Grey significantly called 'the old idea of forming a federal union'.[33] By 1849 acceptance of some form of British North American union was general. Significantly the idea was strong enough in its own right to escape contamination by association with the Canadian tories, who veered between federation and annexation and were blamed for the riots in Montreal in which the parliament buildings were destroyed, just as it had suffered relatively little from its espousal by British radicals a decade earlier.

Even if the provinces had been more receptive, the Russell government was too weak and its colonial secretary too unpopular to carry a general union, as its humiliation over Australian federation proved in 1850. Not until the formation of the Aberdeen coalition late in 1852 could British politics be said to be on a firm enough base to tackle such a question, and there is some reason to think it engaged the hesitant mind of the new colonial secretary, the duke of Newcastle. Federation was already appealing to the precise intellect of Sir Edmund Head as a logical sequel to responsible government, and with negotiations for a trade treaty with the United States, pressure mounting for responsible government in the tiny island colonies, and Newcastle's own antipathy to the monopoly of the Hudson's Bay Company, it was understandable that he should look favourably on 'the consolidation of the provinces into one Government'.[34] There are some faint indications that the duke came close to screwing himself up to take some action on the question. The *Spectator* reported in September 1853 that Elgin's return to Britain on leave would be the occasion for an initiative for a wider union, and Elgin apparently talked the matter over with his leading minister, Francis Hincks, who was strongly opposed to it. Hincks, in fact, went so far as to declare that 'up to this time the scheme of a Union has had more support among eminent British Statesmen than in any other quarter', a view which was endorsed by a Nova Scotian, P. S. Hamilton, who observed in 1855 that colonists generally believed 'many of the leading statesmen of Great Britain are rather desirous than otherwise that a union of these Provinces take place'.[35] Did Newcastle take any action? The only evidence comes from a tart letter from Newcastle to Arthur Gordon ten years later. The bumptious young governor of New Brunswick had been preening himself on his success in persuading politicians to discuss Maritime Union, which he believed to be just around the corner. Newcastle replied:

> so far from you having 'set the measure going' it has been constantly agitated for more than ten years and more than once has appeared quite as near being accomplished as it does now. In 1853–4 I thought the question ripe and actually asked poor Elgin to return and take a new lease of the Gov^t of Canada for the purpose of accomplishing the further union which would be the consequence.

There are some problems in understanding this recollection. There is no trace of any moves towards Maritime Union in 1854, and in any case, Sir Edmund Head, the senior and ablest Maritime governor would surely have been the vehicle for action, not Elgin. Nor can it be said that Maritime Union had been close to achievement at any time in the decade before 1863, although with some hyperbole a claim might have been made for more general union on the basis of the Canadian campaign in 1858–9, and the Nova Scotian resolution of 1861. Moreover, Newcastle's reference to 'the further union which would be the consequence' suggests that he had seen Maritime Union merely as a step to a more general scheme. The explanation for Newcastle's confusion in November 1863 seems simple: he was a sick man, shortly to follow 'poor Elgin' into the grave. He was irritated by Gordon, who had just delivered a particularly brash and savage attack on Monck, and the Canadians over their railway dealings, and he succumbed to an old man's temptation to squash an upstart by hinting at considerations of which the younger man knew not. It is possible too to hazard a guess at what passed in 1853–4. Rogers later noted how conflicting advice could bother Newcastle who 'rather catches at the notion of getting fresh advice, as if the *bulk* of advice made it easier to decide'. Newcastle certainly favoured 'consolidation' in 1853, but faced with the objections of the self-confident Elgin he probably retreated.[36] The lost Confederation initiative of 1853–4 is not one of the more stirring episodes in the march towards Canadian nationhood, but it demonstrates that the ideal of regional union was becoming a generally accepted British aim. Other comment in the mid-1850s gives the same impression: the subject was mentioned, if at all, in passing, as a matter of general agreement or at the very least as a likely item on the political agenda. Thus when Gladstone signalled his availability for the vacant post of colonial secretary with a speech on colonial affairs in 1855, *The Times* was quick to take him to task for omitting any reference to 'the intercolonial question' and wanted to know whether he would 'form the colonies into confederacies'.[37]

It is against this background that the failure of the Canadian federal initiative of 1858 should be seen. It was its timing, rather than its aim, which undid it. For most of the 1850s both British and Canadian parliamentary politics had been dominated by centre-based party alliances. Unluckily these majority groupings both faltered in 1858, giving way – briefly – to the Brown-Dorion ministry in Canada and to Derby's Conservative administration in Britain. A weak minority government in Britain felt too insecure to give a regrouping majority government in Canada the kind of support which its federal initiative required. It is now clear, thanks to the scholarly detective work of B. A. Knox, that the British reaction in 1858 had more to do with its objections to the means employed rather than the end sought by the Canadian initiative. When Derby took office in February 1858, he at first appointed his son, Lord Stanley, as colonial secretary. Stanley was a Conservative because his father led the party, and it was an open secret that 'the entire discrepancy of sentiment and opinion' between himself and the rest of the party would sooner or later force him out.[38] When he expressed enthusiasm for British North American federation, there was thus little guarantee that his colleagues would agree. He came into office at just the moment when Galt proposed resolutions in favour of general union in the Canadian Assembly. Stanley wrote a lengthy and favourable letter to Head, discussing problems in detail, and indicating that he saw no imperial objection to the idea of a federation. Head replied more cautiously, but by the time his letter could arrive in London, Stanley had been transferred to the India Office. In the aftermath of the Mutiny, the problems of Britain's greatest imperial dependency were by far the most pressing – so pressing, indeed, that Stanley failed even to mention his exchange of letters with Head until Merivale enquired about it months later.[39] Thus the governor-general was left in the ambiguous position of receiving encouragement but not necessarily support. In August he played a part in reconstructing the Canadian ministry on a federal platform, only to find that Stanley's successor took a very different view of matters. Sir Edward Bulwer-Lytton, holding his first ministerial post, was beset by worries both personal and political, had the nightmares of facing parliamentary attack because Canada seemed about to run off with a slice of the empire. Fortunately parliament was in recess, but no less a person than the Prince Consort urged Sir Edmund Head's recall. Fortunately the worst outbursts of Lytton's excitability were smothered by Herman Merivale, the permanent official for once exercising a restraining hand. Merivale's deputy, T. F. Elliot, was, however, on hand to stiffen Lytton's hostility to the federation itself. Yet Lytton's disapproval was directed against the means rather than the end. Federation, his official despatch insisted, was a matter of such importance that it 'properly belongs to the Executive Authority of the Empire, and not to that of any separate province, to initiate'. Privately, although he felt that the project would require 'the most anxious deliberation' (but then for Lytton all deliberation was anxious), he had to conclude that 'Confederation' was 'one of the most obvious solutions' to the problem of the Canadian Union, and one which might with careful handling be reconciled to British interests.[40]

Once again, the ideal of regional union was not harmed by association with the obviously sordid intrigues of the 'double shuffle', by which the Cartier-Macdonald ministry resumed office without fighting the usual by-elections. True, most newspaper coverage dwelt more on what Merivale called 'the general air of lunacy which hangs over the whole proceedings' but references to federation itself continued to be friendly, *The Times* for instance regarding the idea 'with more favour than hope'. Galt, who arrived late in September, reported 'that all the press of the country is in favour of my favourite scheme of Confederation'.[41]

In short, British North American union had become an idea
with an autonomous existence in the British mind, not closely
tied to specific considerations, especially of defence and railway
construction, and invulnerable to the machinations of colonial
politicians. One further episode confirms this picture: the aftermath of the defeat of the Canadian Militia Bill in 1862. The bill's
defeat caused considerable shock and indignation in Britain which
only a few months earlier had thrown troops into the province
to defend it against an expected Northern invasion during the
Trent crisis, but it by no means thrust federation to the fore as a
specific remedy. Russell privately considered it as a means to
force the provinces into accepting a junior partnership; Goldwin
Smith publicly preached it as a step to full independence.[42] Galt
went a step further than Russell, arguing that British American
federation might lead to a re-organisation of the whole empire,
on the loose lines of the German Confederation. Probably no
Canadian politician was more likely to raise British ire than Galt,
the architect of the protective tariff of 1859, and Galt hardly
improved matters by breezily telling an audience at Manchester
that it had been Britain's duty to protect Canada during the
Trent crisis. *The Times* did indeed briefly damn all federations,
transatlantic or teutonic, and their supporters too. The *Spectator*
however distinguished between personality and principle, favouring the amalgamation of the provinces 'into one great empire'.
'Everybody pretty well agrees that this is the best chance for
Canada.'[43] The widespread press backing for Confederation after
1864 drew on a long support for the idea.

*   *   *

What kind of regional union did British opinion wish to see
created in British North America? Logically the choice was
between legislative union and federation, but here again allowance
must be made for creative ignorance and confident vagueness,
and on both sides of the Atlantic. P. S. Hamilton complained in
1855 that British North American union was usually described
'as a *Federal* Union, but without any reason being given for the
application of that epithet'.[44] In fact at least two other notional
forms of union can be identified: one, an evolving quasifederation;
the other, a legislative union with federal features, the intellectual
progenitor of the Quebec scheme. The former was the scheme of
Stephen and Howick in 1836–8, revived by Howick as Lord Grey

in 1846, and later described by him as 'if not exactly a federal union of the British provinces at all events some connect^n among them for certain objects of common interest'.[45] Real authority would be gradually and unobtrusively transferred to the inter-colonial body, which would thus develop into a full federal authority. The idea failed to win the approval of the Whig cabinet of the late 1830s for precisely that reason, Palmerston objecting that the central body 'would in fact become a Sovereign as well as a Constituent Power, and whatever it recommended must be done'. 'Such a monster in politics was never yet seen,' Russell observed when Howick made a last attempt to promote the approach in 1839, 'such a provision for confusion never yet created.'[46] If federation was to be considered, it would have to be discussed openly and not introduced by stealth.

The problem with a colonial federal system was not simply that it would be federal, but that it was colonial. Because so much historical writing has focused on Canada's march to self-government, it is easy to overlook the problem that a colonial federation – certainly in the 1830s and 1840s – could only be a mezzanine tier between the existing legislatures and the supervising imperial factor. Colonial tories in particular pointed to the lack of room for federal institutions in the existing system. 'There is no vacant or unoccupied ground for their sphere of action', said Henry Bliss.[47] Few objected to the United States model of federal government as such, but many pointed out that Congress controlled foreign policy and defence, which fell outside the colonial sphere. Durham recognised that it might produce 'a weak and rather cumbrous Government . . . the greater part of the ordinary functions of a federation falling within the scope of the Imperial Legislature and executive'. Whence would a colonial federal government draw its powers? 'If from Parliament, you cease to control these countries, and they become independent; if from the Local Legislatures, you annihilate them', complained T. C. Haliburton. Elgin was to echo this view a decade later: 'a federal can hardly fail to become either a nuisance or a legislative Union'. 'A congress without foreign relations, armies navies and ambassadors would be a very insipid concern.'[48] But gradually this objection became anachronistic. Edmund Head acknowledged in 1851 that a federal legislature 'might employ its spare time in mischievous agitation', but he thought this might be resisted by limiting the length of sessions, or even by convening the central body every second year.[49] Steadily, however, the powers which were to be assigned to the federal authority seemed to increase. Schemes in the late 1830s had envisaged little more than federal control over customs – a sphere which widened a good deal after 1846 – communications, quarantine, postal services and currency. By 1849 Roebuck was adding taxation, copyright and naturalisation laws, the establishment of prairie settlements and of universities to the list. Edmund Head in 1851 thought not only of raising loans but of the assumption of existing colonial debts. Galt in 1858 added lighthouses, fisheries, and control of public lands and Indian affairs.[50] Coordination of the militia had been foreseen by Howick in 1839 and by Roebuck a decade later, but the events of 1861–2 broke the final barrier and a connection – albeit a vague one – came to be seen between federation and defence.[51] Certainly when in 1858 Lord Mulgrave of Nova Scotia advanced the old argument that a colonial federation could control no more than posts, currency and tariffs, an anonymous hand in the Colonial Office added railways, waterways and a Supreme Court to the list.[52]

Nonetheless, the conundrum which Elgin and Mulgrave advanced – that federal union would be inadequate, legislative union unattainable – left its mark on the debate. Outright legislative union certainly appealed to a number of colonial figures, if only because it would eliminate the expense and inefficiency of subordinate legislatures. Furthermore, legislative union would from the outset settle the question which bedevilled American federalism – whether ultimate authority rested in the centre or with the states. Yet attractive though the notion of a total fusion of the provinces might be, it was, as Hincks put it, 'precisely the one which would be most difficult to carry'.[53] British North America was too big for one government, and both French Canadians and Maritimers would resist subordination.

But could some middle way be found between federation and legislative union which might deal with these problems? The intellectual hybrid which became Confederation stemmed from reference to the monarchical constitution of the British empire. Head was perhaps the first to elaborate the idea: in a colonial federation, all legal power would flow down from the Crown rather than up from the people, thus removing any possible challenge to the central power. Any colonial union, he explained to Stanley in 1858, should 'start from the fact that all the Provinces are now under the same Sovereign – not from the assumption that each is a separate state possessing individual & independent rights'. *The Times* developed the idea in its discussion of the 1858 federal initiative. 'They cannot delegate their sovereign authority to a Central Government, because they do not possess the sovereign authority to delegate.' The United States motto, *E pluribus unum*, should be inverted to *Ex uno plura*: a central authority would delegate restricted powers to subordinate local governments, reserving its own supremacy in the process.[54]

Yet the outline of this compromise can be traced some years before the intellectual attempts to justify it. A pamphleteer of 1838 had called for 'one really general government' but with the retention of provincial legislatures '(for merely local purposes of administration)' until improved communications permitted total integration. Durham too was prepared to retain provincial assemblies 'with merely municipal powers' to appease local particularism pending the creation of a more rational system of local government. Howick in 1839 thought that such municipalities would be inadequate to develop internal communications, but by 1847 he had modified his views. When Elgin complained of the instability of political alliances within the small Canadian assembly, Grey concluded that 'a Legislative Union of all the Provinces coupled with an improved municipal organisation' would be the eventual solution. By 1849 he was talking of the need for 'a very much strengthened system of Municipal organisation' to replace the existing local assemblies.[55]

Thus a vague idea may be discerned that a colonial union in a British and monarchical context might be safeguarded against the centrifugal forces rampant in the United States. Here some examination should be given to the origins of the term 'Confederation'. It seems to have emerged as the shorthand term for British North American union during the Canadian discussions of 1858: in April Head was referring to 'the future confederation (or whatever it may be called)', and by September Lytton was using the word without a definite article and spelt with a capital 'C'.[56] Although it was by no means the only term used at this stage, the fact that it emerged as early as 1858 weakens one possible derivation, that of borrowing from the Southern Confederacy formed in 1861 – although the similarity no doubt gave the colonial project a reassuring anti-Yankee aura. Perhaps 'Confederation' emerged to distinguish general union schemes

from the narrower project of a federal restructuring of the two
Canadas alone. Perhaps, too, it was part of that sea-change in
vocabulary which marked the growing self-esteem of British North
America – the process which converted the Halifax to Quebec
railway into the 'Intercolonial', and which tended to talk of
'provinces' rather than 'colonies'. But it is hard to disagree with
P. B. Waite's conclusion that 'the prefix "con" seemed to
contemporaries to strengthen the centralist principle rather than
to weaken it'.[57] Without that pre-existent mental distinction it is
surely highly unlikely that the British would have given such
support to a scheme so apparently federal at a time when the
American Civil War seemed to have discredited all such systems.
Cardwell's reaction to the policy of the Grand Coalition in July
1864 is instructive here:

> I was a little startled when I heard the word *Federation*, for
> Federal Gov^t. has not risen in public estimation recently
> either in America or in Europe. But if I correctly understand
> what your advisers are likely to propose it will not be
> *Federation* in the real meaning of that word but *union* of
> many municipalities under one Supreme Legislature. This
> will exclude altogether the States-rights question which has
> broken up the U. States . . .

Consequently Cardwell could in good conscience assure the agi-
tated Gordon that 'we all agree in favouring a complete fusion, not
a federation' and 'it signifies little what name is employed'.[58]
Gradually this latter sentiment was discarded. Concerned to
elevate the central power, Cardwell even deleted the word
'federal' from a draft despatch altogether – a far cry from thirty
years earlier when Howick had watered down 'federal authority'
to 'federal body' to make it more innocuous.[59] In September
1866 Monck actually apologised for ever having used the term
'federation', explaining at some length its inappropriateness.[60] At
the Westminster Palace Hotel conference in December 1866,
the colonial delegates obligingly substituted 'Confederation' for
'federation' wherever it appeared in the Quebec resolutions. Both
sets of resolutions were put into confidential print in the Colonial
Office, in parallel columns, with changes italicised for easy
reference. Logically the entire word 'Confederation' should thus
have been italicised, but in every case only the first three letters

were so treated.[61] It was a small change, but undoubtedly felt to be a significant one.

*   *   *

Why did British opinion wish to see a regional union created in British North America? Three main areas of motive may be discerned. First, a regional union might either control or accommodate the French. Unfortunately, the incompatibility of these alternative aims tended to torpedo projects founded on either. Secondly, a regional union might provide the framework for extending colonial autonomy, or emerge as a logical corollary of an increasingly wide measure of self-government. At a practical level it might provide the colonies with better government, while on a more elevated plane it might foster some form of 'colonial nationhood'. Thirdly, and most compelling of all, British North American union was seen as a means of creating a check upon the United States. These categories can only be rough. Many enthusiasts were undoubtedly attracted to the idea of nation building for its own sake. They employed arguments which they thought would impress others, and the balance of these arguments changed from the 1830s to the 1860s as the power of the USA grew. Although tidy logic might expect federal schemes to make most headway as Britain sought to reconcile the French and adjust to the transition to self-government, it was in fact not until the late 1840s, when colonial autonomy was secure and French Canada dropped into the hazy background of British perceptions, that support became general. The decisive thread in support for regional union was dislike of the United States and most of the minor arguments advanced – for instance in favour of colonial nationhood and better government – were directed against annexation. In this context, it is pointless to argue whether the British wanted or expected the British North American provinces to become 'independent'. Their precise constitutional relationship with Britain was irrelevant; what mattered was that they remain independent of the United States.

British North American union as a means of solving the imperial quarrel with French Canada was much discussed in the late 1830s. Those, primarily supporters of federation, who hoped to conciliate the French within a framework of British interests, had the ground cut from under them by the rebellions of 1837–8. Those, chiefly supporters of legislative union, who wished to bring in a British population to control the French, had to settle for the immediately feasible target of Canadian Union, however much they may have hoped for its eventual extension. But by 1842, when a French bloc forced its way into office in alliance with English Reformers, it should have been clear enough that the French fact would not go away and that any wider union would merely spread its influence, for good or ill, onto a broader canvas,.

James Stephen was one man who tried to draft a federal scheme which would meet French grievances without requiring the British government to make the politically impossible concession of local supremacy to a hostile community. In December 1836 he had outlined a partition of Lower Canada itself into English- and French-speaking areas, the whole to be governed by a commission drawn from both the Canadas. In January 1837 he extended this to create a commission of five members from each of the four mainland colonies. The committee would come into being when fifteen members were appointed, but its quorum for meetings was eleven: French Canada could neither boycott nor control it.[62] As R. B. Sullivan later remarked, all these schemes to enable the English to control the French were 'founded upon a fallacy', that of 'a supposed unanimity of purpose among the whole British party'. Stephen's plan was half-heartedly adopted by the cabinet but was dropped as opposition politicians began to make headway in Upper Canada and particularly in Nova Scotia.[63] Joseph Howe, who failed to stop Confederation in 1867, unknowingly blocked its predecessor in 1837.

When news of the 1837 rebellion reached London, Russell consulted a former governor, Sir James Kempt, to ask him 'what he thought of summoning the British colonies to redress the balance of the French'. Kempt apparently advised that communications ruled out closer union.[64] Stephen and Howick continued to press for an intercolonial convention – by now of all five provinces – which might constitute itself into a more permanent federal body if it so wished, and as both men hoped. Stephen argued that Britain would gain moral authority by transferring responsibility for the settlement of the Lower Canadian constitution to British North America as a whole, Howick felt that English-speaking colonists would feel less hostile to concessions to French Canada if made through a body controlled by themselves and thereby guaranteeing their economic

interests against 'the asserted anti-commercial spirit of the legislation of the French'.[65] Sir George Arthur, lieutenant-governor of
Upper Canada, was similarly assured that the main purpose of
a strong federal authority would be to prevent French-Canadian
interference with the interests of his province.[66] But the weakness
of this approach in the aftermath of the rebellions was that it still
involved some degree of trust in French Canada: it was liberalism
posing as *realpolitik*. The fact that the radical J. A. Roebuck, who
was agent for the Lower Canada assembly, could espouse the
case made it suspect. To Melbourne he argued 'if England fears
the French Canadians, the way to balance their power is by
means of a federation of the Colonies' which 'would for all general
purposes secure a preponderance of what are termed (though
falsely) English interests' while leaving French Canada with its
own laws and customs. Roebuck was one man for whom British
North American union became a vision to be pursued for its own
sake, and the consistent spur which motivate him was undoubtedly
a wish to check the expansion of the United States, but at this
stage he was equally being loyal to his employers, as he revealed
shortly after to Durham declaring that federation was a 'subsidiary
purpose' to the restoration of elective institutions in Lower
Canada.[67] Hence it was just plausible for opponents to denounce
federation as a surrender to the French.[68] If the 1837 rising made
it difficult for the British to contemplate any form of local
autonomy for the French, its sequel in 1838 made it impossible.
Melbourne concluded that 'we can never suffer the French to
govern or to have much influence in Lower Canada again', noting
pessimistically that this would rule out any form of representative
government, federal or unitary. Yet 'the fundamental principle
that the French must not be reinstated to power in Lower Canada'
clearly weighed more against the first solution than the second,
and there was thus no alternative to the largest feasible legislative
union, that of the two Canadas. Even Charles Buller, who had
started as a federalist, could state in February 1839 that 'the
great argument against a federal Union is that it does nothing to
obtain the main end which we ought to have in view' which was
'the keeping Lower Canada quiet now, & making it English as
speedily as possible'. Arbitrary rule, the only other alternative, was
inadequate because 'an English Assembly would be much more
rigorous in repressive measures than a Governor & Council'.[69]
General federation, which would accommodate the French, was

thus rejected in favour of Canadian union, which would control them.

To a striking extent, the existence of French Canada, which ought to have been a basic element in any British thinking about the provinces, almost totally vanished from later discussion of regional union. Few seemed even to grasp that any move towards wider union would endanger the achievement of the later 1840s, the recognition of Anglo-French partnership in Canada. Elgin had briefly consoled himself in April 1847, when negotiations with the French broke down, that a continuation of communal politics would point to a federation with the English-speaking Maritimes. When the British American League espoused the idea for the same reason in 1849, Elgin, by now successfully presiding over a communal partnership, was totally unsympathetic.[70] Head's outline federal plan of 1851 mentioned, more or less as an afterthought, that the French would recover their autonomy while being placed in an overall minority, and Russell stressed the second element when he revived his support for federation after the defeat of the Militia Bill in 1862.[71] Stanley in 1858 briefly wondered whether the French could not be trusted to rule the Lower Canadian minority, but Galt's advocacy of federation presumably stilled his fears on that point.[72] Overall, however, the French ceased to be not simply a motive but even an element in British thinking about colonial union.

British governments, Stephen complained in December 1837, too often made 'the error of acting upon a policy which is purely occasional and transitional and which does not attempt the anticipation of events'. He favoured a 'forecasting Policy' which would 'deliberately, although of course unavowedly' prepare for a painless transfer of authority to the colonies. His plan for a federation of the Canadas, extended early in 1837 to the four mainland colonies, pointed 'towards a new Congress on the North American Continent'. Even if not a popular conclusion, 'the time must arrive when some such Body may be required to facilitate the relaxation, if not the actual abandonment of a rule, which, in the nature of human affairs, cannot be very protracted . . . . Canadian independence yielded to a Central Body of this kind, may be said to be the Euthanasia of the present Constitution'. [73] Stephen was not an 'anti-imperialist' anxious to 'abandon' the colonies. Indeed, he criticised 'the assumption that between colonial dependence, & national independence, there is no resting place or middle point'. It would be possible to aim for the 'silent substitution' of a partnership to replace 'dominion on the one side, & subjection on the other'. Howick similarly thought that a federal system would 'enable the Home Government gradually to relax the reins of its authority and to substitute a system of ruling by influence for one of direct control.' However, this approach was too subtle for many contemporaries. 'It is at once giving to these provinces the Constitution of the United States,' Melbourne protested, '& leaving the People nothing to do but to ship off your Governor & elect a President'. The Conservative *Morning Herald*, which a decade later was to welcome talk of federation, similarly complained that federation would give British North America one neck for a 'profligate and fortunate demagogue' to strike off the British connection, enabling 'some O'Connell or Papineau' to 'clamber into the president's chair of a new American republic'.[74] The argument that federation should be adopted as a step to independence was most likely in the 1830s to appeal to radicals.[75] Others, however, could be ambivalent. In opposing Howick's quasi-federal scheme in March 1839, Russell argued that in every federation 'the federal power is the supreme power' and asked 'with a neighbouring Congress at Washington, will not the federal body aim at the authority now held by the Mother Country?' But a year earlier, thinking out loud in the House of Commons, Russell had opposed 'immediate independence' for British North America, but had accepted that under undisclosed future circumstances, the colonies might be 'formed into a separate and distinct state, in alliance, offensive and defensive, with this country'.[76]

When Roebuck revived the argument that federation and independence were linked in 1849, its balance was subtly changed. Why not keep the colonies separate? Roebuck asked rhetorically. '*They* would be happy and well-governed – and *we* should be secure in our dominion.' His answer was that the colonies were already moving towards an independence which they were not large enough to sustain. 'Canada, if she once rebelled, must be independent; and when she becomes independent, she must be part of the United States.' Britain must work 'to render the existence of a new confederation not only probable but certain'. British North American union was now a logical sequel to an emerging colonial autonomy, a framework not to provide independence from Britain but to ensure independence from the

United States. Responding to the Montreal annexation manifesto, *The Times* called federation an 'intermediate course' which would give 'the discontented colony independence without forcing her into rivalry or hostility'. It was the 'pressing danger' of annexation which brought Russell to reconsider the federal option. The provinces 'would soon be strong enough to form a state of themselves, but if in strict alliance with this country, I do not think that result ought to alarm us'.[77]

During the 1850s, British North American union continued to be seen as the logical sequel to the degree of self-government already achieved than as the means for widening its scope. Although Stanley in 1858 thought that the provinces would 'at some time more or less remote' become formally independent of Britain, Head's first federal project was based on the assumption that it was not impossible 'that the connection should be maintained for an indefinite period'. Indeed, the supreme power of the external crown was fundamental to his ideas of federal–provincial relations. Lytton believed that the sectionalism of any future federation 'would make them dislike the idea of any native Presidential authority' in preference to a British governor-general.[78]

Thus the logical idea of using regional union as a framework for further colonial autonomy died away to a whisper. Related to it were two more persistent arguments which pointed to union as a means of better government – one that it would provide a structure for cooperation, and the other that the resulting institutions would attract abler political leaders. The *Globe* in 1838 argued that federation would give 'all the advantages of a representative government, while it guards against the mistakes and occasional effects of personal collisions to which small communities are exposed'. Goldwin Smith a quarter century later similarly saw federation as combining 'at once the peace of great Empires, the active intelligence of small communities, the mutual education and discipline of a cluster of independent nations'. Yet, as Elliot cynically pointed out in 1858, while federation would give the colonies a focus for cooperation which they lacked, so too would it provide them with fresh theatre of potential collision. In fact, British concern was less with the institutions than the men operating them. Grey, Blackwood and Newcastle all saw the union of the provinces as the best cure for the faction-ridden pettiness which – to them – characterised so many colonial legislatures. Yet here a number of problems arose. Why should British North American politics be any more elevated simply because its leading figures were gathered under one roof? Murdoch in 1849 could see only one argument for federation: it would bring 'a more extended public opinion and more varied and independent interests to bear on Colonial politics' and create 'more extended and liberal views in the members' as they became conscious of their increased responsibilities. A more realistic conclusion might have been that the more 'independent interests' introduced into the colonial arena, the more people would have to be paid off in some way. Certainly the more prosperous and assured Canada grew, the less she responded to the 'extended and liberal views' which British orthodoxy required on the matter of tariffs. Federation, the *Saturday Review* snarled in 1862, might breed statesmen who did not measure profundity of policy 'by the depths to which it was warranted to dive into the pockets of British taxpayers, and by the refinements by which it could irritate and injure British trade'. If Canadian politicians could not rise to the visionary challenge of governing their great Laurentian province, would they really be improved by the transfusion of the sordid parochialism of the Maritimes? Canada, as Elliot observed, had so little trade with the Maritimes that little but 'barren symmetry' would be gained through assimilating tariffs. It was hardly encouraging that Mulgrave should note in 1858 that a larger union was commonly supported by Nova Scotian enthusiasts with the argument that it 'would place within their grasp, prizes more worthy of their ambition, than any offices to which they could aspire, in their own Province'.[79]

Ministers vaguely hoped that a union of the lower provinces would somehow create one good legislature out of three bad ones, although Blackwood in 1863 gloomily pointed out the population of the Maritimes was much less than that of Canada, then no model of political rectitude. If a wider federation were created without an accompanying Maritime Union, Manners Sutton feared that the best men would be drawn off to the centre leaving the local assemblies pettier than ever.[80] Even if such good men existed would they be elected? Durham had envisaged a federal assembly elected only by the 'better class' of colonists, but narrow franchises had become untenable in the colonies by the 1860s when Gordon bewailed the way in which gentlemen were being driven out of politics by grog-shopkeepers and petty attorneys.

Worse still, to create the elevated polity which would breed the elevated politics, it would presumably be necessary at some stage to win over precisely the breed of parochial politician it was hoped to eliminate. Elgin on his arrival in Canada brought Grey bluntly to earth, telling him that his discussions of the problems involved in uniting the provinces had omitted 'the greatest of them all – vz, the materials with which I have to work'. Bannerman of Newfoundland gloomily responded to the federal initiative of 1858 'there could not be a worse Tribunal for its discussion than Delegates chosen from the Executive Councils'.[81]

Many British observers had set their eyes on some higher level, and here they were in some cases encouraged by the more gentlemanly and tory of the colonials. Durham was heartened to find that 'the leading minds of the various Colonies' supported 'a scheme that would elevate their countries into something like a national existence'.[82] Sir John Harvey tried to take advantage of an intercolonial conference at Halifax in 1849, to bring about a federation, 'the only remedy for the existing state of things because the only measure by which that species of *Nationality*, evidently contemplated by Lord Durham, can be conferred upon them'. This loyalist tradition valued a sense of nationality as a barrier against the United States, not against Britain. A detailed scheme from C. R. Ogden, received with some respect in the Colonial Office in 1850, made 'a National individuality and identity' its aim but took as its slogan 'Colonial Independence, – under the Flag'.[83] British leaders shared these ideas. Peel in 1838 thought that the union of the provinces 'would tend to elevate them in the scale of civilisation', and Russell in 1849 thought federation would give the colonists 'something to look to, which shall be above and beyond the miserable struggles in which they have been so long engaged'. A court official, Lord Edward Howard, pressed on Russell a plan for a British American monarchy, to 'give a *nationality*' to the colonies and make them into a '(so to speak) European power', linked to Britain through 'amicable feeling'. Nationality, then, was not synonymous with breaking with Britain. It too was a means of stopping a drift towards the United States. Canadians, Head concluded in 1853, were not prepared to sink to the level of slave-catchers in an American republic, so long as Britain gave the province 'freedom enough, as we do now & foster her own sense of self-importance . . . especially if any sense of *united interest* in all the British Provinces can be created. Whether Canada belongs nominally or not to England is comparatively immaterial'.[84]

Each of these motives, then, made sense not in a British North American vacuum, but as reflections of a deeper wish to create a continental balance and a barrier against the United States. As early as 1784 Colonel Morse had anticipated that a united British North America might be 'made a formidable rival to the American states'. Stephen in 1836 saw federation as a means of 'raising on the North American Continent a counter poise to the United States', and Howick and Durham both saw it as a means of resisting American influence. The staunchest voice was Roebuck's: British North American federation would 'check and control' the United States, he argued in April 1837. Perhaps he was merely appealing to a common prejudice to deflect criticism from his French Canadian paymasters: certainly his tone grew more strident in 1838, when he urged that 'a northern confederacy' would 'balance the colossal empire' of the USA. But even so, the fact that he thought it worthwhile to appeal to the prejudice would seem to underline its strength. 'Would not the consolidation of a British American Union be a good check on the growth of United States superiority?' asked the Conservative *Morning Post* in October 1838.[85] Yet when Roebuck campaigned for federation again in 1849, there seems little doubt that his chief argument – the need to create 'a counterpoise to the gigantic empire and influence of the United States' – was no mere cover. If the republic swallowed the provinces, it would 'have no frontier to defend' and its 'influence would become dangerous to the liberty of the world' since annexation would be 'fatal to the maritime supremacy of England'. Lord Edward Howard saw general union as 'a counter-balancing power to democracy' while Russell came round to federation in the face of the 'pressing danger' of annexation. *The Times* was also spurred by annexation threats to ask:

> Is it impossible to devise such a Government – whether Royal, Imperial, or Republican – as, by consolidating the three North American provinces, would erect a huge breakwater between us and our nearest but most formidable rival?

What is striking about these sentiments is the anticipation of inevitable American hostility at a period in which the British political nation is normally thought to have been riding on a crest of self-confidence, and when the United States had concluded an external war with Mexico and seemed on the verge of an internal one over slavery. Thus C. R. Ogden could warn in 1850 that an American blow could be aimed 'when England may be fighting with Russia for Her supremacy, nay for her existence as a great Nation, on the plains of Hindostan'.

Such sentiments became more pertinent in the later 1850s, a time of resurgent American diplomatic hostility, when British confidence was dented by the shocks of the Crimean war and the Indian mutiny. Gladstone's friend, the colonial enthusiast J. R. Godley, wrote in 1854:

> the Statesman must be blind who does not see that *the* great peril which overshadows the future of the civilized world lies in the vast power and progress of the United States, coupled as their gigantic material resources are with unbounded energy and inordinate ambition. To raise up to this over-weening power a rival on its own continent, would be a work far more valuable and important to England than the curbing of the power of Russia. Such a rival as British America would be to the United States, necessarily inferior in power, would for its own sake be a faithful ally to England, for on England's friendship and support her existence would depend. If, on the other hand, the British American States remain disunited, they must be annexed one by one to the mammoth republic.

Godley's statement almost certainly sums up the real motive behind British support for British North American union before 1864. Fear of the United States and the wish to curb its expansion combined to point towards a regional union. The formal connection between Britain and the new polity was irrelevant, since it would in any case depend on Britain to survive. As Head noted in 1858, the balance of power was 'no longer a question purely European in its character', and Britain's aim was to ensure that the provinces had 'the power & the will to stand alone' rather than 'swell the strength of the United States'.[86]

This categorisation of British motives, with its emphasis on hostility to the expansion of the United States, is at some variance with the oft-attributed British motive in 1864–7 of abandoning any defensive commitment on the American continent. In fact, it seems more reasonable to see Confederation as assisting a change not in the extent but in the means by which Britain undertook its defence obligations. The dramatic 'withdrawal of the legions' in the late 1860s tends to obscure the earlier and more significant reduction in British garrisons as a result of the Crimean war and the ensuing emphasis on concentration of troops for home defence. So small were the remaining garrisons that Lord Grey in 1861 could cynically suggest to a parliamentary enquiry that their chief function was to guard defence installations against vandalism by the local population.[87] Cardwell was certainly obsessed with the fear that such scattered detachments were a positive invitation to a cheap American military triumph and certainly 'no defence to Canada'. This is not to say that Britain intended to renege on her obligation to protect Canada but rather, as *The Times* observed in 1865, that she did not intend to repeat Napoleon's mistake in Russia. Far from being anxious to dump the new Confederation, *The Times* chillingly remarked 'Canada, in fact, can best be defended by attacking her assailants and forcing them to relinquish their hold'.[88] Britain was a naval not a military power, and an Anglo-American war would not be fought by the army on the hopeless ground of Upper Canada but – to use a modern concept – through a strategy of massive retaliation by the navy. Imperial footholds at Quebec and Halifax were all that this strategy needed. True, some saw Confederation as a step towards a total severance, but most British projectors envisaged some continuing connection and in this they were certainly supported by all the fathers of Confederation, with the possible exception of Galt. Herman Merivale tried without much success to link federation with the ending of a British defence commitment when he gave evidence to the parliamentary committee of 1861. Having recently moved to the India Office he felt free of civil service departmental constraints, and casually injected the possibility of regional union into discussion of colonial reluctance to contribute to the cost of British garrisons. 'If you could organize the North American Colonies into a federation, a different question would arise.' Did he mean that regional union would reduce the need to keep troops in British North America?

I think that if the North American Colonies do federate or amalgamate, it will in all probability be under such conditions as will render the slight tie which still subsists between them and us somewhat slighter, and in that case the probability is that it will not be deemed necessary to maintain troops there any longer.

But asked if this would alter the need 'for troops as a nucleus force against the United States' he admitted that the 'military reasons would remain the same'. And if a British North American union continued to tie itself to British foreign policy? 'If you act on that supposition, you must maintain troops there still.' These conditions were more accurately to describe circumstances after 1864.[89] Yet the possibility that regional union might coincide with an outright break from Britain was appreciated. In August 1862, when Anglo-Canadian relations were at a low ebb, Newcastle was attracted to the importance of fortifying St John's, Newfoundland, especially 'if the other BNA Colonies should become independent and Halifax be *their* Port'.[90]

*   *   *

When did the British expect to see the creation of a regional union in British North America? To say that regional union was seen as a development for the future is perhaps to state the obvious, but nonetheless the stress on it as a long-term and inevitable development is striking. Thus Sir Charles Grey's scheme for a federation within Lower Canada included the hope that Upper Canada would join 'at no distant period' and the other provinces 'ultimately'; Sir John Harvey similarly predicted that the Maritimes would soon join a federation of the two Canadas. To Stephen federation was part of a 'forecasting Policy'; to Roebuck it was an act of 'forethought'.[91] Ministers were perhaps more likely to appeal to the future to avoid decisions in the present: Glenelg thought eventual federation 'a subject for deep and future deliberation'; Russell did not rule it out 'at a fit time'. Peel, in opposition, was more forthright. 'I will not abandon the hope that such a union may some day be formed.' Even Ellice, hostile to immediate federation, thought 'that desirable end' might 'ultimately' be brought about. Ellenborough thought federal union would 'ultimately be necessary', and Buller stood by the Durham view that Canadian Union should in due course be extended to the other colonies.[92]

In the late 1840s Grey acted as if others would pursue his aim. Regional union was 'highly desirable' and 'the probability that

at some future time this may have to be attempted ought never
to be lost sight of'. It was, however, still a 'distant vision' not
likely to come about during his term of office. It was 'not a matter
to be pressed forward in a hurry, all that can be done is to throw
out the general idea & to endeavour to lead mens minds in that
direction'. When others became enthusiastic in 1849, he could
still conclude that general union was 'for the present at least
premature'.[93]

Slow but steady was still the approach of the early 1850s.
Consolidation would 'eventually' solve the problems of petty
governments, Newcastle wrote in 1853. The *Morning Chronicle*
criticised the provinces for failing to work for common interests
'as if isolation, instead of federation, were the object they had in
view'. The *Morning Herald* recalled that it had 'advocated the
union as a thing to be brought about, not immediately, but at
no very distant day'.[94] Manners Sutton in 1855 reported on the
way New Brunswickers seemed keen to move 'in the direction,
which may be supposed to lead to the prospective union of the
British North American Provinces', a despatch which drew a
succinct comment from Merivale: 'This points to federal union.'
Russell, temporarily back at the Colonial Office, merely observed
'a very natural wish, but premature'. Federation, Merivale
recalled of Labouchere, who was colonial secretary from 1855 to
1858, was something which the British should be ready to support
when the provinces asked for it.[95] Stanley in 1858 thought it
would be their 'ultimate form' of government, and more strikingly,
Lord Mulgrave, who opposed the initiative of 1858, could still
predict in a critical despatch that 'ultimately, the British North
American possessions will become one great, and, independent
Country'. Newcastle in 1861 could describe general union 'as an
object to prepare for and eventually effect' even though 'the time
is not yet'. Goldwin Smith was for once speaking with general
support when he claimed that the provinces were 'plainly destined
to form a united confederation'.[96]

The British, then, regarded regional union as a more or less
inevitable future development. Yet that does not explain how
that future was in fact realised. The future is a great reservoir for
procrastination, and the mere strength of the sentiment might
simply have consigned Confederation to the Canadian Kalends.
Related examples are not hard to find. Mid-century Americans
believed they did not need to hurry the annexation of Canada,

because Manifest Destiny taught them that the provinces would inevitably drop in their laps. Late Victorian British statesmen perhaps more willingly assigned the great task of imperial federation to the broad shoulders of posterity. In each case the passage of years made the aim less and less feasible of realisation, even allowing that it had ever been so. What marked the British view of future Confederation was two elements: the existence, in however vague a form, of a timetable made up of necessary preliminary steps and – even more crucial – the collapse or telescoping of that timetable so that in 1864 the British were left in no doubt that the future had arrived.

The 'timetable' can most clearly be discerned in ministerial and official circles, the ones most involved in practical relations with the colonies. It was generally agreed that the basic obstacle to closer union of the colonies was poor communications. Hence the main aim must be the construction of a railway linking Halifax with Quebec. In 1849 Grey described this as 'an indispensable preliminary' to general union, something which would not only pave the way for an effective central government, but create through its construction the point of cooperation which Grey had always intended as the germ of unity. Merivale in 1855 commented that railways were 'an essential preliminary' to political union. In July 1861, according to Edward Watkin's perhaps euphoric recollections, the duke of Newcastle shared his view that British North American union would be 'the necessary, the logical result of completing the Intercolonial Railway'.[97]

Thus far, the timetable simply involved a railway leading to a union. This assumed that the rest of British North America would remain undisturbed until the moment when the railway would make union possible. In fact almost every one of the tacit assumptions had broken down by the early 1860s: thus the Grand Trunk, which was to grow into the Intercolonial, was instead heading for bankruptcy, while the problem of the Hudson's Bay territories, which were peacefully to await their eventual transfer to the general union, called increasingly for an early solution. Most important of all, both the Maritimes and the province of Canada encountered problems of government which could not be left to the ripeness of time. The Maritimes could, however, be incorporated into the timetable. Parliamentary government would clearly not work well in such petty provinces, and they should be united, irrespective of any future link with Canada.

Blackwood, indeed, preferred the smaller union to the larger, in which 'the Lower Provinces w^d. be mere tributaries', and Head in 1857 had swung round to thinking general union impossible. Nonetheless, he argued, Maritime Union 'would not in any way prejudice the future consideration of a more extensive union either with Canada or Newfoundland'. It was Newcastle who incorporated the lesser scheme into the timetable, believing that it would help 'create more nearly a union of equals instead of appending three weak Provinces to one strong one'. The timetable now had three elements. 'I have always been of opinion that the necessary preliminary to a Legislative Union of the Lower Provinces is an Intercolonial Railway, and that the completion of *both* these Schemes must precede a Union with Canada', Newcastle wrote in June 1862, at the moment when he was actually abandoning this stately approach.[98]

A solution to the problems of government in the Maritimes, then, might be incorporated into a step-by-step approach to the union of British North America. A breakdown in Canadian politics, on the other hand, could threaten this whole leisurely approach with a need for immediate action. It had been the urgency of Canada's problems in the late 1830s which had swept aside general federation in favour of Canadian Union, because, as Durham acknowledged, 'the period of gradual transition is past in Lower Canada'.[99] But if the Canadian Union itself failed to work, then general union – of a federal rather than a unitary type – could become an immediate rather than a future consideration. Here Sir Edmund Head's temporary apostasy from the federal cause should be considered. As lieutenant-governor of New Brunswick, Head had taken an informed and sympathetic interest in British North American federation. However, his support lapsed after his translation to Canada in 1854, and by 1856 he had concluded that neither federation nor legislative union of the provinces could be practicable. 'I once thought differently but further knowledge and experience have changed my views', he explained – an interesting comment on the depth of British perceptions in support of such schemes. He had been impressed not simply by the *'perfectly astounding'* prosperity of Upper Canada but by the fact that the dynamic growth of the western section of the province was shifting its entire orientation still further from the Maritimes. His federal project of 1851 envisaged the redivision of the Canadas, but by 1857 he insisted 'the separation of the St Lawrence from the Lakes is an alternative not to be thought of for a moment'. He was yet to realise that that same explosion of Upper Canada was itself forcing a renegotiation of the partnership between the Lakes and the St Lawrence. At the start of 1857 Head was convinced that Canada was 'tolerably well satisfied with her own form of Government'.[100] The elections in December 1857 were to shatter that belief. The two sections of the province began to pull in different directions, and the assumption of a Canadian rock on which a British American edifice might be built crumbled. 'In reality' Head reported 'the dispute *now* is whether the Union was not *federal* rather than Legislative in its character.' If the St Lawrence and the Lakes could not be kept together in the existing Union 'the next – indeed the only hope – would be the formation of some gov^t on a still larger scale more or less like a federation which shall gather up the reins & control the St Lawrence as well as the Western & Eastern waters'.[101] The future, in short, had arrived. 'The question, tho' often considered in a speculative point of view,' Stanley commented 'is new to me, &, I believe, to most English public men, in the practical form which it now seems likely to assume.' As it happened, the future had the good taste to go away again almost as soon as the ministerial crisis was solved in August, but no-one could believe it had retreated to its old distance. The Canadian Union, Lytton concluded, 'will not be long tenable' and Confederation was 'one of the most obvious solutions of the serious problem'. 'All British North America is fermenting, and unless care is taken some bottles will burst', Manners Sutton observed in 1858. When colonial politics reached their nadir in 1862–3, it was pardonable that some in Britain should seem to wish to smash the bottles instead. 'A revision of the Union Act is indispensably necessary' concluded the Conservative politician C. B. Adderley 'but how can it be carried with a Parliament so constructed?' Edward Watkin already believed that the cure for Canada's ills was 'a bigger country – a country big enough to breed large ideas.'[102]

The inadequacy of Maritime politics and the increasing threat of paralysis in Canada threw into doubt the entire timetable, especially as it was becoming less convincing to hope that problems could be left to solution in the ripeness of time. There could be no central government without a railway, but would there ever be a railway without a central government to build it? Questioned, to his obvious embarrassment, by the parliamentary committee of 1861 on the implications of British North American federation, Newcastle would say only 'that of course any plan which threw the Government of all these countries into a united power would facilitate arrangements for the construction of railways' by obviating 'the necessity of mutual financial arrangements which at present are inevitable in the various Colonies through which the line must pass.'[103] In other words, British North American union might be the indispensable preliminary for the railway, not vice-versa.

If the assumptions behind the timetable were breaking down, thus threatening to telescope its provisions, the external challenge of the American civil war was to overwhelm it altogether. Here British ideas about the distant future of British North America fused with conflicting assumptions about the outcome of sectional strife in the United States. Broadly, it seems that most Englishmen before 1861 expected the ultimate disruption of the United States, possibly accompanied by a civil war, but few if any anticipated the actual war which broke out that year. 'That it must become overgrown, and then fall to pieces, was assumed from the time when it was first seen to be growing', the pro-Northern *Daily News* complained in 1864. The British were well aware that sectional conflict existed, and from the late 1840s relied on it to discourage annexation impulses in Canada. Yet they were inclined to dismiss secession threats as typical Yankee (or Southern) brag 'for with such a people talking or writing big words is, in fact, their constitutional safety valve'.[104] If 'as some people anticipate' the American republic disintegrated, then the disunity of the provinces would matter less, Head accepted in 1858, but just three years before the civil war that still seemed 'a pure specula- tion: perhaps a remote contingency'. Even in 1860, Watkin recalled, few Englishmen had realised how close was the conflict. Consequently, notions about the future shape of the continent after the dissolution of the United States were also confused. Grey had consoled himself with the thought in 1848 that annexation would probably precipitate a North-South disruption and many in 1860–1 saw the incorporation of Canada into an anti-slavery union as a likely sequel to Southern secession.[105] Gladstone may even have contemplated using Canada as a bait to secure Federal recognition of the Confederacy: certainly he used the possibility of a new northern confederation as one reason why British money should not be risked in railway guarantees.[106]

One man whose inherent tendency to fluster did lead him to foresee the impact of the war was Newcastle. Warned privately by Seward in 1860 that a Republican administration might try to busy giddy minds with foreign quarrels, Newcastle feared not blustering diplomacy but the sequel of a civil war in which armies 'composed of the scum of all nations' would hold politicians to ransom, tempting them 'to seek for safety to themselves temporary though it would be, by directing this blood red stream on our possessions'. This, in turn, created a greater sense if not of urgency then at least of proximity in relation to general union. In March 1861 Newcastle described it as 'what must eventually be brought about and may be hastened by events arising out of the condition of the rest of the Continent'. It was still, however, something which Elliot felt should be 'generally sought by the colonists themselves'.[107] That opportunity seemed to arise when Mulgrave forwarded a Nova Scotian resolution seeking authorisation for intercolonial meeting to discuss some form of union. Newcastle probably attached more importance to this passing outburst of *bonhomie* than it warranted, but his minute of 22 June 1862 indicates that his timetable was now thoroughly telescoped. He had always believed that both the Intercolonial and Maritime Union had to precede a wider union. 'The latter event may be hastened by the present condition of the neighbouring Country, but I do not expect success to any project which attempts it without *settling* (if not *accomplishing*) both the smaller Union and the Railway'.[108] The civil war, then, had made it necessary to tackle the three steps in parallel rather than in sequence. This telescoping of the timetable also helps to explain why Maritime Union, so important as a catalyst in 1864, disappeared from view immediately after: once Confederation became an immediate prospect, there was no need for the intermediate step.

If Newcastle's despatch was intended to stimulate discussion of intercolonial union at the Quebec conference of 1862, it failed. The subject was regarded, one of the delegates recalled, 'as a matter in the distance'.[109] In the autumn of 1862, with still-amateur Federal armies locked in stalemate with the Confederates, it remained possible to interpret the civil war as time gained for the provinces. By 1864 few could doubt that the North would win. British support for Confederation was based not on a hardheaded ploy to abandon an indefensible dependency, but was more of a psychological response to a long-anticipated crisis. The future had arrived, and this time, the patching up of a Canadian political crisis would not be enough to make it go away. This sense of a foreshortened future can be seen in the response of Lord Mulgrave, who in 1863 had succeeded as Marquis of Normanby. He had opposed federation as lieutenant-governor of Nova Scotia in 1858, but spoke in favour of Confederation in the House of Lords in 1867. He had, however, not so much changed his mind as his perspective. In 1858 he had predicted that 'ultimately' British North America would unite into 'one great, and, independent Country'. In 1865 he was to tell Joseph Howe that his theoretical objections remained unchanged. 'The state of things had however sadly changed during the last two or three years. The US from being a purely Commercial Country has now become a Military warlike & very aggressive power', exuding ill-feeling towards Britain and the provinces '& it is I fear more than probable that the war once over she may evince those feelings in a manner even more unmistakeable'. How could the provinces be defended in the event of a massive American invasion? 'I believe the only safety for the Whole is *Union*, the *Intercolonial railroad* & the erection of certain strong fortifications together with a thorough organiz^n of the Local forces & then with the assistance which I am sure England would under those circumstances willingly render I believe you might rest in peace & bid defiance to the Yankees.' Hence, as *The Times* commented on New Brunswick criticisms of the Quebec scheme, 'under present circumstances even an imperfect Federation is better than none at all'. 'I cannot agree with you in thinking that the reflecting people who wish for a closer Union will wish this occasion to be permitted to pass by unimproved', Cardwell wrote to Gordon. 'When is the Imperial Parl^t. likely to have a better opportunity of enacting that closer union than now?'[110] In fact the sense of futurity did not vanish altogether after 1864: the Confederation of 1867 was seen as an interim settlement. The smaller provinces would surely join, and the local legislatures would wither away in a sense of their own futility. But those were comforting ideas about the development of a Confederation which had itself materialised out of a foreshortened future on the ruins of a collapsed mental timetable.

Any explanation of the success of Confederation after 1864 must take account of British support for the idea of British North American union. Any explanation of British support of that idea must start with the existence of the idea itself. A constructive mixture of sophistication and vagueness, it emerged from the British file on empire to impose its own logic on the bewildering developments of the mid-1860s. The idea did not have to dictate to circumstance, for circumstance could only be understood as announcing that its time had arrived.

NOTES

1. A. P. Thornton, *The Imperial Idea and its enemies: a study in British power* (London, 1959) p. ix.
2. James A. Gibson, 'The Colonial Office View of Canadian Federation, 1856–1868', *Canadian Historical Review*, xxxv, 1954, pp. 279–313; L. F. S. Upton, 'The Idea of Confederation, 1754–1858' in W. L. Morton, ed., *The Shield of Achilles* (Toronto, 1968) pp. 184–207; Bruce A. Knox, 'The Rise of Colonial Federation as an Object of British Policy, 1850–1870', *Journal of British Studies*, xi, 1972, pp. 92–112. The best modern accounts of Confederation are W. L. Morton, *The Critical Years: the Union of British North America 1857–1873* (Toronto, 1964); D. G. Creighton, *The Road to Confederation: The Emergence of Canada 1863–1867* (Toronto, 1964) and P. B. Waite, *The Life and Times of Confederation 1864–1867* (Toronto, 1962). R. G. Trotter, *Canadian Federation: Its Origins and Achievements: a Study in Nation-Building* (Toronto, 1924) and W. M. Whitelaw, *The Maritimes and Canada before Confederation* (Toronto, 1934) remain useful for the whole period. This essay draws upon G. W. Martin, 'Britain and the Future of British North America, 1837–1867' (Ph.D thesis, Cambridge, 1972).
3. Thornton, *Imperial Idea and Its Enemies*, p. 21.
4. Mrs Wilson's remark is in Ch. 38 of Mrs Gaskell's *Mary Barton*, first published in 1848; *Sunday Times*, 27 May 1849.
5. *The Times*, 12 July 1854; 2 June 1863.
6. Trinity College Cambridge, Whewell Papers, 0.18.E1/47, Edward Everett to Whewell, 23 December 1844; Thomson to Russell, 28 May 1840 in Paul Knaplund, ed., *Letters of Lord Sydenham Governor-General of Canada, 1839–1841, to Lord John Russell* (London 1931) pp. 69–72.
7. *Speech of the Hon. Joseph Howe in the Union of the North American Provinces and on the Right of British Colonists to Representation in the Imperial Parliament and to Participation in the Public Employments and Distinctions of the Empire* (London 1855) p.10; Public Record Office, CO 42/656, minute by Blackwood, 20 September 1866, fos 367–368.
8. University of Durham, Grey Papers, Russell to Grey, 16 March 1848.
9. Public Record Office, CO 42/546, minute by Stephen, 3 September 1847,

fo. 217; Martin, 'Britain and the Future of British North America', pp. 31–8.

10. Public Archives of Canada, Elgin Papers, microfilm A-309, Hincks to Bruce, 10 December 1853.

11. William Ormsby, *The Emergence of the Federal Concept in Canada 1839–1845* (Toronto, 1969).

12. *The Times*, 11 January 1849.

13. E. G. Wakefield, *A View of the Art of Colonization* (London, 1849) p. 146. For the 'official mind', see R. Robinson and J. Gallagher with A. Denny, *Africa and the Victorians: the Official Mind of Imperialism* (London, 1965).

14. *The Times*, 6 May 1850; Public Archives of Canada, Monck Papers, microfilm A-755, Cardwell to Monck, 11 August 1864.

15. W. Baillie-Hamilton, 'Forty-Four Years at the Colonial Office,' *Nineteenth Century and after*, lxv, 1909, pp. 603, 601; Cambridge University Library, Add. MS 7511, diary of James Stephen, 20 March 1846; Hughenden Manor, Disraeli Papers, B/XX/He/5, Carnarvon to Disraeli, private, 9 October 1866.

16. Public Record Office, CO 537/137, confidential minute, 30 April 1836, ff. 29–49; University of Durham, Grey Papers, Colonial Papers, 100, 101 (draft), 29 December 1837; Melbourne to Howick, 2 January 1838.

17. Murdoch's memorandum, dated 23 May 1849, is in University of Nottingham, Newcastle Papers, NeC 11276. Its removal from the official files confirms Newcastle's continuing interest in the subject in the 1850s. For the debate on Roebuck's motion, *Hansard's Parliamentary Debates*, 3rd series, cv, 24 May 1849, cols 928–61.

18. R. G. Trotter, 'The British Government and the Proposal of Federation in 1858', *Canadian Historical review*, xiv, 1933, pp. 285–92.

19. Rogers to Miss K. Rogers, 23 December 1864, in G. E. Marindin, ed., *Letters of Frederic, Lord Blachford, Under Secretary of State for the Colonies 1860–1871* (London, 1896) pp. 252–3.

20. *North British Review*, xvii, 1852, p. 27; B. K. Martin, *The Triumph of Lord Palmerston: a Study of Public Opinion in England before the Crimean war* (London, 1924) p. 87.

21. *Dublin University Magazine*, xxv, 1850, p. 161; *The History of The Times* (5 vols, London, 1935–52), ii, p. 131. For an account of Derby's interview with Smith, University of New Brunswick, Stanmore Papers, microfilm no. 2, Sir Fenwick Williams to Gordon, 15 July 1865.

22. Public Record Office, CO 537/137, secret minute, 20 December 1836, ff. 144–69; epitome of proposed Canada Act, 19 January 1937, ff. 196–202; University of Durham, Grey Papers, journal of Lord Howick, 18, 23, 26 January 1837.

23. *Hansard's Parliamentary Debates*, 3rd series, xxxvii, 14 April 1837, cols 1209–29.

24. *Sun*, 18 December 1837; Examiner, 21 January 1838, pp. 32–3; *Spectator*, 3 February 1838, pp. 97–8; *Eclectic Review*, n.s. iii, January 1838, pp. 235–8.

25. Ormsby, *The Emergence of the Federal Concept in Canada*, pp. 14–16; C. P. Lucas, ed., *Lord Durham's Report on the Affairs of British North America* (3 vols, Oxford 1912), ii, p. 304.

26. National Library of Scotland, Ellice Papers, E55, Turton to Ellice, 4 August 1838, ff. 122–3.

27. Ellice attacked the scheme through the *Morning Chronicle*, 17 October 1838, and was identified by *The Times*, 18 October 1838 and admitted in National Library of Scotland, Ellice Papers, E 30, Ellice to Durham (copy), [30 December 1838], ff. 74–6. But shortly afterwards he argued that a federation of the Canadas would leave the possibility of wider union. Public Record Office, CO 880/1, Ellice to Melbourne, private, 24 February 1839, ff. 12–14

28. *Morning Herald*, 20, 22 October 1838; *Morning Post*, 9 October 1838; and cf *Globe*, 8, 10 October 1838.

29. Lucas, ed., *Lord Durham's Report*, ii, pp. 304–23; *Hansard's Parliamentary Debates*, 3rd series, xlvii, 3 June 1839, col. 1264 (Russell); liii, 13 April 1840, col. 1065 (Peel).

30. Public Record Office, CO 42/534, Grey to Elgin (draft), no. 10, 31 December 1846, ff. 369–79.

31. Grey to Elgin, private, 16 June 1847, in A. G. Doughty, ed., *The Elgin-Grey Papers 1846–1852* (4 vols, Ottawa, 1937) pp. 47–8.

32. J. A. Roebuck, *The Colonies of England* (London, 1849); *Hansard's Parliamentary Debates*, 3rd series, cv, 24 May 1849, cols. 928–64; *Morning Post*, 28 May 1849; *Morning Herald*, 25 May 1849; *Morning Chronicle*, 24 May 1849; *Daily News*, 23 May 1849; *Globe*, 25 May 1849; *Examiner*, 26 May 1849, pp. 323–5; *Eclectic Review*, n.s., xxv (1849) pp. 761–2; *Simmonds Colonial Magazine*, xvi (1849) pp. 193–207; *Dublin University Magazine*, xxv (1850) pp. 151–68.

33. *The Times*, 23 January 1847, 31 October 1849; University of Durham, Grey Papers, Russell to Grey, 6 August 1849; Grey to Elgin, 8 August 1849, in Doughty, ed., *Elgin-Grey Papers*, i, pp. 437–8.

34. Chester Martin, 'Sir Edmund Head's first project of federation, 1851', *Canadian Historical Association Annual Report*, 1928, pp. 14–28; Public Record Office, CO 188/119, minute by Newcastle, 7 June 1853, f. 274.

35. *Spectator*, 17 September 1853, p. 885; Public Archives of Canada, Newcastle Papers, microfilm A-309, Hincks to F. Bruce, 10 December 1853; Public Record Office, CO 217/216, P.S. Hamilton to Molesworth, 15 August 1855, ff. 224–7.

36. University of New Brunswick, Stanmore Papers, Newcastle to Gordon, private, 28 November 1863; Rogers to Lady Rogers, 17 June 1860, in Marindin, ed., *Letters of Lord Blachford*, pp. 227–8.

37. *The Times*, 15 November 1855.

38. Ibid., 6 November 1855; J. R. Vincent, ed., *Disraeli, Derby and the Conservative Party: Journals and Memoirs of Edward Henry, Lord Stanley, 1849–1869* (Hassocks, 1978) pp. 153–9.

39. Stanley to Head, 7 April 1858; Head to Stanley, 28 April 1858; Merivale to Stanley, 8 September 1858, in Bruce A. Knox, 'The British Government, Sir Edmund Head, and British North American Confederation, 1858', *Journal of Imperial and Commonwealth History*, iv, 1975–6, pp. 206–17.

40. Hertfordshire County Record Office, Lytton Papers, D/EK/01, Lytton to Prince Albert (copy), 9 September 1858; D/EK/01, memorandum by Merivale, 6, 22 September 1858; R. G. Trotter, 'The British government

and the proposal of federation in 1858'; Public Record Office, CO 42/ 614, Lytton to Head (draft), no. 55, 10 September 1858, ff. 297–300, partly printed in G. P. Browne, ed., *Documents on the Confederation of British North America* (Toronto, 1969) p. 2; Lytton to Derby, 7 September 1858, in Bruce A. Knox, 'Sir Edward Lytton and Confederation 1858', *Canadian Historical Review*, liii, 1972, pp. 108–11.

41. National Library of Wales, Harpton Court Collection, C/2028, Merivale to Lewis, [23 September 1858]; *The Times*, 3 September 1858; Public Archives of Canada, Galt Papers, vol. 7, Galt to Mrs Galt, 30 September 1858, pp. 2382–5.

42. Public Record Office, Russell Papers, PRO 30/22/31, Russell to Newcastle, copy, confidential, 12 June 1862, ff. 97–8; Goldwin Smith, *The Empire* (Oxford, 1863) pp. 101–2, 199–200.

43. *Daily News*, 28 September 1862; *The Times*, 29 September, 1 October 1862; *Spectator*, 23 August 1862, pp. 932–3.

44. P. S. Hamilton, Observations upon a union of the colonies of British *North America* (Halifax 1855) p. 25.

45. Public Record Office, Russell Papers, PRO 30/22/8A, Grey to Russell, 8 August 1849, ff. 62–5.

46. University of Durham, Grey Papers, Palmerston to Grey, 4 January 1838; Public Office, Russell Papers, PRO 30/22/3C, memorandum by Russell, 28 March 1839, f. 998–1001.

47. Henry Bliss, *An Essay on the Re-construction of Her Majesty's Government in Canada*, (London, 1839) p. 101.

48. Lucas, ed., op. cit., ii, p. 304; Elgin to Grey, private, 7 May 1847; same to same, private, 3 September 1849, Doughty, ed., op. cit., i, 34–7, ii, 463–6.

49. C. Martin, 'Sir Edmund Head's first project of federation', p. 24.

50. Roebuck, *Colonies of England*; C. Martin, 'First project'; Cartier, Ross and Galt to Lytton, 23 October 1858, in O. D. Skelton, *Life and times of Sir Alexander Tilloch Galt* (Toronto, 1920) pp. 239–42.

51. Howick to Durham, 7 February 1839, in A. G. Doughty, *Report of the Public Archives for 1923* (Ottawa, 1924) pp. 338–40; Roebuck, op. cit., pp. 176–8.

52. Public Record Office, CO 217/221, Mulgrave to Lytton, confidential, 30 December 1858, ff. 556–78.

53. Cf Bliss, *Essay*, pp. 104–5; Public Archives of Canada, Durham Papers 27, Merritt to Durham, 4 October 1838, ff. 262–73; Newcastle Papers, microfilm A-309, Hincks to F. Bruce, 10 December 1853.

54. C. Martin, 'First project'; Head to Stanley, 28 April 1858, in Knox, 'The British Government, Sir Edmund Head, and British North American Confederation', pp. 212–15; *The Times*, 3 September 1858.

55. *The Canadian crisis and Lord Durham's mission* (London, 1838) pp. 42–8; Lucas, ed., op. cit., ii, pp. 320–22; Howick to Durham, 7 February 1839, in Doughty, *Report of the Public Archives for 1923*, pp. 338–40; Grey to Elgin, private, 16 June 1847; same to same, 22 September 1849, Doughty, ed., op. cit., i, pp. 47–8, ii, pp. 470–1.

56. Head to Stanley, 28 April 1858, in Knox, 'The British Government', pp.

212–15; Lytton to Derby, 7 September 1858, in Knox 'Sir Edward Lytton', pp. 110–11.

57. Waite, *The Life and Times of Confederation 1864–1867*, pp. 37n.–38n.

58. Public Archives of Canada, Monck Papers, microfilm A-755, Cardwell to Monck, private, 16 July 1864; University of New Brunswick, Stanmore Papers, microfilm no. 1, Cardwell to Gordon, private, 14 October 1864; same to same, private, 12 November 1864.

59. Public Record Office, CO 42/643, Cardwell to Monck (draft), no. 84, 2 November 1864, f. 132; University of Durham, Grey Papers, Colonial papers, no. 101, 29 December 1837.

60. Public Record Office, CO 42/656, Monck to Carnarvon, confidential, 7 September 1866, f. 335–59, draft printed in W. M. Whitelaw, 'Lord Monck and the Canadian Constitution', *Canadian Historical Review*, XXI, 1940, pp. 298–306.

61. Public Record Office, CO 880/4, confidential print, vii, f. 51–7.

62. Ibid., CO 537/137, secret minute, 20 December 1836, f. 144–69; epitome of proposed Canada Act, 19 January 1837, f. 196–202.

63. Memorandum by Sullivan, [1 June 1838] in C. R. Sanderson, ed., *The Arthur Papers* (3 vols, Toronto, 1957–9) I, pp. 178–81; Public Record Office, CO 537/137, minute, 2 November 1837, f. 210–15.

64. Russell described his enquiry to Kempt in University of Durham, Grey Papers, Russell to Howick, 31 December 1837, and Kempt's reply in *Hansard's Parliamentary Debates*, 3rd series, XLVII, 3 June 1839, col. 1264 and CV, 24 May 1849, cols 955–6.

65. University of Durham, Grey Papers, Stephen to Howick, 28 December 1837; Colonial Papers, no. 99; Royal Archives, Melbourne Papers, Box 7/56, Howick to Melbourne, private, 2 January 1837 [sic for 1838]. Material in the Royal Archives is quoted by gracious permission of H. M. The Queen.

66. Colborne to Arthur, 25 June 1838, in Sanderson, ed., *Arthur Papers*, I, pp. 205–6.

67. Public Archives of Canada, Roebuck Papers, MG 24 A 19, vol. 2, file 8, Roebuck to Melbourne (draft), [29 December 1837]; Roebuck's memorandum to Durham in Roebuck, op. cit., pp. 191–220.

68. E.g . *Morning Chronicle*, 16 October 1838.

69. Melbourne to Russell, 11, 23 December 1838 in L. C. Sanders, ed., *Lord Melbourne's Papers*, (London, 1889) pp. 441–2, 444; Public Archives of Canada, Durham Papers, vol. 28, memorandum by Buller, [February 1839], pp. 194–9.

70. Elgin to Grey, 26 April 1847; same to same, private, 6 August 1849, in Doughty, ed., op. cit., I, pp. 33–4, 440–4.

71. C. Martin, 'First project', pp. 24–5; Public Record Office, Russell Papers, PRO 30/22/31, Russell to Newcastle, copy, confidential, 12 June 1862, f. 97–8.

72. Stanley to Head, 7 April 1858, in Knox, 'The British Government', pp. 210–11.

73. University of Durham, Grey Papers, Stephen to Howick, 28 December 1837, quoted in H. T. Manning, 'Who ran the British empire?', *Journal of British Studies*, V, November 1965, p. 100; Public Record Office, CO

537/137, secret minute, 20 December 1837, ff. 144–69, and cf. epitome of proposed Canada Act, 19 January 1837, ff. 196–202.

74. University of Durham, Grey Papers, Stephen to Howick, 28 December 1837; Colonial Papers, 100, 29 December 1837; Melbourne to Howick, 2 January 1838; *Morning Herald*, 22 October 1838.

75. E.g. Henry Warburton, *Hansard's Parliamentary Debates*, 3rd series, 1̄, 25 January 1838, col. 484.

76. Public Record Office, Russell Papers, PRO 30/22/3C, memorandum, 22 March 1839, f. 12–14; *Hansard's Parliamentary Debates*, 3rd series, x1, 16 January 1838, col. 41.

77. Roebuck, op. cit., pp. 169–70; *Hansard's Parliamentary Debates*, 3rd series, cv, 24 May 1849, cols 928–43; *The Times*, 31 October 1849; University of Durham, Grey Papers, Russell to Grey, 6 August 1849.

78. Stanley to Head, 7 April 1858, in Knox, 'British government', p. 210; C. Martin, 'First project', pp. 17–18; Lytton to Derby, 7 September 1858, in Knox, 'Sir Edward Lytton', pp. 110–11.

79. *Globe*, 8 October 1838; Smith, *The Empire*, pp. 199–200; memorandum by Elliot, 4 November 1858, in R. G. Trotter, 'The British government', pp. 285–92; University of Nottingham, Newcastle Papers, NeC 11276, 23 May 1849; *Saturday Review*, 4 October 1862, pp. 396–7; Public Record Office, CO 217/221, Mulgrave to Lytton, confidential, 30 December 1858, ff. 556–78.

80. Public Record Office, CO 188/119, minute by Newcastle, 7 June 1853, fo. 274; Bodleian Library, Oxford, Clarendon Papers, C-70, Labouchere to Clarendon, private, 30 September 1857, f. 100–1; Public Record Office, CO 188/137, minute by Blackwood, 19 February 1863, fo. 365; CO 188/131, Manners Sutton to Lytton, private and confidential, 2 October 1858, f. 428–42.

81. Durham to Melbourne, 17 July 1838, in S. J. Reid, ed., *Life and Letters of the First Earl of Durham, 1792–1840* (2 vols, London 1906) ii, pp. 222–6; Public Record Office, CO 188/137, Gordon to Newcastle, confidential, 31 December 1862, ff. 341–65; Elgin to Grey, 26 April 1847, in Doughty, ed., op. cit., i., pp. 33–4; Public Record Office, CO 194–153, Bannerman to Lytton, no. 83, 11 October 1858, f. 380–1.

82. Lucas, ed., op. cit., ii, pp. 305–6; and cf. Upton, 'Idea of Confederation'.

83. Public Record Office, CO 217/202, Harvey to Grey, no. 133, 10 August 1849, f. 77–8; CO 42/570, Ogden to Grey, 25 October 1850, f. 244–50.

84. *Hansard's Parliamentary Debates*, 3rd series, 1̄, 26 January 1838, cols 557–8; University of Durham, Grey papers, Russell to Grey, 6 August 1849; Howard to Russell, 7 August 1849, enclosed in Russell to Grey, 19 August 1849; National Library of Wales, Harpton Court Collection, C/1531, Head to Lewis, 29 December 1853, quoted by D. G. G. Kerr, *Sir Edmund Head: a Scholarly Governor* (Toronto, 1954), p. 113.

85. D. Brymner, *Report of the Public Archives for 1884* (Ottawa, 1885) pp. xxvii–lix; Public Record Office, CO 537/137, confidential minute, 30 April 1836, f. 29–49; *Hansard's Parliamentary Debates*, 3rd series, xxxvii, 14 April 1837, cols 1209–9; 1̄, 5 February 1838, col. 770; *Morning Post*, 9 October 1838.

86. Roebuck, op. cit., pp. 188–9; University of Durham, Grey Papers, Howard to Russell, 7 August 1849, enclosed in Russell to Grey, 19 August

1849; Russell to Grey, 6 August 1849; *The Times*, 31 October 1849; Public Record Office, CO 42/570, Ogden to Grey, 25 October 1850, Ogden to grey, 25 October 1850, f. 244–50; Godley to Adderley, 25 August 1854 in *Extracts from letters of J. R. Godley to C. B. Adderley* (London, 1863) pp. 214–16; Head to Stanley, 28 April 1858, in Knox, 'The British Government', 212–15.

87.   C. P. Stacey, *Canada and the British Army 1846–1871: a Study in the Practice of Responsible Government* (rev. edn., Toronto, 1963) pp. 88–91, and cf. *The Times*, 12 December 1854; evidence of Earl Grey to Select Committee on colonial military expenditure, *UK Parliamentary Papers*, 1861, xiii, pp. 69–466, 9 May 1861, q. 2619.

88.   Public Archives of Canada, Monck Papers, microfilm A-755, Cardwell to Monck, 16 July 1864; *The Times*, 20 March 1865.

89.   *UK Parliamentary Papers*, 1861, xiii, pp. 69–466, evidence of Merivale, 6 May 1861, qs 2221, 2222, 2390, 2391, 2392. Donald Creighton, *John A. Macdonald: the young politician* (Toronto, 1952) notes the apparent lack of connection between Confederation and defence in official and ministerial memoranda in 1864.

90.   Public Archives of Canada, Newcastle Papers, microfilm A-309, Newcastle to Bannerman (copy), private, 9 August 1862.

91.   *UK Parliamentary Papers*, 1837, xxiv, report of Sir Charles Grey (17 November 1836) pp. 246–8; Public Archives of Canada, Durham Papers, vol. 18, confidential memorandum by Harvey, 16 August 1838, pp. 378–90; Public Record office, CO 537/137, confidential minute by Stephen, 30 April 1836, f. 29–49; *Hansard's Parliamentary Debates*, 3rd series, xxxvii, 14 April 1837, cols 1209–29.

92.   *Hansard's Parliamentary Debates*, 3rd series, xl, 2 February 1838, col. 484 (Glenelg); 16 January 1838, col. 41 (Russell); 26 January 1838, cols 557–8 (Peel); 26 January 1838, col. 560 (Ellice); 1; 9 July 1840, cols 565–6 (Ellenborough); l; 29 May 1840, col. 740 (Buller).

93.   Grey to Elgin, private, 13 June 1847, 2 June 1847, in Doughty, ed., op. cit., i, pp. 47–8, 37–9; Public Record Office, Russell Papers, PRO 30/22/8A, Grey to Russell, 8 August 1849, f. 62–5.

94.   Public Record Office, CO 188/119, minute by Newcastle, 7 June 1853, f. 274; *Morning Chronicle*, 12 September 1853; *Morning Herald*, 3 November 1853.

95.   Public Record Office, CO 188/124, Manners Sutton to Russell, private and confidential, 20 April 1855, f. 251–3, minute by Merivale, 10 May 1855, f. 253, and Russell, n. d., fo. 413; CO 42/614, minute by Merivale, 31 August 1858, f. 295–6.

96.   Stanley to Head, 7 April 1858, in Knox, 'The British Government', pp. 210–11; Public Record Office, CO 217–221, Mulgrave to Lytton, confidential, 30 December 1858, f. 556–78; University of Nottingham, Newcastle Papers, N. C. 10885 Newcastle to Manners Sutton, (copy), private, 8 March 1861, pp. 41–5; Smith, op. cit., pp. 101–2.

97.   Public Record Office, Russell Papers, Grey to Russell, 8 August 1849, f. 62–5; CO 188/124, minute by Merivale, 3 July 1855, f. 205–15; Edward Watkin, *Canada and the States: Recollections 1851 to 1886 (London, 1887) p. 65b*.

98. Public Record Office, CO 188/131, minute by Blackwood, 20 October 1858, f. 442; Public Archives of Canada, RG 7, G 10, 2, Head to Labouchere, copy, separate, 29 July 1857; Public Record Office, CO 217/230, minute by Newcastle, 22 June 1862, f. 255–6.
99. Lucas, ed., op. cit., II, p. 306.
100. Public Archives of Canada, RG 7, G 9, 32, Head to Labouchere, 3 September 1856; National Library of Wales, Harpton Court Collection, C/1546, Head to Lewis, private, 9 June 1856; Alice R. Stewart, 'Sir Edmund Head's Memorandum of 1857 on Maritime Union: a Lost Confederation Document', *Canadian Historical Review*, XXVI, 1945, pp. 417, 414.
101. Head to Stanley, 28 April 1858, in Knox, 'The British government', pp. 212–15; Public Archives of Canada, J. C. Dent Papers, Head to Hincks, (copy), private, 31 October 1858, enclosed in Hincks to Dent, 12 January 1883.
102. Stanley to Head, 7 April 1858, in Knox, 'The British Government', pp. 210–11; Lytton to Derby, 7 September 1858, in Knox, 'Sir Edward Lytton', pp. 110–11; Public Record Office, CO 188/131, Manners Sutton to Blackwood, private, 30 October 1858, f. 453–8; Public Archives of Canada, Monck Papers, microfilm A-755, Adderley to Monck, 12 June 1862; Watkin, *Canada and the States*, p. 23. Even in 1858, the Canadian ministry was careful only to approach, not confront, the future. The governor-general's speech, on 16 August 1858, invited the Maritimes 'to discuss with us the principles on which a bond of a federal character . . . may perhaps hereafter be practicable'. Whitelaw, *The Maritimes and Canada before Confederation*, p. 128.
103. *UK Parliamentary Papers*, 1861, XIII, pp. 69–466, evidence of Newcastle, 16 May 1861, q. 2968.
104. *Daily News*, 24 December 1864; *The Times*, 16 December 1850.
105. Head to Stanley, 28 April 1858, in Knox, 'The British government', pp. 212–15; Watkin, op. cit., pp. 16–17; Grey to Elgin, private, 27 July 1848, in Doughty, ed., op. cit., I, pp. 206–8.
106. Public Archives of Canada, Newcastle Papers, microfilm A-309, printed memorandum by Gladstone, 14 December 1861. This seems to strengthen the testimony of Goldwin Smith, *My memory of Gladstone* (London, 1904), pp. 43–4 against the exculpatory apologetic offered by Paul Knaplund, *Gladstone and Britain's imperial policy* (London, 1924) pp. 91–2.
107. Watkin, op. cit., p. 16; University of Nottingham, Newcastle Papers, NeC 10885, Newcastle to Head (copy), private, 5 June 1861, pp. 134–44; Public Record Office, CO 42/626, minute by Newcastle, 13 March 1861, f. 22–4; minute by Elliot, 9 March 1861, f. 16–21.
108. Public Record Office, CO 217/230, Mulgrave to Newcastle, no. 47, 21 May 1862, f. 251–3, and minute by Newcastle, 22 June 1862, f. 251–6.
109. Waite, op. cit., p. 50, quoting William Annand.
110. Public Record Office, CO 217–221, Mulgrave to Lytton, confidential, 30 December 1858, f. 556–76; Public Archives of Canada, Howe Papers, MG 24, B 29, Normanby to Howe, 17 February 1865, pp. 263–78; *The Times*, 5 April 1865; Public Record Office, Cardwell Papers, PRO 30/48/6/39, Cardwell to Gordon (copy), private, 7 January 1865, f. 37–40.

A New Brunswick newspaper admitted: 'we have all at different times had our dreams of a future when the British possessions in America should become one great nation. For the first time we are being brought face to face with the reality'. *Evening Globe* (Saint John), 29 August 1864, quoted by Waite, op. cit., p. 63.

For other discussions of the British role in Confederation, see 'Confederation Rejected: the British Debate on Canada 1837–1840', *Journal of Imperial and Commonwealth History*, xi, 1982, pp. 33–57; 'Launching Canadian Confederation: Means to Ends, 1836–1864; *Historical Journal*, xxvii, 1984, pp. 575–602; 'Lost Confederation Initiatives, 1846–1847; *Bulletin of Canadian Studies*, vi(2), 1983, pp. 25–35.

3 The Imperial Historian as 'Colonial Nationalist': George McCall Theal and the Making of South African History

D. M. SCHREUDER

Every doctrine of imperialism devised by man is a consequence of their second thoughts.

A. P. Thornton, *Doctrines of Imperialism* (1965) p.47

I am here concerned with just such a *considered* second thought. In particular, the very considered and complex imperial second-thoughts of George McCall Theal (1837–1919), critical pioneer historian of colonial Southern Africa.[1] After an extended teaching, administrative and archival career, Theal came from the 1880s to draft a massive multi-volume *History* of this huge colonial region. Here he set out, in somewhat plain narrative form over the course of nearly 5000 pages, his interpretation of the cumulative European impact on Southern Africa.[2] Taking the late 19th century as his personal vantage-point, he portrayed that colonial experience in terms of a unique, emerging 'new society' of white 'civilising' settlement. Claiming to offer an impartial and scientific account of the making of 'South Africa', he in fact developed a highly personal view of that history of imperial contact and conquest. And here his 'doctrine of imperialism' – as A. P. Thornton might characterise it[3] – ultimately transpired to be a personalised doctrine of 'colonial nationalism'.[4] This particular vision of assertiveness of local identity, based on the white settler community, saw colonial 'home rule' as contingent political strategy – contingent upon the cultural unity of the colonists and their place within a wider system of Empire.[5] Theal had created a *History* which offered a cohesive, validating, intellectual force in the evolution of a mythology of white colonial nationality and dominion.

Theal's colonial vision was to be highly potent, both within his time and since.[6] It was official colonial history with a vengeance. It flattered fellow colonists by casting them in the heroic role of nation-makers and world civilisers. It also offered an interesting rationale, which I shall explore below, for the convergence of Dutch and English traditions, towards a single united white governing 'caste'. More still, Theal's work became of fundamental importance to the public culture of the white colonial élite because of his capacity to link his powerful evocative conceptualising vision of a new society of white settlement, with a positively Rankean passion to create an historical narrative from the most comprehensive and scientific network of documentary, archival and oral evidential supports.[7] It may now read as a monumental essay in national mythologising; but it is also infused with an elaborate infrastructure of minute documentary data. Theal's technique was, in fact, to construct his narrative by carefully arranging, for cummulative effect a minute mosaic pattern of dates and events, only occasionally interlaced with personal commentary or analysis. The overall effect is that of an enormous archival deposit of historical veracity bearing down upon the reader. Before the age of the cross-indexed record-card, Theal had already created a *History* which was not least a select compendium of thousands of such 'cards'. Many contemporaries, following a more traditional and positivist view of history, took Theal's volume to be simply definitive.

Theal himself was immensely proud of the fact that his mature historical writings had been developed in close relationship to his monumental archival explorations. For it was he indeed who, not least, interested the colonial government in publishing its records; and who laboured enormously hard, in collecting and transcribing those documents, including European archives, bearing on the early history of colonial southern Africa. The result was a series of colonial documentary volumes, in the form of a series of *Records* – akin, for example, to the contemporary *Historical Records of New South Wales* (published in seven volumes, 1893–1901). These were, in fact, inspired by certain European documentary publications: 'In Europe whole series of ancient papers are continually being printed . . .' as Theal pointed out in 1895, adding the rule that if this 'should be done in South Africa, each paper should appear *verbatim et literatim*, and no translation should be given without the original at its side'. He succeeded remarkably well, certainly at the cost to his health, but also certainly to the great advantage of his reputation and his career. No less than 36 volumes of *Cape Records* were to be published by 1905. In addition, he collated 9 volumes of earlier *Records of South East Africa*, as well as a collection (3 volumes) of *Basutoland Records*. His name was personally attached to them all and his major *History* existed as a parallel creation. Characteristically, he commented in the introduction to his short, popular, *Story of South Africa* (completed in September 1893) that those chapters not based directly on his gradually emerging volumes of the 'great' *History* which rested upon his archival work – could not be seen to have 'the same claim to be regarded as *absolutely* correct'. The archivist in Theal apparently did not doubt that a definitive history *could* be created, once the documents had been assembled. Theal is sometimes these days portrayed as the quintessential legitimising historian of white invasion and white supremacy in southern Africa. That may be so. But his power, as public intellectual force, lay elsewhere: in his potentially more dynamic role, as the zealous archivist with a 'national' mission, able to draw from both European archives and African oral tradition.

It was Theal, in fact, who historically invented white 'South Africa'. And he did this largely through the multi-volume *History*, published in clusters of volumes from 1886 to the Great War. Here he portrayed the sweep of history on the veld, ultimately going back *before* the coming of the white man, to the existence of the transhumance peoples of San and Khoikhoi, to the impact of the arrival of the Bantu-speakers – the great groupings of Nguni and Sotho especially. Volumes were also devoted to the earliest European contacts in the Portuguese era of Vasco da Gama, with a growing concentration however on the Dutch presence after 1652. The British conquest and expansion in the nineteenth century occupied the later volumes, though his narrative ended abruptly in the 1890s, and on a rather flat note, as he ran to the end of the 'open' official documents. There, in fact, he left his account, standing like an incomplete bridge, the narrative projecting out from the frontier and colonial side of the last century, towards the 20th century future and the making of the South African Union in 1910 – an event satisfyingly and significantly contemporaneous with Theal's last volumes. But the vision in the *History* is by then quite clear. It mirrors the unification movements of the 1890s and 1900s, with the Anglo-Boer War occupying a special retrospective moral role, – in warning of the dangers of white-white conflict, of imperial interference, and of Dutch (Afrikaner)–English antipathy. (More popular studies by Theal point to how he would have handled the early 20th century.)

What Theal projected is a modern white polity called 'South Africa', as a great dominion of European settlement, served by black labour from the tribal reservations, and ruled by a white elite drawn from *both* Anglo-Saxon and Dutch traditions. Indeed, he saw this élite as potentially representative of an almost Bancroftian capacity to find the genius of its nationhood within the cultures and historical experience of its founding colonial peoples. Not only had they confronted an enormously difficult frontier environment, the very stuff of new settlement society history, as well as dealing with the most powerful native opposition to that expansion in the history of settlement – the nine Eastern Cape wars with the Bantu-speakers become South Africa's '100 years war'. But, more than that, the colonists had gradually come to terms with each others' cultures. The Dutch and English foundation – Louis Hartz's ideal European 'fragments' established overseas[8] – had ultimately made for a unique colonial community, now at the point of finding its nationhood. History, and his *History*, entered the public domain as the revelation of this inherent pattern of cultural and political development.

*   *   *

Of course, the fact that a white colonial author should project such a view from within a white colonial society, in the prelude to the making of the white state of 1910, will not perhaps seem like much of a revelation to students of a pluralistic empire. In his luminous study of the writing of Canadian history, Carl Berger has reminded us of Herbert Butterfield's enjoinder, to be aware of the unsuspected factors behind national historiographical traditions, so that we might confront them.[9] And this seems a

fair rationale for examining the writings of G. M. Theal in terms
of white South African national history. But, in the case of Theal,
those so-called 'unsuspected factors' are rather plain. Indeed, the
author himself is at pains to point to them as the *strength* of his
argument. The *leitmotif* of Theal's work is about as hidden as
Macaulay's thesis on page 1 of the volume of *his* more famous
'*History*'. In fact, however, Theal's writings reflect a more complex
content and social reality than the bald one which I have so far
outlined, both as regards Theal's own background and his early
relationship to Africa and the African peoples.

   To start with, it is surely of interest to know that this intellectual,
founding father of white 'South Africa', was not born a 'South
African', as he himself would have clarified it. Rather, he was a
Canadian, 'born and bred'.[10] He did not come to the Cape until
his early adult years (aged 24); and it appears that his migration
was touched with chance. In addition, it should immediately be
noted that Theal was not just 'a Canadian', as the biographical
entries would so often have it. Rather, as he frequently stated in
his own text, he was a very particular Canadian, being a
'Maritimer' from the Atlantic Provinces; and within the Maritime
context, descended from an even more particular social and
intellectual tradition. His family were 'United Empire Loyalists'
of Saint John, New Brunswick, an avowed 'Loyalist City'.[11] In
trekking away from republican America in the 1780s, the Loyalists
had shown the closest of sympathies with the Imperial connection.[12] This had determined their ultimate role in the Revolution,
just as it affected their role thereafter in the public life of British
North America. Far from being 'home rulers', they counted dear
their British connections. And far from evincing a Canadian
nativist nationalism, as the earliest of the English-speaking
inhabitants of the later Dominion, they largely showed a notable
coolness towards the Confederation movement of mid-century
which brought together the political élites of lower and upper
Canada to make the nation of 1867.[13] The Maritime provinces
were, indeed, closest to Britain on the Atlantic seaboard of North
American settlement societies: and the young Theal grew up in
that social and political milieu.

   These are not promising beginnings for a frontier 'nationalist
historian' of colonial southern Africa. And there is more apparently unpromising information to note. Firstly, it has been
demonstrated by Merle Babrow, that Theal's earliest writings in

Africa – some scattered articles in missionary journals, and a small school text published by the Lovedale Mission Press – do not evince several of the major conceptual propositions with which his mature writings are associated.[14] Indeed, it can be shown that over a number of critical issues and individuals, he held views opposite to those which are expressed in the later massive *History*. This apparent lack of continuity in his writings, indeed what appears to be the disjointed aspect of his life and thought, is daunting to comprehend biographically; yet it is also fascinating for students of colonial societies. We have given far too little attention to the 19th century antecedents of the modern historiography of the overseas settlement societies as written by the colonists themselves. And yet, for every Seeley who is well documented in the metropolitan imperial scene, there was often a Theal abroad whose history should be explored if we are indeed to understand the real nature of colonial cultures. Moreover, as John Burrows has argued, in introducing his justly acclaimed study of Victorian historians, *A liberal descent* (1981), we should indeed be concerned with historiography 'in the sense defined by Burkhardt, as a record of what one society finds of interest in another'; for the deposit of historical writings provides a valuable historical source in itself – 'one of the ways in which a society reveals itself, and its assumptions and beliefs about its own character and destiny, is by its attitude to, and use of, its past'. This perception is as true of the metropolitan as of the colonial society. It should also be noted, as Dr C. C. Saunders has acutely observed, that Theal took African societies and their histories very seriously indeed. His volumes may indeed chronicle the progress of European colonization in southern Africa, but they do not ignore either the role of African politics in the inter-action of authors, nor do they work from the ethnocentric view of some nineteenth century historians, that African societies had no history. For Theal, Africans had their own culture and their own sense of history. He regarded it as extremely important to incorporate an accurate account of that inner history in the *History*, and he was not daunted by the lack of written records. Before the more recent historiographical revolution in African history involving the collection and deployment of oral source materials, Theal had already embarked on this 'method'. He also initiated the interesting procedure of inviting African comment on his early writings as this affected Nguni society. In the second edition Preface to his *Compendium of South African History and*

Geography (January 1876) Theal indeed nicely sets out how the self-trained historian, which he was, had confronted the problems of sources and of perspectives in writing the chapter on the turbulent Eastern Cape Frontier, particularly as this drew from African history.

> In the present edition, the chapters referring to early Kaffir history will be found to be much more complete. . . . The writer, finding it impossible to form a satisfactory conclusion concerning preceding events in any other manner, applied to various antiquarians throughout Kaffirland, and by comparing their accounts with Colonel Collin's report and the statements of Barrow and Lichtenstein, is enabled to lay before his readers a coherent narrative of the principal events in the history of these people since their ancestors crossed the Kei. Kaffir proper names are spelt in this book as they would be by an educated native . . . The first edition was read by some hundreds of natives, among whom were many of the teachers of mission schools on the frontier, and as it is confidently anticipated that this issue will have a still larger circulation among them, it is but fair that anything in the history of their people – even to the spelling of the names of the chiefs of old – should be accurately given.

This concern was to endure. In 1882 Theal published a substantial volume which reflected his interest in both African culture and in oral sources – *Kaffir Folklore: a Selection from the Traditional Tales Current Among the People Living on the Eastern Border of the Cape Colony, with Copious Explanatory Notes* (second edition, 1886) – and which he introduced with the striking remark that,

> Of late years a great deal of interest has been taken in the folklore of uncivilized tribes by those who have made it their business to study mankind. It has been found that a knowledge of the traditionary tales of a people is a key to their ideas and a standard of their powers of thought. These stories display their imaginative faculties: they are guides to the nature of the religious belief, of the form of government, of the marriage customs, in short, of much that relates to both the inner and outer life of those by whom they are told . . . Without this a survey is no more complete than, for instance, a description of

the English people would be if no notice of English literature were taken.

Equally interesting is Theal's claims for the authenticity of the oral native sources:

> It is necessary to say a few words concerning the care that has been taken to give absolutely not a single sentence in any of these tales that has not come from native sources. Most of them have been obtained from at least ten or twelve individuals residing in different parts of the country, and they have all undergone a thorough revision by a circle of natives. They were not only told by natives but they were copied down by natives. The notes only are my own. I have directed the work of others, but have myself done nothing more than was necessary to explain the text. For this I can claim to be qualified by an intimate knowledge of the Kaffir people, gained through intercourse with them during a period of twenty years, and while filling positions among them varying from a mission teacher to a border magistrate.

These recorded stories and myths are set by Theal within an extensive 'Introductory chapter regarding the Kaffirs' in which an anthropology of explanation is offered, working from the premise that such a volume 'may be found useful, as throwing light upon the mode of life of a people who differ from ourselves in many respects besides degrees of civilization'.

In writing the multi volumed *History*, Theal drew extensively from his early collected oral sources. Large sections of the *History* are devoted to careful accounts of African political history, and to accounts of indigenous social standards and beliefs. In 1905 he accepted a commission to edit for publication the manuscript left at death by G. W. Stow (1822–82), the pioneer ethnologist (and geologist) of Southern Africa. 'It needed only a hasty look through the packets', of the bulky MS conveyed to Theal by Miss L. C. Lloyd, who had purchased the "volume" from Stow's widow, 'to impress me with the conviction that no production of such value upon the native race of South Africa had yet appeared and I was therefore most anxious that it should be published.' Thus the scholarly world received from Theal the famed text of *The Native Race of South Africa : a History of the Intrusion of the Hottentots and*

Bantu into the Hunting Grounds of the Brahman, the Aborigines of the Country. Within two years, in May 1907, the third edition of Theal's *History of South Africa before the Conquest of the Cape Colony by Great Britain in September 1795* was published, and he took this opportunity of changing its title to *History and Ethnography . . .*, because – 'I have added so largely to the information previously given concerning the Brahman, as the aborigines of the country, the Hottentots, and particularly the Bantu immigrants . . . Theal's history of colonisation was not to be built upon either ignorance or utter neglect of African indigenous politics and culture.

In plain terms while Theal was to provide the classic colonial interpretive history of the rise of the white South African state, it was accomplished from a complex personal perspective which included 'Loyalist' beginnings in Canada, and a pioneer concern for African perspectives in a colonial environment of several ethnic groups.

*   *   *

There is no proper biography of Theal to reconcile both these external and internal complexities in the individual. But enough is known of Theal to provide pointers of explanations, partly in the outline of his career, more still, I will argue, in the pages of the *History* itself.

George McCall Theal was born coincident with the formal start of the Victorian Age in 1837.[15] The 'Thealls' (spelt with two 'ls' until his father's generation) had been in the New World since the last years of the reign of Charles I. They had initially gone to Connecticut and there Joseph Theall had become a prominent member of the community. In the 1690s they are found in New York State, having purchased lands from the Iroquios, around the village of Rye. The Revolution deeply affected the family as the 'protest' and angry debate turned to dissent, and then at last to rebellion against the Imperial connection. Eight members of the family are known to have reached Nova Scotia in 1783. They included the 18-year-old Samuel, grandfather-to-be of the historian. Later they are found in Saint John, the Loyalist City par excellence. The family, however, still apparently kept up close American connections. Samuel, for example, married a Philadelphia girl, and much of the commerce of Saint John was still conducted with New York. Moreover, it was Samuel's eldest son, William Young Theal, who was sent to Philadelphia, and later New York, for training as a doctor. He returned to the Loyalist community and worked as a medical practitioner in the Saint John, and then in the Cockaigne area to the north in Acadia. On a hill, in the old Saint John Loyalist Cemetery, many of these Theal's are gathered in a crowded family plot. One prominent Theal is missing.

George McCall Theal had initially grown up in Saint John, though in fact much of his early education was in a small academy in the lowlands of Shediac County on the Acadian coast, run by the Rev. Alfred Horatio Weeks, and a single assistant master, a Mr. Miller. The Cockaigne Academy attempted, according to B. T. Tennysen, to replicate the English public school system, of which Principal Weeks was a product.[16] Theal himself has left a vivid but critical account of his education in the Academy: a poor shadow of *Tom Brown's School Days* (1857), being a mixture of classical studies and corporal punishment.

> All classes were taught in one large room, which was warmed in winter by an immense stove in the centre, round which desks were ranged . . . the reverend principal was conscientious, and as he really believed that to spare the rod was to spoil the child, he tried to do his duty regardless of his muscles. I [once] asked my old class mate if he remembered the punishment inflicted on a particular occasion. . . for what would now [1895] be regarded as a trifling fault. I have need to, he replied, and baring one of his wrists he showed me a large mark which he has borne ever since as a result of it. Yet the reverend principal was not naturally a cruel man. He was a very strict disciplinarian, but he could say kind words and act generously enough outside the schoolhouse. He made me a present of a pair of skates once . . .

> The school [however], being a place of terror, it was a natural result that no one went to it of his own free will. If a boy did not know his lessons, he would argue that he might as well play truant for one day, as the punishment for the one offence would be no worse than for the other. And there was [thus] frequently a strong temptation to play truant, even when a boy could repeat his home task, but knew he would likely be belaboured for something else.[17]

In these truant days, Theal himself apparently enjoyed a wide range of compensatory activities : helping make maple sugar in the spring, collecting wild berries, fishing, even hunting a wolf, and visiting schooners freshly arrived in port from Europe and the overseas world of the Atlantic. With these attractions 'on one side', as he put it, 'and the rod on the other, the pupils of the Cockaigne Academy often turned away from the path that led to knowledge'.

When he *was* in school, Theal was certainly drilled in the basics of what was then taken to be the education of a young gentleman. He claimed that his curriculum was typical of the time: indeed, 'a good specimen of a Canadian public shool . . . regarded as of first class'. But was this common of most British colonial schools?

I have yet to . . . enumerate the subjects taught. The usher [Mr. Miller, the assistant] took spelling, reading, geography, arithmetic, what was called philosophy and . . . once a week there was a lesson in one of the principal languages of the country and then it was bare reading without any explanation whatever. The geography lessons were home tasks, and were nothing more than the repetition by each boy of a certain quantity of matter in a book . . . The philosophy meant answering by rote a series of questions from a long catechism . . . the arithmetic was better . . . we really got some explanation of rules. The principal took the Latin and Greek languages, history and penmanship . . . they used to set a copy for us to follow, and then warm with his cane the hands of those whose performance was not to his satisfaction.

It is above all interesting to learn what the future historian was to learn about the past under the subject of 'History':

The history taught was that of Greece, Rome and England, but we learnt little more than lists of events and names of rulers. Of the life of the Greek people, of the effects of the Roman institutions upon modern nations, and of everything in fact that would be really useful for us to know, we remained ignorant. The great movements of our times, the stirring events of modern Europe and America, even past occurrences in Canada, were utterly ignored. We could repeat the legend of Romulus . . . but we never heard in school of Frederick the

Great or of George Washington, except indirectly as their actions affected England. A knowledge of the Latin and Greek languages was . . . the first and highest object of a schoolboy's life, and consequently a very large portion of time was taken up with those studies . . . [Indeed] the day I entered I had a copy of the Eton Latin grammar put into my hands.[18]

From this Academy he moved to complete his education at the Saint John Grammar School, then under the principalship of Dr James Paterson, whose portrait in the official *History* of the school (covering the period since 1805 and published in 1914) is fearsome, but whom Theal recalled affectionately. The emphasis was still apparently on the classics: we learn that more time was devoted to Latin than to all other subjects put together, and that he had to be coached privately by a Mr O'Donell in mathematics – 'an eccentric but very estimable' Irishman, in Theal's memory – or he would have been numerically illiterate. Yet Dr Paterson apparently inspired the youth : 'I owe [him] what little knowledge I had when I entered upon the duties of [adult] active life [in 1855] . . . his idea of a school was that it should be a place of preparation for a boy to educate himself . . . he pointed out, too, the good for admiration, and cast scorn upon the mean and bad, till every boy felt an enthusiasm to do what was right'.[19] It is perhaps an oblique tribute to Dr Paterson when we find the mature Theal qualifying his concept of 'scientific history' – unbiased and based on archival data – with the unusual remark, buried in volume III of the *History*, that the duty of an historian 'is to expose to scorn the evil deeds of the upright . . .'[20] Just how such heroes and villains are identified was of course to be somewhat more complex in that *History*.

Upon leaving the Saint John Grammar School he travelled surprisingly widely. For example, he took ship to the African Cape in the schooner '*Jonathan Levitt*', named for his maternal uncle, owner of the vessel. After other youthful adventures, young Theal sailed again, this time to West Africa, where he appears to have worked for a short period in his uncles's trading-post in Sierra Leone. These various youthful adventures and voyages, as well as later journeys to Britain, suggest a restless spirit of independent adventure in the youth. It also may be of significance to know that his father wished him to enter Anglican orders. Theal himself was an avowedly earnest individual all his life, with what may be termed an evangelical–protestant inclination. It should be noted that his father's younger brother was an Anglican priest; and indeed, rector of the parish church at Cockaigne not far from the Academy of the Rev. Weeks. But Theal himself doubted any 'calling' as a priest, and declined to obey his father on this matter. Instead, he set out on another ocean adventure after a period of work in America – this time he was intent upon following the route of Captain Cook.

Theal was never to see Australia.[21] He lingered at the Eastern Cape, took temporary employ at a small farm school at Knysna on the coast; later he walked on to British settler territory proper, namely the Albany district. A bookish and earnest young man he was to spend the next few years in a series of jobs which reflected his character, starting with a period as a bookseller in King William's Town, the major British garrison settlement on the troubled Eastern Cape frontier. After that we keep catching glimpses of him in the mid-1860s, as a journalist. He later remarked that he had since young harboured as his real ambition to live by his own writings. He now made a fair, but ultimately failing attempt, to live his dream. Most notable, he worked on a local newspaper in the Victoria East area at Maclear, where British farmers and trek-Boer lived side by side in the region of the snow-capped Sotho mountains, having learnt the local Boer language sufficiently well to publish in *Het Hollands Nieuwsblad*. Later he is found as proprietary editor of the *Kaffrarian Recorder*, published from the port town of East London, for the interior Border area.

After two years as editor a local economic crisis drove him to office work, then again to school-teaching, this time at Dale College, a non-denominational grammar in King William's Town. He appeared to be settling. He became a prominent member of a local protestant congregation – interestingly Presbyterian and Calvinist, rather than Anglican and Tractarian; and he published occasional pieces in Cape literary journals. But he was soon to be on the move again. He followed the cry of 'Diamonds' in the 1870s to the great Kimberley 'Field' which eventually made the fortune of Cecil John Rhodes. It did not do the same for Theal. He was here in a good majority, of dispirited diggers. After some 18 months of intense excitement, he left 'the Fields', and accepted an appointment at that remarkable African educational institution, Lovedale Mission at Alice in the Eastern

Cape. Founded by Scottish Presbyterians in 1842 as a mission, trade school and seminary, it had become a critical centre of evangelical Humanitarianism in the region. The institution was looking for an individual who combined a knowledge of printing, journalism and teaching, plus a protestant faith. They found it all in George McCall Theal. He joined the staff in 1871 and remained until the end of the decade, though he still enjoyed some further wanderings – to Scotland in 1874, and to Central Africa in 1877.

At last we can claim to discern something of the future historian, as detailed in the recent pioneer biographical studies of Christopher Saunders.[22] Theal's literary inclinations and ambitions found release in the monthly publication of the Mission journal, *The Christian Express* (originally *The Kaffir Express*). He also took the opportunity to print and publish a small monographic pamphlet of his own, an evocative sketch of some 64 pages, entitled *South Africa, as It Is*, January (1871). It was a combination of geography, popular history and simple observation, suitable for classroom or family reading room. A few years more at Lovedale as a teacher, and the opportunity to pursue some library researches, resulted in what should be regarded as his first publication of major significance. This was now his book, *Compendium of South African History and Georgraphy*, of 176 pages (1874) covering the colonisation of the region from 1652. A second volume was published in 1876, and was larger again in size; a third followed in 1877 of 454 pages. The teacher and writer had come together and made a text for general consumption. 'This book', as the Preface to this first edition explained in January 1874,

> is published in the hope that it will supply a want very generally felt, that of a cheap and accurate description and history of the land we live in. The descriptive portion of it has already been before the public, in the pamphlet, "South Africa as it is", which, at the time of publication (January 1871) was most favourably commented upon by the leading organs of the colonial press. Accuracy and brevity have been the points chiefly aimed at. One object kept in view was to point out the moral as well as the material advancement of the country.

Theal was particularly pleased that his volume drew African readers and that he could claim that it had 'the advantage of being correct from the Kaffir point of view' (p.iv). He could make such an assertion, that his narrative included data from 'the other side of the frontier', as modern idiom might have it, because of his mode of research, based on his personal experience of Africa. 'Before I entered the civil service of the Cape Colony in 1877', as he wrote autobiographically in the Preface to his 1907 volume of *History and Ethnography of South Africa* . . . ,

> I had been engaged for many years in studying the traditions, habits, and power of thought of the Bantu tribes of the south-eastern coast, and the knowledge gained thereby led, on the outbreak of the ninth war with the Xosas, to my being requested by Governor Sir Bartle Frere [1815–84; in South Africa 1877–80] to fill a post then considered to be one of considerable difficulty . . . I had also collected among the different Bantu tribes a number of folklore tales, some of which were published in magazines, and others at a later date in a small volume issued in London [in 1882].

Theal could also claim to have based his African genealogies on African sources, a point he was quick to make where other writers produced alternate histories of African chiefdomships. For example, A. H. F. Duncan's 'Outline History of the Barolong to the end of the year 1884', and which appeared in the British Imperial bluebook c.4889 of 1886 (Duncan being a member of the British colonial Bechuanaland Land Commission), drew this interesting commentary from Theal, in 1887, concerning a difference in important genelogies:

> Mine was compiled in the first instance from those furnished by Montsiwa [sic; died 1896, chief of the Barolong] to Governor Sir Henry Barkly; they were then sent to various Barolong chiefs and councillors for revision, and have been submitted to a great many authorities since, without any alteration being made in them. The differences arise from Mr. Duncan using the word *son* in the European sense, and I in the native significance . . . If the native rule be not followed in such instances, the history of the tribes becomes involved in inextrica-

ble confusion ... Under such circumstances, it seems to me
that native ideas ought to be respected ...

A particular disagreement over the family descendants of Chief
Ratlou led Theal to declare his research sources: 'I have ...
before me several lists of Ratlou's descendants, drawn up by
natives, and in all of them Moshete is represented as Goutse's
son.'

Care in his African sources of indigenous authorities was
matched by a general interest in the African dimension of frontier
inter-action and conflict. In the unlikely place of the Preface to
his volume of *Chronicles of Cape Commanders, or an Abstract of Original-
Manuscripts in the Archives of the Cape Colony Dating from 1651 to 1691,
Compared with Printed Accounts of the Settlement by Various Visitors
during that Time. Also Four Short Papers upon Subjects Connected with
the East India Company's Governments at a Later Period, Reprinted from
Colonial Periodicals and Notes in English, Dutch and French books
Published before 1746 Containing Reference to South Africa* (428 pages,
1882), Theal makes a significant general statement of interest
concerning the importance of the African dimension in the
colonial history of the Cape. The rich archival deposits of the
early VOC presence at the Cape have not been properly
deployed partly because of their sheer bulk and uncatalogued and
uncoordinated nature, with no proper archival policy, but also
for a deeper reason:

There was another cause for the neglect of the Cape Archives.
Not only is their volume vast, but in their contents the minutest
details of petty and obscure events are mixed up with matter
altogether foreign [to European readers]. They are thus
intolerably heavy, except to one who has the means of gathering
information from words which to ordinary students are
meaningless. When, for instance, one meets with relations of
the intercourse between Batuas, Obiquas, Chobonas, and many
others, if one knows what people these words refer to, a flood
of light is thrown upon pages that would otherwise be very
wearisome reading. The greater the acquaintance with any of
the native races of South Africa that one has, the more
information will he be able to extract from the Cape Archives,
and the less dull will they appear to him.

He himself could therefore claim to have brought that light to the use of the archival deposits, and indeed that his *Chronicles of the Cape Commanders* . . . contained not merely 'an account of the origins of European power in South Africa', but also 'of the condition of the Native Races when white men first came into contact with them, and of the nature of the intercourse between Europeans and Natives during a period of 40 years'.

The patient reader of Theal's lengthy multi-volume *History* is also rewarded with aspects of his early ethnographic concerns and his collection of African oral evidence, usually unobtrusively deployed without a precise source indicated – though just occasionally in his few footnotes he actually quotes or paraphrases oral sources provided him by African witnesses. A good example is Theal's close account of the internal struggles for dynastic power among the Xhosa in the 1790s, between Ndlambe and Gaika, which was clearly enriched by talking to the aged widow of one of the major participants – Tutula, a wife of Gaika – who was still alive in 1873, and whom Theal interviewed in that year.[23] An even more striking example is the way in which he apparently verified aspects of the data in his narrative with a major African figure. The same patient reader of volume IV of the *History* will find this fascinating footnote concerning the 18th century history of the Xhosa:

> The chief Kreli was regarded as the most learned antiquary of his tribe, and nothing pleased him more than to discuss events of the past. He was good enough to listen patiently to my account of his people as here given, which he confirmed as correct, and added to it information concerning the burial place of his ancestors. Of the origin of the tribe he knew nothing, but was aware that at some not very distant time it came down from the north.[24]

Theal's early writings are marked indeed by a sympathetic perspective towards African culture and the African condition on a colonial frontier of expansion and conflict, though the 'Lovedale Theal' still concurred in the colonisation of Africa, and the advantages to Africans of protestant Christianity and economic development, not least through Lovedale's combination of Christian teachings and artisan training. But Theal's early history still evinced a strong concern for the manner in which the process of acculturation took place, and showed a distinct empathy towards the protective agencies of Humanitarianism concerned for African rights in the process of colonial development. Above all, there is no overt sign of the colonial nationalist in these early writings.

It could indeed be argued that until the late 1870s Theal's life, and the evolution of his thought, had been part of an 'unfolding' in which it is possible to connect the Empire Loyalist and Anglican to the Lovedale teacher and imperial scholar. Thereafter, this is less obviously so. A series of developments, both personal and public, soon swung his life and thought into a new plane of existence.[25] 'After a long residence on the Cape Frontier in a position which brought me into constant contact with the different races', as Theal recalled in 1887 in a Preface to his *History of the Boer in South Africa* . . .

> on the outbreak of the Kaffir War, towards the close of 1877, I was requested by the Government to undertake a diplomatic post requiring special knowledge of native character. Having succeeded in performing the duties entrusted to me, when the war was over I asked for and obtained the charge of the Colonial Archives preserved in Cape Town. During the period from March 1879 to January 1881, I prepared a volume of Abstracts of Early Cape Records, which was published by the Government, and I collected a quantity of material for a History of the Foundation of the Cape Colony. Transferred again to the Native Department, I returned to the frontier and acted as magistrate at Tamacha until the close of the Basuto War, when I obtained leave of absence for six months and proceeded to the Hague to complete by research in the Archives of the Netherlands the information required for my early Cape History . . . Upon my return from Europe the Cape Government instructed me to collect, arrange, and publish all the authentic records that could throw light upon the history of the Basuto tribe. [And while] . . . engaged in this work, which occupied my time until March 1884, a very large amount of correspondence relating to the Emigrant Farmers passed through my hands

The historical writer was in the making. Having left Lovedale to take up this series of administrative appointments, ranging from resident at the coast of Chief Oba Ngonyama, and labour agent in the Western Cape farm districts, Theal was significantly using his African knowledge to serve the Colony and not the humanitarian agencies per se. He was bitterly disappointed in these years at failing to be appointed parliamentary librarian, but the alternative, of permanent civil service appointment, in fact gave him access to the wider archives of the Cape in both the metropolitan and regional administrative depots.

A pattern was soon established. The transcription of original and unpublished historical documents for public consumption proceeded over the rest of his career, starting in 1881 with his *Abstracts of Debates and Resolution, of the Council of Policy, from 1651 to 1687*, and followed by 3 volumes of *Basutoland Records* (1883), and the even larger *Records of the Cape Colony* and *Records of South-Eastern Africa* – totally a monumental 40 hefty volumes of documents, drawn from domestic and European archives, covering a staggering 25 000 pages of transcription in print. Yet that was only one aspect of Theal's activities. Of even greater significance was his episodic but increasingly fruitful use of the archival materials in historical essays and small monographic volumes. For a full-time civil servant he managed a flow of publications enough to put a modern academic's c.v. to shame. For example, between 1882 and 1888 he appears to have published a book or essay a year, starting with the collected volume entitled *The Chronicles of the Cape Commanders . . .*, as well as his edition of oral traditions of the Xhosa, *Kafir Folklore*. In 1887 he again published two studies : his innovative *History of the Boers in South Africa . . .* as well as *The Republic of Natal*. The original Lovedale *Compendium . . . of history and geography* was revised in an enlarged edition. And the massive *History* was anticipated by the accumulation of vast documentary materials and the obvious need to correct the separate, episodic narratives coming from Theal's pen.

The main conceptual argument and framework for such an extended narrative *History* was also foreshadowed by two further developments in Theal's life, and both depended on changes in the public domain. First there was the simple reality that he had come to live in the heartland of the Cape colonists: not surprisingly he appears to have been now even more drawn into the values and perspectives of the old Durban settlement community. Lovedale and Humanitarian perspectives were gradually lost as Theal was assimilated into the Cape ruling élite. By the time he came to draft the first volume of the *History* he had moved somewhat from both his Maritime and his missionary background: the *History* became indeed something of a declaration of Cape colonial citizenship. Yet beyond mere social intercourse and official employment affecting his world view, it should also be noted that it was hardly coincidental that the particular phase when he 'migrated' to Cape Town from Lovedale, the years 1877–80, were crucial in political terms. It was a phase of fundamental political flux and re-alignments in the public scene of southern Africa as a whole; and the Cape was deeply affected by these major events – evolving imperialism, Afrikaner nationalism and African resistance.[26] Starting with the sudden British annexation of the Transvaal Boer republic (in April 1877) Theal suffered, along with other 'loyal colonists', increasing disillusionment with the conduct of the Imperial Factor. Then came the British Imperial confederation attempts, propagated by Conservative and Liberal Secretaries of State alike, from Carnarvon to Kimberley. These apparently high-handed attempts at Imperial intervention, followed by the disaster of the British military campaign against the highveld Boers, ending in the ignominy – for the Victorian army and state – of Majuba (February 1881) hardly placed Great Britain in a favourable light. The Cape Dutch grew restive over this Imperial posturing, with its mixture of belligerence and jingoistic fervor: English-speaking colonists became distinctly cool towards an Imperial policy which mixed such insensitivity to colonial aspirations with such incompetence.[27] Theal was surely not at all alone in suffering a sense of shame over the behaviour of the Imperial Factor; nor singular in moving closer to the Cape Dutch as fellow colonists. Even the imperial Secretary to the Cape Governor was to record in his later 'memoirs' that it was these events which had moved him to re-think his imperialism.[28]

The years 1878-81 saw indeed a new political accord emerging for the first time in the Cape between the Afrikaner rural interests and the English-speaking commercial classes. The ultimate expression of that accord was the development of a major political block in the Cape Assembly between Jan Hofmeyr's *Afrikaner Bond* and the parties of British capital led by Cecil John Rhodes. Hofmeyr's definition of an 'Afrikaner' included all white citizens who regarded Africa as their home, regardless of home language; Rhodes' imperialism was in fact a form of 'colonialism', which stressed Cape identity over service to the Imperial Factor.[29]

Theal's *History* was ultimately to draw from that political accord, and attach to it his growing personal identity with Cape colonial interests and the cultural intermingling of the Dutch and British communities in the making of this 'new society'.

This movement in Theal's thought, and identity of interest, can in fact be discerned in the gradual but crucial shift in his writings, both in topic and perspective. The monumental work on the Cape *Records*, for example, drew Theal into a totally new relationship with colonial history and of the Cape *Dutch* beginnings. Not only did he now relinquish the world of Lovedale, with all its inherent perspectives in humanitarianism, together with its particular relationship with African societies, and personally come to dwell in the colonists capital with all *its* values and perspectives; but, Theal also came to a totally new appreciation of the history and character of the Cape Dutch. This was to be absolutely fundamental in his *History*, and it marks a vital shift in the *mentalité* of the historian. The significant emphasis is not that he merely took up a white colonial view, but that he came to identify so strongly with an entity he termed 'South Africa', and which he took to be founded not alone by the British, but first of all by the Dutch. Several of his minor publications in the 1880s had begun to signal this crucial change in both his historical perspective and, probably, also his own personal identification with what he often referred to as 'the nation of my adoption'. His essay on the Dutch colonization of the Cape (1879), a study of the Dutch commanders, and a small book on the trekker movement of emigrant Boers, all gave outward sign of this inward movement of mind and sentiment: the Loyalist and the 'Lovedale Theal' was dissolving into the Cape historian; or, as he would have preferred it, the historian of 'South Africa'.

The first five volumes of the *History* were in fact published in 1886, and they revealed how he had come to adopt the dual role of Cape colonial historian *and* projector of a concept of 'South Africa' based on Cape Dutch foundations. By 1896 volumes VI–IX of the *History* had been published, and the British 'second-foundation' securely attached to the Dutch origins. Volumes X and XI allowed Theal to play Thucydides, and write about his own times, as if these were at an equal point of perspective to the historian. Here the colonial nationalist is most marked, with an increasingly critical tone towards British imperialism as he discussed what he now characterised as 'metropolitan interference' in the life of the colonial polity and its culture. The Empire Loyalist's position had come full circle. He was now a colonial nationalist and 'home ruler'. In 1891 he was appointed to the special and extraordinary post of 'Colonial Historiographer'. Here was a happy recompense for his rejection as Cape Librarian in 1881; *and* also a suitable recognition of the transition in his thought and status. He had now moved from mission teacher and writer, to public orator of colonial society. Equally appropriately, in 1892–3 he published the large and definitive 'Geslacht Register der Onde Keepsche Familien'; in Theal's words, a 'complete genealogical register down to 1800 of every European family that settled in the Cape Colony before that date', the materials for which had been 'collected by my late friend, Mr. Christoffel Coetjee de Villers', which were 'unarranged at the time of his death', but which were now 'put in order by me – assisted by Mr. W. J. Vlok . . .' in 3 large crown quarto volumes and 1596 pages of colonial piety.

*   *   *

Is is incontrovertible that Theal's new official role as Cape civil servant and archivist-extraordinary was closely paralleled by a changed perspective – or 'tone' as he himself admitted – in his history, and the shaping of the *History* itself. Yet what has so far not been explored or appreciated by scholars is how he actually reconstructed his perception of South African society and history. And to make that analysis we have to analyse the content of the *History* itself.

This issue is intellectually of the greatest interest, as it involved so much more than any simple switch of loyalties, from the Humanitarian to Settler point-of-view. Theal had worked to accomplish something far deeper, and, I suspect, something more personal. This involved confronting the issue of *place* and *identity* in the new white colonial society. Not only was there the problem of dealing with a regional and historic dispersal of whites, in a range of colonies and republics, but there was the deepest issue of all – the problem of cultural pluralism among the whites of southern Africa. The Dutch and English foundations surely stared at Theal constantly in the history of the Cape, as well as in the daily life of the Western districts in which he moved. Here was a British colony in which the majority of the whites were not

English-speakers. What then of the future of a 'South Africa' as a modern nation? In addition, there was another related question, often neglected by subsequent historians, concerning the *third* group of pioneer white settlers in southern Africa more largely. Where did the Portuguese belong in the history of this huge sub-continental area, in that future for the region as a domain of the white settler? Theal's *History* is distinctive because these were the very questions central to the construction of his thesis and explanation.

It should also be stressed that Theal's *History* rested on an intellectual set of presuppositions which are much more complex than the hagiography of a white settler patriot. Put simply, Theal's scientific view of the making of his *History* was matched by what he appears to have taken to be 'social scientific laws' of historical formations and developments. He also saw his *History* as performing the vitally useful role of making colonial society self-consciously aware of the *meaning* of its past. In Theal's *History* there was offered a series of historical lessons with direct significance and utility for the making of the modern South African community and state. Theal's *History* became an excellent early exemplar of Professor Harrison Wright's evocative idiom, of South African historiography as essentially shaped by the 'burden of the *present*'.

In the last resort, Theal's *History* is not great history, albeit on a great scale – not because it is dominated by an E. H. Carr-like 'dialogue with the present', or even for its teleological implications; but primarily because it rests on such debatable conceptual frameworks. Yet, if it is ultimately as valuable for what it tells about Theal as about history, then it is still an historical document of enormous interest and value in allowing us to probe the milieu in which he lived; and to contemplate the function of the historian as nation-maker, in one region of the colonial New World.

For analytic purposes here we might conceive the *History* as developing around four interlocking presuppositions. First, there is the relatively simple matter of Theal's view of history as a science, which then draws in the more complex matter of his notion of the historian as impartial observer and commentator. The documents provide the raw truth; and the responsible historian constructs the accurate narrative portrait of the past, with favour and animus towards none. 'In preparing the book', he wrote in 1893 of his *Story of South Africa*, 'I was guided by the principle that truth should be told, regardless of nationalities or parties, and I strove to the utmost to avoid anything like favour or prejudice.'[30] He was later to inform a correspondent that he had declined a commissioned history of the Dutch East India Company, *because* 'I must be free to write what I believe to be the truth, altogether regardless of the opinion of any man or Society of men, otherwise the work would not be congenial.'[31]

Theal indeed saw himself as possessing very special personal advantages in addressing the conflicted history of the peoples of Southern Africa. He argued forcefully in the Preface to his 1887 study of *The History of the Boers in South Africa* . . . that 'something more than bare knowledge is needed in writing history'. This was:

> Determination to be strictly impartial, freedom from prejudices which might involuntarily affect that determination, are equally requisite. I believe that I possess these qualifications, at any rate I have done my utmost to work in that direction. I have no interests to serve with any particular party, and I am on friendly terms with all. Though a resident in South Africa for more than a quarter of a century, I am by birth a Canadian, the descendant of a family that sided with the king at the time of the American Revolution, and afterwards removed from New York to New Brunswick with the other Royalists. The early years of my life after boyhood were spent in the United States and Sierra Leone. Thus no ties of blood, no prejudices acquired in youth, stand as barriers to my forming an impartial judgement of events that transpired in South Africa a generation ago.

Moreover, the good historian did not need to place a personal interpretation on controversial events. The proper documentation spoke for itself. 'Having thus stated what the material at my disposal has consisted of, and that circumstances have placed me in a position to write without bias, I must leave to others the decision as to the manner in which I have carried out the work'.

Theal was fascinated with the apparent cummulative power of empirical data to 'reconstruct' the past. The administrator and archivist in him constantly warmed to the historical possibilities inherent in the documentation. The fact of being so often the pioneer in either establishing a public history, or of correcting the loosely based attempts of others (even G. W. Stow's pioneer ethnographic work is quietly criticised, on the grounds that 'Mr. Stow never had an opportunity of research in the colonial archives' to the detriment of the narrative), allowed Theal both a certain hubris as to the authority of his history, and also encouraged his penchant for a belief in the 'scientific' truth about the past inherent in the archives. He was not naive in being unaware of questions of motivation in actors of the past : but he rested his interpretation strongly upon the capacity of exhaustive archival research to tell 'what really happened.' For example, when introducing his *History of the Boers in South Africa: or The Wanderings and Wars of the Emigrant Farmers from Leaving the Cape Colony to the Acknowledgement of Their Independence by Great Britain* (London, 1887, in 392 pages with 3 maps), he tells of how it was based on the fact that he had come across 'a very large amount of correspondence relating to the Emigrant Farmers' –

> I found that the most important of these documents, those which were of greatest historical value, had never appeared in bluebooks. In these papers the motives of the various actors could be clearly traced. After reading, comparing and digesting them, the only labour in writing the history of the emigration was that of guiding the pen.

Theal's administrative career as a Cape civil servant reinforced his philosophic view about the inherent significance of the detailed archival record. 'Every reader naturally wishes to know with what authority the book in his or her hands, if it professes to be a history, has been written', Theal asked pointedly in the Preface to his succinct volume on *The Progress of South Africa in the Century* (Washington & Ottawa, 1902). 'What, it is asked, were the author's sources of information?' Theal was quick to answer his own questions in his characteristically emphatic manner:

> My sources of information are archives, in which I have been making researches for a quarter of a century, many hundreds of printed volumes upon South Africa in various languages, and an intimate acquaintance with the country and its people, European and natives.

He also added a revealing autobiographic commentary, providing his own personal view about the 'facts' of history.

During 14 of the most active years of my life it was my duty to supply the head of the Native Affairs Department of the Cape Colony, in which I served as first and chief clerk, with abstracts of the contents of collections of documents on every variety of subject relating to the Bantu tribes. Such abstracts necessarily contained nothing but facts, as they were to be acted upon by the heads of the department, and favour, prejudice, or imagination could find no place in them. Training in such a school has the advantage of making one very careful as to accuracy, but it has the disadvantage of preventing – or at least of not encouraging – a graceful style of writing. The first object is to state nothing but facts that can be proved, and the second to state them in plain language that cannot be misinterpreted. Ornamentation of sentences or paragraphs comes in nowhere.

Writing history in such a fashion indeed posed considerable challenges of self-denial on the part of the historian in responding to the human and political dimensions of the past – 'In this volume I have made some few remarks that would have been out of place in such an abstract as I have described above' – yet Theal held determinedly to his view about the possibility of a 'scientifically' exact history,

> . . . the book has been prepared exactly as it would be written for the head of the government to act upon, no matter what his political views might be. *It contains the indisputable truths of South African history*, and each individual is left to colour to suit his own inclinations, whether in favour of English, Dutch, or Bantu. As far as human power goes, it is absolutely free of partisan spirit.

Not so surprisingly, in the larger *History*, Theal's fascination with history exhibiting itself through the apparent exactitude of past records becomes one of its most characteristic dimensions. He was hardly alone in this approach : the late 19th century witnessed a so-called 'scientific revolution' in history whereby documents would at last reveal the past 'as it had been'. Theal's text rests the spare narrative on the underpinnings of such researches, and in the few footnotes he occasionally discusses, often at length, not so much the merits of his sources, or the alternate views of other writers, but such empirical issues as exact dating of events, or the condition of particular documents; or his own search for manuscripts, relics, even personal visits to certain historical sites. The quality of the documentation is the issue, not whether it is reliable or adequate as a basis for 'reconstructing the past'. The most extraordinary or revealing example is perhaps a footnote in volume II, which begins with the classic Theal remark, 'It would be interesting to know the exact date on which Diaz sailed . . .'; and then concludes, in close print, a whole page later, only to be taken up again, over the course of 6 pages, at the conclusion of the chapter![32] In other places, Theal worries aloud, and at length, over past currency values, the precise place of explorer's landing points, whether a certain day of the week, or another, was involved in such an event; even the rigging and navigation of ships is a subject for close detailing, surely derived in part from a 'Maritime' background, but also an essential part of his view of history as detailed documented truth. The most sympathetic thing that can be said is that Theal as historian had a special archivist's 'feel' for documents, and often saw them as having a validity all of their own. Discussing the role of the secretary to Cape governing council under the VOC (the Dutch East India Company), Theal quite suddenly breaks his spare, plain narrative, with an unusually vivid sentence about the records themselves, as left by one of these long-dead Dutch civil servants (and also echoes his own school training?):

> One of his most necessary qualifications was that his penmanship should be good; and now after the lapse of more than two centuries and a half, the beautiful black letters which the early secretaries wrote can be read by those who know its characters almost as clearly as print.

Yet more revealing and significant is to observe how Theal dealt with revisions of his definitive *History*. He took criticism of interpretation, or judgement, very ill. Factual detail however could always be improved, though he handles such revisions in a revealingly characteristic fashion. 'Note', he says at the bottom of page 22 of volume III, of the revised 1913 edition of the *History*, in dealing with Jan van Riebeeck and the Cape colonial foundation of April 1652.

The alterations in two pages of this chapter from the previous editions are due to the publication in Amsterdam in 1912 of Professor E. C. Godée Molsbergen's volume, *De Stichter van Hollands Zuid-Afrika Jan van Riebeeck*. That author found in the archives at the Hague a journal kept by the junior merchant Leendet Jansz from the 25th of March to the 14th of September 1647 which I had not seen, and which is certainly of great importance. I was engaged [in] making researches and copying documents and charts at the Hague on three different occasions, amounting altogether to about a year, but that was a mere fraction of the time that would be needed to exhaust all the material to be found there. Professor Godee Molsbergen, in confining himself to the life of one man, was able to gather a good deal of fresh material, and has produced a very interesting book of 297 pages. *But, the account given by me remains in nearly every respect undisturbed, as it is based upon the original documents of the period in the archives in Cape Town as well as in Holland*, though of course it can be enlarged.

Here too was Theal's explanation for the highly significant change in his writings over the years concerning critical questions involving humanitarianism and the missionaries in particular. He was all too aware that the 'Lovedale Theal' had expressed views somewhat more sanguine than the critical author of the nation-making *History*. 'Regarding the acts of the various missionaries', he wrote in the 1887 Preface to his *History of the Boers in South Africa . . .*, 'there is certainly a difference in tone of this volume and of my "Compendium of South African History", written sixteen years ago [at Lovedale, in 1871]. I had not then read the mass of missionary correspondence in the colonial records nor the comments upon their complaints and the refutations of many of their statements made by officers of the Colonial Government'. More recent scholars – not least W. M. MacMillan 1885–1974 in his classic *Bantu, Boer and Briton* (first edition, 1929) and J. S. Galbraith, in his exhaustive study of imperial policy on the eastern Cape frontier in *Reluctant Empire* (UCLA, 1963) – have examined the documentation afresh and come to views distinctly different from Theal's *History*. Buttressing Theal's conscious and conspicuous emphasis on documentation as a main defence of his interpretation was a second important aspect of his 'scientific' approach to *History*. This concerned that particularly 19th century fascination with what were taken to be 'laws' of social evolutionism. Theal's concern with 'race', culture and ethnicity as historical determinants, is pervasive in the *History*. Indeed, essential to his ideological perception of the pattern of the Southern African past, was his only partially articulated yet fundamental set of beliefs, in a variety of racial theoretics. His whole mentalité was so veined by a concern for 'race', 'colour' and 'ethnicity' that it is almost impossible to isolate for analysis. He appears to have absorbed into his world view all manner of race theory: from craniology – the San hunters and Khoikhoi herders, for example, are compared in terms of skull size, to explain responses to the West[33] – to an interest in ear lobes, bone formations and blood analysis – he was fascinated with the degree of 'Arab blood' in the Bantu societies of south-east Africa, and how this affected their qualities as cultures able to cope with European expansion. The grander race explanations, concerning the ranking of 'races' (akin to the 'Great Chain of Being') also intrigued him, as part of the pseudo-Darwinian explanations of history itself developing through the growth and extinction of the fittest ethnic 'nation'.

Theal indeed ultimately saw modern history as quintessentially defined in terms of an age of civilising, European expansion – which he significantly characterised as the 'great progressive movement of the Caucasian race'.[34] Such expansion therefore had very considerable meaning. 'Upon a conquering nation rests an enormous responsibility: no smaller than that of benefitting the world at large'.[35] Theal often evinced a sense of human conscience about the losers in the story of progress by European conquest. The Lovedale teacher was not utterly dead. But, like Winwoode Reade's famed *Martyrdom of Man* (1872), in Theal's *History* humanity indirectly moved to the sound of the crushed bones of less-adept societies. This is most blatant when Theal comes to consider the fate of the San peoples and their complex but fragile cultures faced by the advance of Cape trek-boer. I quote from volume four, concerned with the frontier interactions in the 18th century:

> The settlement of the Europeans in the country was disastrous to the aborigines. Bushmen were still numerous along the interior mountain range, but in other parts of the colony there were hardly any left. One may feel pity for savages such as these, destroyed in their native wilds, though there is little

reason for regretting their disappearance. They were of no benefit to any other section of the human family, they were incapable of improvement . . .[36]

Even those African peoples deemed capable of 'improvement', in Theal's terms, also found themselves subject to his historical 'laws' of social development. History apparently stood between individual Africans and immediate acculturation. European attitudes to capital and labour – 'habits of industry', in Theal's idiom – were 'the result of pressure of circumstances operating upon the race through hundreds of generations'. Theal was in no doubt as he expressed in his *Kafir Folklore* . . . (1882) that the African was inherently capable of joining the 'civilising' development of the world – 'His intellectual abilities are of no mean order, and his reasoning power is quite equal to those of a white man', and equally that 'there is no difficulty whatever in expressing any ideas in the Kaffir language' – but African culture as such held individuals in the thraldom of an unprogressive, irrational and far from moral order of society: 'Ingenious as they are, the men are far from being industrious. A great portion of their time is spent in visiting and gossip, of which they are exceedingly fond. They are perfect masters of that kind of argument which consists in parrying a question by means of putting another. They are not strict observers of truth, and, though not pilferers, they are addicted to cattle lifting . . .'.

The same perspective is pressed when Theal is considering the fate of freed black slaves. They often, disappointingly, in Theal's account, 'reverted to type' – so validating his notions of ethnicity and progress in history:

At first [under Dutch rule at the Cape] blacks were enslaved on the plea that they were heathens, but a profession of Christianity, coupled with a knowledge of the Dutch language, sufficed to free them and to place them on a level in civil rights with their former masters. As time wore on [however], it became apparent that in most instances emancipation meant the conversion of a useful individual into an indolent pauper and a pest to society. . . . Experience showed that a freed slave usually chose to live in a filthy hovel upon coarse and scanty food rather than toil for something better . . . He put nothing by [in money] and when sickness came he was a burden upon the public. Such in general was the negro when left to himself . . .[37]

Theal also occasionally applied a similarly harsh view to Africans who had in his own time experienced a Christian conversion. In a footnote that shows an appreciation of the crucial issue of continuity and change in colonial situations, as this affected Africans, he yet also firmly revealed how his ideas of melioration and civilisation are seen to operate over a long, almost Darwinian, process of generations. Africans at the Mission are portrayed as having minds 'shackled by hereditary superstition even while earnestly striving to seek the truth'. And he then also inserts this intriguing personal statement below an asterisk in the main text of volume five of the *History*:

> In the case of most [African] converts – perhaps all – it would be a mistake to suppose that our form of Christianity entirely replaces the Bantu belief. Even in the third generation of professing Christians, the old religion often exhibits its presence in a way that startles observers. It has not even been dormant, much less was it dead. Instead of the new doctrine eradicating and completely filling the place previously occupied by his hereditary religion, the profession of our faith by a Kafir seems only to give a Christian colouring [sic!] to his belief. The one undoubtedly leavens the other, but, if I have observed these people correctly, ancestral worship and fetishism will only be completely removed by a series of rejections, taking place with long intervals of time between them. I refer to the converts in general; there are individuals to whom these remarks may not be applicable, though even of this I have doubts.[38]

Those last few words must have stung his former African and Christian colleagues at Lovedale. Yet Theal is committed to that stance as part of his larger perception of African cultures within a general view of ethnicity. Indeed, only a few pages further on, in the same volume, he drops the arresting remark, in the context of the British raising a Khoikhoi frontier corps in 1819, that '*naturally* the [Cape] colonists disliked to see men of an inferior race trained to the use of arms . . .'. It is the use of 'naturally' in that context which is so revealing, let alone the concept of inferior races.[39] Similar comments are, in fact, deposited over the length of Theal's many volumes. He took it as absolutely 'given' that what he was describing in his narrative was not merely a clash of cultures, or polities in Southern Africa, but the impact of a superior civilisation upon the traditional culture of vanquished people. Theal indeed worried over the consequences of applying British legal codes to this colonial context – 'a country inhabited by men of the highest and of the lowest races, all absolutely equal before the law'.[40]And he ultimately wearied of the whole revolutionary concept of equality of individuals before the law. 'So little was understood of the working of the minds of barbarians!'[41] At the base of it all, as Theal stated in the Preface to his *Kafir Folklore* was the 'degree of civilisation'.

The 'barbarians' were, however, at least *sui generis* in Theal's racial hierarchy : they *were* open to improvement, such 'improvement to be most effective should be gradual rather than sudden' (1913). He had few such hopes of those groups of *mixed* race in Southern Africa. If 'purity of race' was a key to progressive evolution, then impurity of race was a key to social decline. As early as volume two, Theal is informing the reader on the deleterious consequence of race mixture. We learn, as a general point, that the Portuguese who invaded East Africa in 1505 had such an easy path because of the lack of indigenous resistance on the part of the local Arab agencies.[42] And why?

> If they had been pure Arabs, or pure Persians, there is no doubt that they would have preferred risking their lives [than] to submitting tamely, but they were of mixed blood and the hearts of most of them waxed exceedingly faint'.[43]

In turn, the decline of the great Portuguese maritime empire is not least traced to the race consequence of the conquerors too closely integrating the conquered into their domestic society. Indeed,

> never has a mistake or crime led to more disastrous results, for the introduction of negroes or labourers on estates belonging to the nobles and religious orders in Alemtejo and the Algarves, the decline of the kingdom in power and importance may largely be attributed. The effects were not visible for many years, but no one can come into contact with the lower classes in Southern Portugal today without being impressed with the

fact that both the Europeans and the Africans have been ruined by mixture of their blood.[44]

Again and again does Theal return to the negative point, that miscegenation is the enemy of not merely colonial progress, but even of civil society itself. We learn that in the mid-18th century Cape frontier, 'nearly every case of cruelty by colonists was committed by men who either had coloured blood in their veins or who had mixed with the uncivilised coloured people on terms of equality';[45] we read of the reasons why mixed-race Griqua people failed to civilise and pacify their frontier regions, despite missionary assistance –

> They dressed in European clothing, used the colonial Dutch language and in many respects conformed to European customs . . . but from their [black] mothers they had inherited an amount of restlessness, indisposition for prolonged industry, and want of frugality, that tended to prevent their advance in wealth or comfort in mode of living.[46]

And we learn of the distinction between the 'pure Asiatic settlers on the African coast', who were 'grave and dignified, though courteous in demeanour', and 'the mixed breeds', who 'had all the superstitions of both races from which they descended'.[47]

Above all, we are given a most damning account of Portuguese expansion in Africa, centred around the failure of this major European colonising power to hold true to its civilising mission. Indeed, according to Theal, 'long before the close of the 16th century they had ceased to be participants in the great progressive movement of the Caucasian race'. The reasons for this decline are highly revealing:

> Rapacity, cruelty, corruption have all been laid to her charge at this period, and not without sufficient reason. But apart from these vices, her weakness under the Castillian kings was such that she was incapable of doing any good. When an individual is too infirm and decrepit to manage his affairs, a robust man takes his place, and so it is with States. The weak one may cry out that might is not right, but such a cry finds a very feeble echo.

One crucial sign of Portuguese infirmity was its absorption of the conquered peoples into the coloniser's society. 'No other Europeans have ever treated negroes so mildly as the Portuguese, or been so ready to mix with them on equal terms', he declares in discussing the decline of Portugal in the 1570's.

> But even in Estremadura, Alemtejo and the Algarves it was impossible for the European without losing self-respect to labour side by side with the African . . . . The slaves, on embracing Christianity, had various privileges conferred upon them, and their blood became mixed with that of the least energetic of the peasantry, until a new and degenerate stock, frivolous, inconstant, and incapable of improvement, was formed. In the northern provinces . . . a pure European race remained, fit not only to conquer but to hold dominion in distant lands, though too small in proportion to the entire population of the country to control its destinies.[48]

Fatal to Portuguese power was the social reality that 'even among the upper classes there was not that aversion to alliances with blacks that to a large extent protects the northern races from deterioration'.[49]

Not that this 'deterioration' belonged alone in the metropolitan homeland. On the very ocean-going Portuguese vessels, which connected Africa and Lisbon, black labour and black temptation soon existed, 'and then decay set rapidly in . . .'[50]. And once settled in Africa, the Portuguese ultimately lost their sense of distinctive Caucasian strength and mission. In Theal's plain language,

> The Portuguese, whether soldiers or traders, were in South Africa so circumstanced that they degenerated rapidly. A European female was very rarely seen and nearly every white man consorted with Bantu women . . . Cut off from all society but that of barbarians, often until towards the close of the 16th century without ministrations of the Church, sunk in sloth . . . no lives led by Europeans anywhere could be more miserable than theirs.[51]

Even when the Catholic Church did ultimately intervene in this African mission field, it failed to hold the Portuguese true to their role in the Caucasian movement of overseas expansion:

There were energetic men of the Dominican order in South Africa at the close of the 17th century, but the spirit of languour in which Portugal and her foreign possessions were steeped embraced the great body of the friars also. Further, many of these were Asiatics and Eurasians, and a few were Africans, not half weaned from another creed, all quite unfit to carry on mission work unless under close supervison of white men.

The 18th century showed no better prospect. By then 'so many members were either Asiatics, or Africans, or mixed breeds, that little zeal could be expected from it'.[52] Theal's ultimate verdict on Portuguese colonial activity is bleak in the extreme, mirrored only by his dismissive summation of Portuguese Christian missionising:

> And so, between wars, invasions and want of competent teachers, Christianity [actually] declined in Portuguese South Africa, and among the Bantu quite died out . . . This was the condition of things after intercourse between the Caucasian and black races extending over 300 years.[53]

Theal's final words on the Portuguese, at the close of volume II of the *History*, are simple, but damning. By 1700 the Portuguese were 'no longer a nation of explorers'.[54] Indeed, when introducing his separate story of *The Portuguese in South Africa, with a Description of the Native Races between the River Zambesi and the Cape of Good Hope during the Sixteenth Century* (January, 1896) Theal made all too plain his view of the relative significance of the Portuguese as against the Dutch in the colonial settlement and development of the region: 'The Portuguese in South Africa are not entitled to the same amount of space in a history as the Dutch, for they did nothing to colonise the country. I think that in this little volume I have given them their just proportion' (Preface, p.8).

Africa, in Theal's *History*, was by 1600 drifting back to its old barbarian rhythms given the Portuguese colonising failure. But in Theal's grandly unfolding narrative, a crucial new, and positive phase was about to begin after the Portuguese failure. 'In the next volume', he writes with assertive pleasure, 'the progress of a real European colony will be traced, a colony full of life and energy, capable of growth, and of occupying no small place in the world's history . . .'.[55] It is not hard to anticipate what is to happen. The Dutch have arrived, at last, in volume III. Calvinism and capital are about to make their imprint on Africa. We ultimately learn that, among the Dutch, 'pride of race was part of their nature'.[56] The frontier experience accordingly does not dilute the energy which resides in their exclusive ethnicity: 'The repugnance with which uncivilised coloured people were regarded by the Dutch had this good effect, that it preserved the colonists from contamination of blood'.[57] Theal is aware of the miscegenation which still did take place – he is after all writing in the Cape with 'Coloured people' about him – but the consequences of these liaisons are placed firmly outside the ruling Cape Dutch social order:

> There were indeed in the border district a few hundred individuals born of Hottentot mothers by European fathers, but they were not permitted to associate with even the poorest and roughest families of graziers. They were servants, or they were provided by their fathers with a few head of cattle, and then moved away northward to live by themselves. In later years, these people formed the ruling element in the little Griqua clans.[58]

Equally, while acknowledging that the Batavian empire itself was one which was less self-conscious about colour than about Christianity, and that some of the early Dutch administrators were individuals of probably mixed ethnic parentage, Theal argues that the real foundations of the Cape colony were laid not so much in the commercial years of Van Riebeeck, and his moderate incursions, but in the later settlement period of Tulbagh, in the 18th century. And here a crucial factor was the cohesiveness of the colonists as an ethnic group in their interaction with Khoikhoi clans and large Bantu-speaking groupings. In particular, Theal is concerned to make a crucial distinction between servants of the VOC at the Cape, and free burghers who came to settle and colonise the Cape. He saw the beginnings of modern South Africa as symbolically attached to 1657, and not 1652: 'In February 1657, nine of the Company's servants took their discharge, and had small plots of ground allotted to them along the Liesbeck River at Rondebosch. *They were the first South African colonists in the true sense of the word*'.[59]

In time, where environment had finally overcome the Portuguese, and certainly tried the Dutch, it had ultimately witnessed their triumph as a colonising people. They had thus validated their place in the Caucasian movement over the world. Theal occasionally, indeed, interrupts his narrative to provide genealogical lists of these heroic founding families. Below the first of such a list, in volume III of the *History*, he remarks significantly for example,

> In the records many more names than those here given are found, but they are of individuals who did not remain long in South Africa. The law of survival of the fittest was here in full operation, and those who were not adapted to become useful colonists were speedily obliged to return into the Company's service. The men might indeed be said to have been discharged on probation [from the VOC] and, in addition, to this process of selection, a wastrel was very unlikely to obtain a wife among the farmer's daughters, so that the permanent colonists were a picked body of steady and well conducted men.[60]

The family of this historian enter Theal's *History* in volume four when the first Schreuder emigrated to the Cape. This paper allows me a family response to Theal.[61]

Part of Theal's ethnic and cultural interpretation of the foundation of South Africa was an unspoken assumption about protestantism. It is there in a negative sense when he speaks disparagingly of the Catholic colonising powers, such as the Portuguese; and it is there in a positive manner, when he contemplates the migration of French Hugeunots, and of the northern Germans, to join the original Dutch founding group. Far from diluting the sterling qualities of the Dutch colonists, the protestant French and German settlers are seen as important and complementary ancillary groups, who reinforced the attributes of the founders. The Hugeunots of 1688 are personified in terms of their protestant pastors, 'men of earnest faith, of great bravery, of entire self-devotion'; individuals indeed of singular 'force of character'. As to the German settlers, they are depicted as having come fron singularly 'good stock' – 'from the borderland between the high and low Teutons'.[62] Theal records his approval of the fact that in the case of these various new protestant groups at the Cape, 'care was taken . . . to mix them together [with the Dutch] so that nationalities would speedily become blended'. Indeed, they were absorbed into the founding group in a particular manner –

> The Germans were, almost without exception, men who were married to Dutch women. Inter-marriages between the Hugeunots and other colonists were common, and in another generation, distinctions of nationality were entirely lost.[63]

Elsewhere he remarks pithily, 'Thereafter, all were Afrikanders (sic)'.[64]

Here was the very beginning of Theal's conception of modern white South Africa. And here, too, in these early centuries, was laid the basis of a colonial society of settlement, comparable with any in the grand history of European expansion:

> Their views of rights and liberties were not indeed those of today, because they were men of the seventeenth, not the twentieth century. But they possessed a full share of the sturdy spirit of independence which led the people of the Netherlands on more than one occasion within that century to risk life and property in defence of freedom . . . And assuredly the men who built up the European power in South Africa were, in those qualities which ought to command esteem, no whit behind in pioneers of any colony in the world. They brought to this country an unconquerable love of liberty, a spirit of patient industry, a deep-seated feeling of trust in the Almighty God: virtues which fitted them to do the work marked out for them by Providence in the land that to their children was home.[65]

In addition, these 'founders' remained conscious of their ethnic identity and of their role as Europeans in the overseas world – thus bequeathing another legacy to the future South Africa in relation to its non-European peoples. The natural environment, together with the frontier conflict in Africa, as the colonists interacted with the indigenous peoples, produced its own powerful reinforcing determinants:

> observation and experience had taught them [by 1800] that these [African] races who did nothing for the world's good were inferior to their own, and they did not, and could not, set the same value upon the life of one of them as upon the life

of a civilised white man. There were instances of harsh treatment of coloured people, but upon the whole the white colonists of South Africa were not more cruel than other Europeans in similar circumstances were at that time. To their feeling of superiority of blood it is due that the present colonies [1893] are not inhabited by a nation of improvident and worthless mongrels.[66]

In Theal's historical vision, these early Dutch simply created better than they knew, and it becomes the task of the historian to illuminate such a social significance in the scale of world events.

The records of the colonists and their industries are the symbols of a community so small that its history would scarcely be worth recording, if it had not occupied such a commanding position, if it were not that from it the present Union of South Africa has grown, and if it had not been in contact with the barbarism of a continent.[67]

That last metaphor, the contact with 'the barbarism of a continent', also provides the key to the third major feature of Theal's writings that I would notice. This concerns his general conception of European expansion as African conquest, and which formed a natural extension of his racial theoretics. Subsumed in this issue is Theal's moral legitimisation of the 'right to the land' in the process of conquest. Theal saw Western imperialism as more than the expansion of the European economy and state-system. Rather, he cast it more grandly, within a more elevated theme – as the cutting edge of the civilising of mankind. In Theal's view, here was what he happily termed 'the law of progress'. And by this he meant both the evangelising of European values, by individual commercial or christian agencies, as well as the spread of European society itself in overseas settlement: the provision of both emulative models and systems of progressive rule. Commenting upon the capacity of individual Africans from the Xhosa clans to make a career within colonial society – such as Tiyo Soga, William Koyi and John Bokwe, who in fact became Christian missionaries – Theal provided this classic summation of his views:

The Xosas, like all other Bantu, are of mixed blood, and among their ancestors must have been Asiatics of high intelligence. The men here named may have owed their qualities to atavism, but even if so, they serve as models for their people to work up to, and in course of time an elevation must take place. If by mischance they were left to themselves they would not advance, but with civilisation facing them, and the leaven of a higher life working in the minds of some of themselves, they must conform to the law of progress.[68]

Theal himself placed greatest faith in the expansion of European settlement as the best hope of an improving revolution in African society. 'Without colonisation on a sufficiently large scale to make the higher indisputably the ruling race', as he put it as early as volume two, in bewailing the langour of the Portuguese approach, 'no part of Africa can be brought within the domains of civilisation by Caucasians'.[69] When he was writing these volumes, in the 1890s, Zimbabwe was, of course, being conquered by the British South African Company of Cecil John Rhodes and partners; and here Theal was in no doubt how its future history *should* be written.

There is an opportunity for introducing civilisation far into the heart of Africa, in the only way in which it can successfully be done, that is by means of European settlements sufficiently strong to rule without danger of revolt, and to be able at the same time to act with justice and kindness towards the native race.[70]

Indeed, this was Theal's prescription for the progressive historical development of a Dominion of white settlers in the region. The challenge of the 20th century was to fulfill the promise and the achievement of the original white 'founders' –

The continuation of the *Story of South Africa* [sic] . . . will be an account of either brilliant successes or disastrous failures, there will be little of mediocrity in it. The prospect certainly seems bright at present [in 1893], but a stream of European immigrants of the right stamp is needed to make it continue so. In the movement northward [into Zimbabwe], the sons and daughters of the Cape Colony are taking an active part, and there are no people on earth more fitted than they to be the pioneer settlers of a new land. The nationalities from which they spring are not those that recede, and the fusion that is taking place – nothwithstanding there is still a small section of both Dutch and English who regard each other with hostility – is not diminishing the vigour . . . But they are too few in number to occupy and hold the great interior plateau. As they go forward, men and women from Europe – of the class that wins success by industry, perserverance, and prudence – must come in and fill the places they leave, if South Africa is to have a really brilliant future.[71]

Again and again does Theal return to his underlying theme of a 'South Africa' made in the image of the founding peoples, that special 'fusion' of Dutch and English characteristics which are to confront and 'civilise' Africa itself. By natural implication, the hope for Africa lay in imitation of 'the European mode of living'. Those African resources, either political or cultural, which prevented that process from taking place are condensed in Theal's *History*. Elemental to his social view was ultimately the notion that the conquest of Africa by the forces of white colonial civilisation was an extension of the general force of world progress. Theal's characterisation of the famed and critical Anglo-Zulu War of 1879 is pointedly plain: 'The question was simply whether civilisation or barbarism was to prevail in the country'. [72] For behind the continued existence of the House of Shaka, in the form of King Cetshswayo, Theal detected forces antithetical not merely to the colonists but to Western expansion and the 'laws of progress'. The reason why Natal was not advancing 'as other British possessions were advancing was lack of European immigrants in large numbers and European capital, but neither one nor the other was attracted to a land so largely occupied by barbarians, and with a powerful barbarian military state on its border ever menacing the security of life and property'.[73] The Zulu war became accordingly, in Theal's idiom, 'a necessity'.[74] Cetshwayo was condemned not alone because he ruled Zululand autocratically, but because 'he cannot have had a moral right to be a perpetual menace to others'.[75] The Zulu leader had become an enemy of that larger force of progress and which ultimately affected even his own peoples. Theal's summation of the results of the Zulu War neatly draws out the lesson involved:

In this manner the most formidable of the military powers that had their origin in the early years of the nineteenth century was overthrown, to the great gain not only of Natal, which colony was now able to make a great bound forward in prosperity, but of every black man in South Africa.[76]

Theal was all too aware that a tragedy was inherently involved for the 'losers'. His text is often marked by a compassionate comment on a vanquished African leader. He remarks of the destruction of Makoma, for example, that

> if one of another race sympathises with him, what must the Gaikas have felt when the tidings reached them that he had died as a dog dies? What must Tini, his son, have felt?[77]

And yet: this chief and every African traditional leader, *has* to be seen by Theal within that larger force of progress. His epitaph was accordingly preordained: 'The fate of Makoma is an illustration of what must happen when civilisation and barbarism come into contact, and barbarism refuses to give way'.[78] A similar verdict was duly pronounced over other Xhosa leaders who opposed the march of the Cape up the coastal lands of the Nguni in the later-19th century. 'Such is the fate of a barbarian ruler who endeavours to resist the progress of a civilised neighbour, he must go under'.[79] The conquest of Pondoland was similarly treated: 'At the beginning of 1894 the colonial authorities regarded the condition of things in Pondoland as such that the country and people must be brought at once under the control of civilised men'.[80] The Scramble for Africa in the same decades was played out in the region of Southern Africa with a vengeance. Theal came to see colonial expansion over African lands and societies in terms of the clash of progressive and retrogressive forces. To the moot question of 'why imperialism' he responded vigorously:

> The answer is that they were taken over from sheer necessity . . . There was no other way of keeping order among them. The danger to be apprehended from extending [colonial rule] . . . was great, but the danger of leaving them to themselves was greater. Prevented from destroying each other in war and on charges of dealing in witchcraft, they would increase at an amazing rate; [however] under European rule old tribal feuds

would be forgotten, so that one section could not be used to keep another in submission; but it might [rather] be hoped that as new generations came into existence they would learn to appreciate more and more the benefits of peace and righteous government, and would be content to live as obedient subjects. And so they were taken over, and the most strenuous efforts that were possible . . . were put forth to lead them onward in civilisation and prosperity.[81]

Theal's mature imperialism was governed, of course, by his ultimately critical attitude towards traditional African culture. 'The reclamation of the people from barbarism, for their own good . . .' accordingly became an ever more marked aspect of the narrative, as the white polities expanded across the veld, and as the age of the chiefs was gradually eroded by the advance of the colonial frontier-agencies. Here lay the moral justification for imperialism; or, as Theal put it, 'the right of civilised men to take possession of land occupied by such a race . . .'. A great historical inevitability was here detected by Theal: 'to the present day no one has devised a plan by which this can be done without violence'.[82]

Almost incidentally Theal introduces into popular circulation one of the most pervasive myths of white colonial historiography in South Africa, namely that the settlers and the Africans entered the region largely concurrently in the 17th century. In a footnote, at the end of volume five, we indeed learn that 'neither the Hottentots nor the the Bantu are aborigines, and consequently are not entitled to be called natives more than children of European colonists born in South Africa are'.[83] And in his popularising *Story of South Africa*, Theal offers a map which delineates this concurrent partition of Southern Africa between the colonising Europeans and the defensive Bantu-speaking groups.[84] The point conveyed is a simple but critical message in terms of settlement and colonisation: the native societies have no more natural right to the land of Southern Africa than the colonists. And accordingly, in the light of the capacity of the Europeans to civilise and redeem Africa from both 'barbarism' and economic subsistence, the right of justice tips historically in favour of legitimising white conquest and settlement. This becomes all the more important as Theal's narrative unfolds to depict 'South Africa' as one of the major new societies of the new world – not a peculiar state of minority rule which diverged sharply from the pattern of, say, Australia or Canada.

Primarily indeed Theal rests his argument for the legitimacy of European expansion on global forces of change and of progress. He sees this as even more true through the 19th century, as Southern Africa was drawn into the advanced industrialising phase of Immanuel Wallenstein's 'world system'. The mineral revolutions of the 1870s and 1880s on the highveld finally confirmed the meaning of the imperial impact in Theal's view: 'we have been brought under the law that impels Europeans to struggle for knowledge and power, and have fallen into line with the most energetic communities of our race'.[85]

This stress on the colonial polity as agent of conquest and civilising progress is quintessentially Theal. Here he is at his most didactic and most patriotic. Here he is also most revealing of the last of the major suppositions which I suggested underpinned the massive *History*. For ultimately, fundamental to his whole enterprise – delineating the overall meaning of the colonial experience in southern African history – was his propagation of a particular conception of the making of the white state. Even before the formal state-making of 1910, Theal had committed himself to portraying southern African history in terms of the rise of a new nation, a unique 'new society' of overseas settlement, which reflected both its diverse European immigrant composition and its frontier experience in history. Not for him the flat notion of 'South Africa' as a political compromise among the white élite from regional colonies, in the face of the huge overall African majority. The road to 1910 was rather the high road of a new and evolving colonial nationality – the making of a particular 'national identity', rooted in historical experience, and shaped not merely by environment, but by the greater forces of human evolution, those favourite 'laws' of social progress. A distinguished historian of the Australian state once asked, 'who are the fathers?' of the new society.[86] If such a question were to be posed of the 1910 state in South Africa, G. M. Theal should be included alongside Smuts, Botha and the delegates to the national convention. For it was Theal who had provided the public culture with the intellectual justification of the English-Dutch idiom of a new state.

Theal was indeed to hang his whole *History* from the hook of 'nationalism'. The era of the Dutch, and even VOC rule, had made the first and sure beginnings of this natural foundation. The coming of the British in the 19th century had secured that achievement, in terms of colonisation and settlement. And then, very gradually but ineluctably, history had seen a convergence of 'Afrikaners' and Victorians. It is hard not to smile when Theal first introduces the British into his narrative, after the glowing Dutch foundation has been described. We might expect a disjunction. But no, he has a theory ready to hand to make the transition seem an effortless, 'natural', historical event. History is again on the side of his *History*. 'The surrender of the Cape Colony to the British forces', he happily tells us,

> brought together two branches of the same race, for conquerors and conquered were of one stock. Of all the nations of Europe, the inhabitants of the Northern Netherlands are the closest in blood to the people of England and Scotland.[87]

'Afrikaners' and British had initially viewed each other with some small suspicion: 'Though in the most important feature their characters were the same, each regarded the variations in the other as blemishes, and often made more of them than was fair or honest.'[88] *But*, the common environmental experience, and social interaction in a colonial world, soon meant that history had its way:

> And yet, with all these harsh opinions of each other, there was really so little difference between English people and *South Africans* [note: it's the Dutch who are the real founders] that as soon as they came together, matrimonial connections began to be formed. The attractions of blood were stronger after all than the prejudices born of strife and want of knowledge.[89]

The English indeed leavened the rude 'colonial character', as Theal described the Cape Dutch founding frontier society, with 'education of a healthy kind'; and the Cape Dutch, in return, gave to South African society as a whole 'several virtues possessed in a very high degree' – self-reliance, courage and tenacity of purpose – 'in which they were without equals'.

Heros and villains in this epic had undergone something of a revolution since Theal's pioneer historical narrative in the *Compendium* of the early 1870s. The Dutch now occupied a new and central role: the Cape Dutch had become the Pilgrim Fathers, creating that orderly basis for the emergence of a colonial society; the expanding Cape Dutch of the frontier, either as treking Boers or as Voortrekkers, had become the pioneer civilisers, opening the interior of Africa. The stalwart English farmer, and honest man of business, joined this colonial progress, absorbing the qualities of the founding emigrants, and adding the framework of a great empire of commerce, administration and power: 'the advantage of being connected with a realm vastly more powerful than their own fatherland'.[90]

At the top of Theal's list of critics of the nascent nation was now the Humanitarian lobby in the imperial capital, and its several representatives at the Cape. Previously Theal had written largely from within the Humanitarian tradition at Lovedale. Now he was convinced that this tradition was not a true guide to the key issue of race-relations in plural South Africa. In his marked shift of perspective it is important to note that Theal is not merely altering the balance of his position: in the 1870s he is sympathetic to the Humanitarian interest; in the 1890s he presents the settler view. His intellectual 'conversion' involves something deeper than a switch in environments. The reason he is ultimately so critical of the Humanitarian position, and especially towards certain key representatives of that tradition – such as the missionaries, Philip, Livingstone and Mackenzie – is because he interprets their opinions and actions as those of enemies to his emerging 'new society' of Dutch–Anglo–Saxon South Africa. He is not merely bristling with patriotic irritation at the imperial outsider who criticises colonial practices; he is rather seeing in them the critics of the evolving new 'national' community to which he is committed. The Humanitarian exposé of *Boer* practices concerning labour and frontier policies thus cuts to the quick of Theal's sense of new patriotism. The Dutch are not the rude first settlers of South Africa, to be civilised by the later British colonisation. They are 'the founders', the 'first South Africans'. To criticise them is implicitly to suggest a less than complete commitment to the idea of 'South Africa'. Writing in his 1887 *History of the Boers in South Africa* Theal was careful to remark that 'no one will find a word in this volume condemnatory of mission work *properly, so called*, for no one can be more favourably disposed towards it than I am'. But of course Theal's charge against certain Humanitarian agencies in South Africa was that their conception of mission work had exceeded its evangelical and educative role to become political and partisan. It was the old cry of 'rid me of this meddlesome priest' in a colonial setting.

This theme is admirably revealed in Theal's portrayal of Dr. John Philip (1775–1851), Superintendent of the activities of the non-conformist London Missionary Society in South Africa from 1822; and whose two volume *Researches in South Africa* (1828) had attempted an exposé of frontier labour practices, especially as regards the Cape Coloured people.[91] Philip is shown in Theal's volumes to be singularly instrumental in influencing the Imperial Government to promulgate Ordinance 20 of 1828, which secured civil rights for 'free persons of colour' in the Cape – and this over the real majority opposition, and understanding, of the colonists at the Cape. How could this have happened? Theal's explanation is curiously simple: 'as the great philanthropical societies of England supported him [Philip] he was virtually master of the position'. But far from simple consequences followed for the Colony –

> In July 1828 an ordinance was issued which relieved the Hottentots and other free coloured people from the laws concerning passes and the apprenticeship of children, and placed them in all respects on a political level with Europeans. From that time the colony was overrun by idle wanderers to such an extent that farming could hardly be made to pay, and the coloured people were falling back in the scale of civilisation; but when an attempt was made years later to get a vagrant act proclaimed, Dr. Philip and his party opposed the measure so strenuosly that it had to be abandoned.[92]

Indeed, at that critical period of the 1830s, when Dutch and English settlers were coming to an appreciation of each other as colonists, it was Dr. Philip who took, up the issue of race and frontier relations, and worked as an enemy of the new society. Colonial frontier expansion in the 1830s, so necessary for white security and African civilisation, was to be denied. 'This plan of settlement commended itself to the great majority of the colonists and of the missionaries, who hoped that under it the Kosas would make rapid advances towards civilisation and that property on the border would be secure.'[93] *But*:

There was ... in Cape Town – five hundred miles from the Kaffir frontier – a party under the leadership of the reverend Dr. Philip, that entirely disapproved of the governor's plans. It was composed of only a few individuals, but it had powerful support from abroad. This party desired the formation of states ruled by Bantu chiefs under the guidance of missionaries, and from which Europeans not favoured by missionaries, should be excluded. It maintained the theory that the Kosas were an eminently docile and peaceably disposed people, who could easily be taught to do what was right, and who must therefore have been provoked to take up arms by great wrongs and cruelties. The utmost fear was expressed by its members that the Bantu tribes would perish if exposed to free intercourse with white people.[94]

A false departure in Imperial policy resulted, not least in terms of the noted despatch of 26 December 1835 which abandoned the recently acquired frontier area between the Keiskama and the Kei rivers in the Eastern Cape.

The contents of this despatch spread consternation widely over South Africa. Outside of Dr. Philip's little party at Cape Town there was but one opinion: that it destroyed all hope of the preservation of order, and placed life and whatever property was left in the eastern districts at the mercy of the Kosas.[95]

Above all, Philip is indicted for interfering in the 'natural' evolution of race relations in colonial Southern Africa. Here the colonial nationalist in Theal subsumes the settler views on not only white supremacy, but on a supremacy which involved colonial development and progress through a combination of African land and labour exploitation.

The elevation of the coloured races was then a leading – and surely a praiseworthy – idea in England, but, unfortunately, the great philanthropic and missionary societies had made up their minds as to the precise manner in which this should be effected, and condemned as unchristian all views that differed from their own. Applying their principles to South Africa, the formation of large Bantu states under missionary guidance and

British protection was what they desired, and the reverend Dr.
Philip, the exponent of their views, was urging this scheme
upon the Cape Government. Time has shown how faulty it
was, but no one even in this country could foresee the full
extent of harm it would cause to the black people as well as
to the white. The devastations which the Zulus and Matabele
had wrought were unknown in Europe, and therefore when
intelligence reached England that many thousands of the men
of those tribes had fallen before the farmer's guns, public
opinion was shocked. No one suspected that the destruction of
those fierce warriors meant life to all other black people in the
country.[96]

In short, Philip's Humanitarianism was not in the interest of any
section of the colonial society. Writing in the 1890s, Theal still
had this harsh verdict to make on events and policies of half-a-
century previously:

> It is only within the last ten years that the disastrous effects of
> policy towards the Bantu tribes initiated by Dr. Philip and put
> into operation through the enormous influence which he
> possessed with the philanthropic societies, have been
> obliterated, if, indeed, in the case of the Basuto tribe they can
> be said to be obliterated even now. During the intervening
> years the government was put to infinite trouble, and the
> progress of the colony in prosperity and of the black races
> towards civilisation was greatly retarded by the measures which
> he devised and his powerful supporters carried out. A quarter
> of a century after his death his name could not be mentioned
> in the eastern districts of the Cape Colony without calling forth
> denunciation . . .[97]

Theal's hostile view of Philip was not, it should be stressed, a
kind of personal literary vendetta against an individual. The
missionary movements more largely, and individual missionaries
in particular, are assessed in terms of whether they met or failed
the test of being acceptable to colonial wisdom on the critical
issues of race, labour and the frontier. Before Philip there had
been Van der Kemp and Read, both LMS servants, who
intervened on 'the wrong side' in the issue of race relations in the
first decade of the British presence and were duly censured by

Theal: indirectly they 'caused a lasting unfriendly feeling between the colonists and the missionaries of the London Society'.[98] Later, it was the renowned Dr. David Livingstone who earned Theal's approbrium. Livingstone is portrayed as indeed 'the greatest explorer of modern times', but it is noticed that 'Dr. Livingstone was a strong partisan of the Bantu, and did his utmost to oppose the claims of the emigrant farmers [of Boer trekkers] to dominion over the clan with which he was living, so that his statements are those of an advocate rather than those of a judge. He represented [chief] Setyelli as wholly in the right, and the farmers as wholly in the wrong: but any impartial writer who examines Setyelli's own account of the matter . . . must come to a different conclusion.'[99] Later still again, in the era of the Scramble for Africa after 1880, it is the Rev. John Mackenzie who failed to work with the new society in the making, and instead acted as the partisan critic of the colonists. 'The government and people of the South African Republic were strongly opposed to Mr. Mackenzie's appointment [as Deputy Commissioner in the British Protectorate of Bechuana-land in 1882] on the ground that he was a partisan of the Bantu whether they were in the right or wrong . . .'. Bishop Colenso of Natal was also to receive a like judgement from Theal concerning Anglo-Zulu relations in the 1880s. As we learn: 'his championship of the Bantu whether they were right or wrong arose from his feeling that they needed protection, as they were unable to defend themselves . . . But his judgement in this respect was not always correct and indeed want of judgement was his weakest point'.[100]

In essence, it was this hostility of the British Humanitarians to the pattern of race relations established by the founding Dutch colonists which Theal felt increasingly bound to comment upon as part of his propagation of a community of Afrikaner-English convergence as the quintessential South African society. 'It is not a pleasant admission for an Englishman to make', as he writes plainly at the opening of chapter XV of his *Story of South Africa* when dealing with the critical 1826–35 period, the very prelude to the Great Trek,

> but it is the truth, that it would be difficult to find in any part of the world a people with so much cause to be discontented as the old inhabitants of the Cape Colony . . . There was no sympathy whatever shown towards them by the authorities in England, in fact there was a decided antipathy, which was

fostered by the so-called philanthropic societies, then at the height of their power. The most outrageous stories concerning the colonists were circulated by men who bore the title of Christian Teachers – and nothing was too gross to be believed in England, – until the word Boer (Dutch for farmer) came to be regarded as a synonym for an ignorant and heartless oppressor of coloured people. It was useless for the governers to report differently, or for the courts of law to pronounce the stories libellous: the great societies condemned "the Boers", and the great societies represented and led public opinion in England.[101]

By the 1890s Theal had so thoroughly come to absorb the classic white colonial view of African societies that he could summarise the Humanitarian case as essentially one which 'laid down a theory that the coloured races were in all respects except education mentally equal to the European colonists, and that they were wrongfully and socially oppressed by the white people of the government',[102] and had an ultimate influence on policy that was deleterious both for the colonial 'new Society' *and* for the non-European peoples themselves – 'The effect was something like giving a child of ten years of age the rights of a full grown man'.[103] In plain terms, the L.M.S. had become an enemy of the colonists.

Theal is also alert of course to non-religious or civil agencies who were antithetical to the colonial point of view, as he would see it. His hostility to interfering 'high imperialists' of the later 19th century had been pre-dated by his negative verdict on Dutch officials such as H. C. Maynier, who attempted to regulate race relations in the frontier district of Graaf Reiniet from the basis of principles of justice found to be in discord with that of the local trek–Boer population.[104] Maynier's interventions had led to Boer disaffection, and Theal is in no doubt on which side his *History* would stand in relation to these events of the 1780s. We quickly learn that Maynier was an individual who 'professed to believe that the Xosas were incapable of acting with duplicity', a view based on his non-South African intellectual heritage – he was 'deeply read in the works of the French philosophers of the day'; and, 'in defiance of what observations should have taught' had 'professed to believe that simplicity and innocence are virtues of barbarian life'.[105] Clearly, here was not the kind of 'founder' required of a new colonial society. Maynier summarily leaves the *History*.

Theal's narrative has a cumulative balance sheet of positive and negative events by which he charts the emergence of his new society of settlement. The Great Trek becomes, perhaps a little surprisingly for an English-speaking author, a positively great event, in revealing the heroic qualities of the founders, and also a great mark against the ill-informed interference of the Humanitarian school of British missionaries. Equally, events such as Transvaal annexation (1877), the Jameson Raid (1895) and the Anglo-Boer War (1899–1902) all become further near catastrophes, which might permanently have divided British and Afrikaners in the evolution and making of the colonial society. Ultimately, however, not even the best efforts of meddlers – from Dr. Philip to Lord Milner – can defy the force of their emerging national identity. Little wonder. Not only is this South African state the product of sturdy Anglo-Saxon settlers, but its beginnings can be seen to rest with Dutch colonists who 'were of the same blood as the men who withstood the great power of Philip II of Spain [and] who laid the richest part of their country under water rather than surrender it to Louis XIV of France'. The same former Empire Loyalist could now cast the future history of one of Her Majesty's dominions around the phenomenon of a colonial nationality, rooted in the spirit of a Dutch–English convergence, and focussed on a political strategy of 'home rule'.

Theal indeed took the elevated view that this was exactly what was involved in the grant of responsible government to the Cape colonists in 1872. He saw rule from Whitehall as ineffective at 6000 miles distant, dangerously arbitrary and open to the lobbying of pernicious Humanitarian Societies, especially against the Boer frontier-farmers. At last the British realised that 'the best course they could adopt would be to let the affairs of the Cape Colony be settled by its own people'. This provided, in Theal's view, a strong feeling of loyalty to the crown, while leaving South African politics properly in the hands of its own white society. The advantages were certainly material: 'Since the management of its affairs has been in the hands of its own people, the . . . Colony has made an enormous stride in prosperity.' They were also practical: at last an 'effective' frontier and native policy was followed. But, above all, they had deep meaning for the nature of the colonial society itself: self-government had made the local parliament 'more truly representative of the people, and it has removed a serious obstacle to the perfect blending of the colonists of Dutch and British blood, which is now happily in rapid progress'.[106]

*   *   *

The Anglo-Boer War at the turn of this century was to cause George McCall Theal considerable distress. His distress had something in common with that of the founding professor of my Australian Department, George Arnold Wood, who also came to question both the morality of the war and its effect upon the imperial idea itself.[107] But in the case of Theal, his dilemma extended beyond criticising imperial policy while a citizen of the empire. Theal had developed strong pro-Boer sympathies, even if he dissented from 'Krugerism'. This came to light in the fierce debates which broke out over the war both in Britain *and* in the other colonies of settlement which had contributed to the imperial war effort, with 'colonial' contingents of soldiers and in material. Most embarrassing of all for Theal, powerful criticism of his position came from his homeland of Canada itself.

In 1895 Theal had taken deep pleasure in the fact that Queens University, in Kingston, Ontario, had honoured him with a D. Litt., not least in recognition of his *History*.[108] And in the citation Theal had been specially commended for writing a *History* which expressed the *colonial* point of view. Indeed, it was suggested that he was uniquely fitted to write such a *History*, as he had been born into a colonial world, and was therefore more attuned to the character and spirit of an overseas settlement nation than the writers of the metropolitan state. Now, in 1900, it appeared that he was found to be *too* sympathetic to that sense of colonial identity, in the form of the Afrikaner (Dutch) leanings in his *History*. Worst of all, from Theal's point of view, the main attack on his conception of South African colonial nationality came from the pen of the professor of English at Queen's University.

In a work called *Britain's Title in South Africa*, Professor Cappon went to considerable lengths to expose the underpinnings of Theal's *History* as providing a biased and one-sided account of the colonial history of the region. In particular, Cappon was at pains to identify the manner in which he believed Theal's *History* to have favoured the role of the Cape Dutch and the highveld Boers, at the expense of the British imperial role, not least over critical issues concerned with race-relations and the 'right to the land'. Cappon's view of the 1899 war was in terms of a belated attempt at intervention by the Imperial Factor, after almost a century of appeasement of the colonists over issues of race and civil rights.

Theal was clearly furious at the charges. His lengthy reply to Cappon's critical book was published in the *Toronto Globe* on Saturday, 24 August 1901, during the last phases of the war for the highveld. Theal was defiant of Cappon's charges of being pro-Boer, and proudly spoke of his friendship with leading Afrikaners, such as President Reitz of the Orange Free State – though he was more guarded over Oom Paul. He lashed out, in classic Theal fashion, at the Humanitarians who had poisoned world opinion against the white colonists of Africa – and now, by inference, duped Professor Cappon, who was characterised as merely echoing 'the sentiments of the abolitionist press' of the early 19th century. Theal also debunked the notion, pressed by Cappon, that white colonisation in South Africa had been established over earlier African title to the land. In particular, Theal was determined to present an historical characterisation of the crucial Cape frontier areas in which Bantu-speaking indigenous societies had no special natural prior claim to the land. Cappon had specifically argued that certain African clans 'had fed their flocks and hunted buffalo on the banks of the Sandy River long before a Dutch Boer had trekked beyond the Breede'. But Theal quickly exposed such simple historical geography:

No one with an unprejudiced mind who had made close research into the history of South Africa could have written these sentences. *The Europeans were advancing from one side, the Kaffirs from the other; they met at the Fish River.* If the Europeans had arrived there ten years sooner they would have occupied the land as far as the Kat [River] without opposition. If the Kaffirs had arrived there ten years sooner they would in the same manner have occupied the Zuurveldt. The claim of each rested upon prior occupation. In 1780 ... some other small clans of Kaffirs invaded the Zuurveld and drove many of the Europeans away; and in 1790 the Chief Ndlambe, with a large body of followers, entered the district and completed the conquest. Constant expansion, war and plundering followed until 1812, when the whole were expelled by Governor Sir John Cradock.

A few missionaries, claiming for the Kaffirs far more than those people ever claimed for themselves, made an outcry against this expulsion, and used language concerning it like that of Professor Cappon. Ndlambe, however, barbarian as he was, based his claim on conquest alone. How many generations would there have been between 1789 and 1812? The claim through the Chonaquas did not hold good, except for a fraction of Cungwas' clan, that had the whole territory below the lower Fish and the Keiskama as its proper abode. There are some people, however, and Professor Cappon is evidently one of them, who are either mutually incapable of judging impartially between whites and blacks or too prejudiced in favour of the latter to do so.

Equally important, Theal was determined to dispute Cappon's view that there was significant distinction to be drawn between Afrikaner and British settler practises concerning race-relations and, notably, over the issue of Labour. 'The truth is this', replied Theal in adopting his most belligerent colonial nationalist stance,

> most of us English in the Colony are at one with the [Cape] Dutch in this matter. We look upon the natives as the natural source of rough labour, and we believe that they cannot be raised in the scale of civilisation without first being taught to work. But we go about compelling them to do so in a different manner. The Dutchmen in older times said straight out [to Africans]: "You must work". We [rather] plan our legislation to compel them to do so and in our self-conceit we imagine that . . . [Africans] do not know what we are aiming at . . . They are awake to our aims, and they have no more real love for us than they have for our Dutch neighbours.

Theal saw the issue of labour as critical, for it symbolised both the race exclusivity of the white community, and the common identity of the colonists in the face of outside criticism. In the very long term, it was over race and nationalist issues that the 'South African Republic' was indeed finally declared in 1961;[109] and here Theal had already partially anticipated the basis of that potential rupture with the empire–commonwealth when he answered Cappon in 1901. 'What is the future of the present

British Empire to be?' he asked rhetorically at the conclusion of his fierce columns. Given that it could not be 'kept together with the sword', only two alternatives existed. The first was to accept the fact of colonial nationality, and let the new societies of settlement rule themselves as they determined best for their polities. They were 'no longer dependencies', in Theal's view, 'but component parts of a great empire, joined together by love and interest'. Indeed, 'in the great colonies already the word dependency rankles'. The future of any empire lay in recognising colonial nationalism, with 'home rule'. Richard Jebb had been anticipated.[110]

The alternative path, in Theal's suitably loaded language, was 'disruption'. And that was the direction which Theal argued was delineated by Professor Cappon's book. For not only did Cappon's views threaten 'disruption', by advocating an unwelcome and unwise interference on the part of the Imperial Factor in the life of emerging settlement nations, they flew in the face of the force of white colonial nationality and identity. The result would *not* be a strengthening of Britannia, but rather the destruction of that natural unity, that convergence of Dutch and British settlers, which had come to characterise the colonial society of Theal's *History*. 'There can be no question that Professor Cappon's book is on that side [of disruption]', was Theal's parting shot at his fellow Canadian. He was to add a final sentence, however, which stood alone from this detailed refutation of his critic, and which yet so well revealed Theal's own spiritual journey – from empire loyalist to colonial nationalist.

> A body of people like the Dutch inhabitants of the Cape Colony – the truest representatives in existence of the sturdy and stubborn sea beggars of three centuries ago – cannot be misrepresented and reviled, and then be expected to love and unite with their assailants.

Writing elsewhere in 1902 Theal declared himself the most loyal servant of crown and empire: 'As a Canadian of Loyalist descent, I naturally wish to see the extension and solidification of the Empire ...' – though he had added guardedly 'where that can take place without wrong or injustice to others ...' this caveat had special meaning in the context of South Africa.

British imperialism in the age of Milner had ultimately to reconcile itself with the 'destiny' of South Africa.

> Let us hope that the time of passion and bloodshed may speedily pass away, and that the restoration of peace and concord in South Africa may be followed by the still closer political union of the states widely severed by land and sea, that have shown themselves at heart to be one ...[111]

The colonial nationalist in Theal, the historical nation-maker, indeed now pressed a particular vision for 'South Africa' in the 20th century.

> South Africa is a land of good hope. Every notable advance that has been made has been preceded by a period of deep depression. God grant that the present – the greatest trouble that it has ever known – may be followed by the perfect reconciliation of the two kindred peoples who occupy the soil, by which alone it can attain the highest point of happiness and prosperity.[112]

Theal lived until 1919. He therefore enjoyed the gratification of witnessing the successful unification movement which created the 'Union' of 1910. His *History* had been fulfilled. In both the withdrawal of the 'imperial factor' from South African domestic politics, and in the apparent reconciliation of 'Dutch' and 'British' communities, he took considerable pleasure. The idea of the nation in the *History* had become the Union of South Africa. Concluding the eighth, revised edition of the *Story of South Africa* – now entitled *South Africa: the Union of South Africa, Rhodesia and All Territories South of the Zambesi* – in June 1916, Theal could not resist the opportunity to make these very points. Despite the damage to English/African relations in the years from the 1895 Jameson Raid, through the Anglo-Boer War to the departure of Milner in 1905, a decade of disasters in Theal's eyes, a vital reconciliation of the colonists had still taken place. 'One good effect of the war was that it created in England a feeling of greater respect for the Dutch-speaking farmers than had existed before', as Theal the 'South African' put it in pointing to the significance of Afrikaner reconciliation:

They proved themselves valiant, if stubborn opponents, in
many instances they had acted chivalrously, and, in sporting
language, they had played the game and kept it up well.
For such a people the feeling could only be one of admiration.
Co-operation between them and the English-speaking people
now became possible, for such prejudice overseas caused by
the misrepresentations of former times could no longer exist.

Immediately after the terms of peace were signed, the fullest
confidence was in each other shown by those who had just
been enemies, and all combined in a strenuous effort to repair
as much as possible the damage that the war had wrought.[113]

Theal accordingly regarded the British Liberal Government's
decision to devolve authority to self-governing South African
colonies after 1906 – the controversial 'magnanimous gesture' –
as 'certainly the best thing that could be done'. He did not
at all see it as condemnation of the British war aims of 1899–
1909 or a capitulation to Afrikaner nationalism. Rather, the
home ruler and nation maker in Theal cheered the result.

It placed the leaders of the men recently in arms against
Great Britain in political power, as had been foreseen, for
General Botha became prime minister of the Transvaal, but
it turned them into firm adherents of connection with the
widespread British nation.[114]

Certainly, Theal did not share the contemporary critical view
that the magnanimous gesture, and the subsequent passage of
the South African Act of unification in the imperial parliament,
was a failure of British policy. Rather he took the reverse view:
it was an act of highest statesmanship. Least of all did Theal
see 'union' as a failure of imperial trusteeship towards African
subjects of the crown in South Africa – the Crown 'handing
over' Africans to the white settlers of the region. Neither the
opposition to union of African protest groups, nor the criticisms
of certain radicals in the Westminster Parliament – 'Abandon
hope all ye who enter here' was suggested as a new slogan to
be painted over the British empire – moved Theal at all.
Instead, it drew from Theal this settled view about both

'white–white' and 'white–black' relations in a future 'South Africa':

> The interests of these colonies were the same, and they were inhabited by closely related people, so that there was no reason why they should not become a single state now that the grant of responsible government to the Transvaal and the Orange Free State made voluntary union possible. Instead of pursuing four different policies with regard to the British, as had previously been the case, a single system dealing with those people, kindly and justly, but firmly, could be carried out, and this was, and would long remain, the most important question to be dealt with everywhere in South Africa, the advantage of union of the European governments would be great.[115]

Theal's interest in African society remained, but it was placed within the framework of white nation-making. Looking to the last great African rising, the Bambatha rebellion in Natal in 1906, Theal argued that it showed, despite European 'improvement in the condition of a large number of the Bantu', this had still not 'eradicated their desire to be free of European control . . .'. And the local Union of the colonists was crucial: 'No other overseas possession of Great Britain had so difficult a question as this to deal with, and a stronger government than any of those then existing was needed for this purpose.'[116]

Unification provided this possibility of nation-making; and the response of the Union to the challenge of the First World War – involving South African confrontation with the Germans in South West Africa, for example – suggested more than promise. The personal journey of the Canadian Empire Loyalist to independent 'South Africa' was complete.

> For the first time in our history, on a large-scale English and Dutch speaking men lived together in the same camp, drilled together, formed close friendships, and, as the casualty lists showed, shed their blood together for the same cause. This is hopeful indeed for the future of South Africa.[117]

George McCall Theal's considered 'second thoughts' about empire in South Africa had become an integral part of a personal declaration of 'second identity'.[118]

NOTES

1. There is no definitive study of Theal as historian, and no biography. I have relied on the following: A. J. Boeseken, entry on Theal in *Dictionary of South African Biography*, vol. IV (Pretoria, 1981) pp. 645–8, and 'Theal as Baanbreker: 11 April 1837–17 April 1919', *S. A. Argiefblad*,I (1959) pp. 33–42; and 'Theal en sy Bronne', *Historia* (March 1964). Merle Babrow has commented on the latter article in 'A reply to Dr. Boeseken', ibid. See also her very valuable M. A. Thesis (U.C.T., 1962) 'A Critical Assessment of Dr. George McCall Theal'. In addition see R. F. M. Immelman, 'George McCall Theal: a Biographical Sketch', in 1964 reprint of G. M. Theal, ed., *Basutoland Records*. I. D. Bosman pioneered the study of Theal, in his *Dr. George McCall Theal as die Geskiedskrywer van South Africa* (Amsterdam, f1932). The most significant recent work on Theal is contained in the extremely important articles by Dr. C. C. Saunders of Cape Town, which I have found invaluable – 'George McCall Theal and Lovedale', Paper presented to the 11th Annual Conference of the *Canadian Association of African Studies* (Unpublished, but kindly sent to me by Dr. Saunders); 'The Missing Link in Theal's Career: the Historian as Labor Agent in the Western Cape', *History in Africa*, 7 (1980) and 'The Making of an Historian: the Early Years of George McCall Theal', *S.A.H.J., No. 13. Nov., 1981*, and personal communication. There is a brief entry on Theal in E. Rosenthal, ed., *Southern African Dictionary of National Biography* (London, 1966) p. 374, which omits important aspects of detail; he has not yet been included in the *Dictionary of Canadian Biography*. I have also consulted a range of obituaries on Theal. A useful retrospective item on Theal appeared in the *Saint John Evening Times*, 25 May 1935. Theal is placed in the context of South African historiography in the valuable essay by L. M. Thompson, in R. W. Winks, ed., *The Historiography of the British–Empire–Commonwealth* (1966), pp. 212–36. The British domestic historiography of empire in the 'Theal years' is now attracting attention: see, J. G. Greenlee 'A Succession of Seeleys; the "Old School" Re-examined', in *Journal of Imperial and Commonweath History*, IV, 3 (1976) pp. 266–82, and Luke Trainor, 'Historians as Imperialists – Some Roots of British Imperial History, 1880–1900', *New Zealand Journal of History*, vol. 15/1 (April 1981) pp. 35–48. Richard White has provided a fascinating comparative perspective on nationalism in another 'region of recent settlement', in *Inventing Australia: Images and Identity* (Sydney, 1981) where he remarks that 'We must remember that historians can be image-makers too' (p. viii).

2. I have used a personal copy of Theal's *History* for citation – the eleven-volume revised edition of his work which he initiated, known as the 'Star Edition', and published by George Allen & Unwin of London, reprinted in 1964 by Struik of Cape Town. And hereafter simply cited as *History*. I have also made use of Theal's companion study, the single volume *Story of South Africa*, (London, 1894), part of the 37-volume 'Story of the Nation

Series' published by T. Fisher Unwin of London; I have quoted from my own copy of the first edition. By 1916 Theal's 'Story' had gone into six editions.

3.   A. P. Thornton, *Doctrines of Imperialism* (New York, 1965).

4.   An excellent comparative example is Carl C. Berger, 'Race and Liberty: the Historical Ideals of Sir John George Bourinot', *The Canadian Historical Association Report*, 1965, pp. 87–104. I thank him for sending me his paper.

5.   Douglas Cole, 'The Problem of "Nationalism" and "Imperialism" in British Settlement Colonies', *Journal of British Studies*, x (1971) 160–82.

6.   T. R. H. Davenport, *South Africa: a Modern History* (London, 1977) p. xiii notes that 'The study of South African history [was] so dependent in the early part of this century on the work of George McCall Theal . . .'. See also, Boeseken: 'Theal as Baanbreker', op. cit.

7.   The documentation is, of course, in the main text. Theal's volumes are almost entirely innocent of footnotes – either to provide documentary references, or to cite other historical authorities. He relies on his 'facts' to give his narrative authority.

8.   Louis Hartz, *The Founding of New Societies* (Yale, 1964); see the fascinating Introduction; and the excellent chapter on 'South Africa' by L. M. Thompson pp. 178–218. Professor Thompson has in addition provided the definitive study of *The Unification of South Africa 1902–1910* (Oxford, 1960).

9.   Carl Berger, *The Writing of Canadian history: Aspects of English–Canadian Historical Writing: 1900 to 1970* (Toronto, 1976) p. ix.

10.   Helen Harper Steeves, 'George McCall Theal', in *Dalhousie Review*, 1936–37, vol. 16:2, pp. 171–5, kindly supplied by the New Brunswick Museum Archives Section, History Department.

11.   E. C. Wright, *The Loyalists of New Brunswick* (Federicton, 1955). I thank Dr. Esther Wright for her most generous response to my query about Theal family genealogy.

12.   W. S. MacNutt, *New Brunswick: a History, 1784–1867* (Toronto, 1963); J. Hanney *History of New Brunswick*, 2 vols (St. John, 1909); M. Whitelaw, *The Maritimes and Canada before Confederation* (Toronto; rep., 1966). For Saint John see the useful succint account by George Nader, *Cities of Canada* (Canada, 1976) ii, pp.55–76.

13.   See D. G. Creighton, *The Road to Confederation: the emergence of Canada 1863–67* (Toronto, 1964); J. M. S. Careless, *The Union of the Canadas: the Growth of Canadian Institutions* (Toronto, 1968).

14.   Babrow, 'A Critical Assessment of George McCall Theal', (Thesis) op. cit.

15.   Steeves, 'Theal', op. cit. is most useful on his early life.

16.   B. T. Tennyson, ed., 'Schooldays, Schooldays . . . Cocagne Academy in the 1840s'. Documents, in *Acadiensis* (September 1976), vol. v, no. 2. See also G. M. Theal, *Notes on Canada and South Africa* (Cape Town, n.d.) which reprinted his articles from *The Cape Illustrated Magazine*.

17.   Ibid., 'Schooldays . . .'.

18.   Idem. Given the style of Theal's later *History* it is not surprising to learn that the historians whom he admired included Edward Gibbon, as well as the historian of the Dutch republic, J. L. Motley, and the chroniclers

of the American frontier, W. H. Prescott and E. F. Parkman. See *D.S.A.B.*, op. cit., 645.

19. *A History of the Saint John Grammar School, 1805–1914*, compiled by members of The Saint John High School Alumnae, with an Introduction by H. S. Bridges, Superintendent of City Schools. (Saint John, N.B. 1914) p. 64.

20. *History*, III, 413.

21. Boeseken, 'Theal as Baanbreker', op. cit., for detail of his early career in the Cape. See also *A.Y.B.*, op. cit., pp. 645–6.

22. Saunders, 'George McCall Theal and Lovedale', op. cit., is very valuable.

23. *History*, V 57, fn.

24. *History*, IV, 155, fn.

25. See the incisive article by C. C. Saunders, 'The Missing Link in Theal's Career', op. cit.

26. See C. W. de Kiewiet, *The Imperial Factor* (London, 1937); C. F. Goodfellow, *Great Britain and South African Confederation, 1871–84*, (Cape Town, 1961); T.R.H. Davenport, *The Afrikaner Bond* (Cape Town, 1966) and his *South Africa: A Modern History* (London, 1977) chs 6–9.

27. D. M. Schreuder, *Gladstone and Kruger: Liberal Government and Colonial 'Home Rule', 1880–85* (London, 1969).

28. See the unpublished 'Memoirs' of Sir Graham Bower, Rhodes House Library, Oxford; Afr. MSS collection, currently being prepared for publication by J. E. Butler and D. M. Schreuder.

29. D. M. Schreuder, *The Scramble for Southern Africa: the Politics of Partition Reappraised, 1875–96* (Cambridge, 1980).

30. *Story of South Africa*, Preface, p. vii.

31. Boeseken, 'Theal as Baanbreker', 3.

32. *History*, II, 28ff.

33. *Story of South Africa*, 3.

34. *History*, II, 331.

35. *History*, II, ibid.

36. *History*, IV, 381.

37. *History*, III, 464.

38. *History*, V, 332, fn.

39. *History*, V, 344.

40. *History*, V, 491.

41. *History*, IV, 11.

42. *History*, II, 27.

43. *History*, II, 188.

44. *History*, II, 27.

45. *History*, IV, 118.

46. *History*, V, 481.

47. *History*, II, 80.

48. *History*, II, 278.

49. *History*, II, 276.

50. *History*, II, 176.

51. *History*, II, 238–9.

52. *History*, II, 460.

53. *History*, II, 462.

54. *History*, II, 404.

55. *History*, ii, 450.
56. *History*, iv, 179.
57. *History*, v, 205.
58. *History*, ibid., fn.
59. *Story of South Africa*, ch. V, 32.
60. *History*, iii, 504.
61. *History*, iv, 86 in 1746, to be precise.
62. *Story of South Africa*, 52.
63. Idem.
64. *History*, iii, 455: Theal dates this to 1707.
65. *History*, iii, 373.
66. *History*, iv, 375: '1795'.
67. *History*, iii, 372: 1691.
68. *History*, x, 28: 1877.
69. *History*, ii, 463.
70. *Story of South Africa*, 386.
71. Ibid., 387.
72. *History*, x, 3: 1879.
73. *History*, x, 225: 1873.
74. *Story of South Africa*, 304.
75. *History*, x, 229: 1878.
76. *History*, xi, 28: 1879.
77. *History*, x, 29: 1877.
78. *History*, ibid.
79. *History*, x, 96: 1878.
80. *History*, x, 220: 1892.
81. *History*, x, 172: 1885.
82. *History*, iii, 482: 1715.
83. *History*, v, 510, fn.: 1828.
84. *Story of South Africa*, p.7.
85. *History*, x, ch. 1: 1873.
86. J. A. La Nauze, 'Who are the fathers?' *Historical Studies*, xiii (1968). See also of course the definitive study by Professor La Nauze, *The Making of the Australian constitution*, (Melbourne, 1972).
87. *Story of South Africa*, 112.
88. Idem.
89. Ibid., 116.
90. *History*, iv, 210: 1806.
91. W. M. Macmillan, *Bantu, Boer and Briton* (rev. ed, 1963); J. S. Galbraith has questioned the influence which Philip really had on policy in *Reluctant Empire: British Policy on the South African Frontier, 1834–54 (California 1963)*.
92. *Story of South Africa*, 178: '1826–35'.
93. Ibid., 191.
94. Idem.
95. Ibid., 193.
96. Ibid., 220.
97. *History*, v, 504: '1828'.
98. *Story of South Africa*, 146.
99. Ibid., 335.

100. *History*, xi, 217: '1884'.
101. *Story of South Africa*, ch. XV., p. 175.
102. *History*, v, 505.
103. *History*, v, 507: 1828.
104. J. S. Marais, *Maynier and the First Boer Republic*, (1944). See also, Herman Gilliomee, 'Democracy and the Frontier,' *South African Historical Journal*, 6 (1974) pp. 30–51.
105. *History*, iv, 242–3.
106. *Story of South Africa*, 387.
107. R. M. Crawford, *'A bit of a Rebel': the Life and Work of George Arnold Wood* (Sydney, 1975).
108. James Barber, *South Africa's Foreign Policy, 1945–70* (Oxford, 1973), Part 3.
109. T. H. B. Miller, *Survey of Commonwealth Affairs; Problem of Expansion and Attrition, 1953–69* (Oxford, 1974), pp. 126–66.
110. Richard Jebb, *Studies in Colonial Nationalism* (London, 1905).
111. G. M. Theal, *Progress of South Africa in the Century* (The 19th Century Series), (London, Edinburgh, Toronto and Philadelphia, 1902) p. 500.
112. *Ibid.*, p.510.
113. G.M. Theal, *South Africa: the Union of South Africa, Rhodesia and All Territories South of the Zambesi* (8th ed, 11th impression, 1916) p. 418.
114. Ibid., p. 420.
115. Ibid., p. 422.
116. Ibid., p. 423.
117. Ibid., p. 428.
118. The idiom has been given authority by Professor Richard Cobb.

4 The *Raj* as Daydream: the Pukka Sahib as Henty Hero in Simla, Chandrapore, and Kyauktada

EDWARD INGRAM

> They were there because they were there.
> A. P. Thornton, *Imperialism in the Twentieth Century*, p. 57

Rudyard Kipling was a less popular author in the colonies and brought his readers less comfort than G. A. Henty; an intriguing claim tucked away by Professor Thornton in his file on Empire.[1] The reason for Henty's greater popularity lay in the character of his heroes. Whereas Kipling's heroes, being Pukka Sahibs, fulfil themselves toeing a line, Henty Heroes are men who will never fail to dominate their surroundings. Noel Annan might say that this difference matches the difference between Henty as Little Englander and Kipling as Anglo-Indian (rather than empire-builder); between Henty as Whig historian and Kipling as would-be French sociologist, the one following Macaulay in the search for progress, the other Durkheim in the search for stability.[2] Both men explain how existing political and social structures can be maintained most effectively, but they write about different worlds. Their worlds are, of course, frequently to be found in the same place at the same time.

Rummage a little further into Professor Thornton's file and one will find out why this is so in a critique of D. O. Mannoni's *Prospero and Caliban*.[3] According to Mannoni, the lure of the

159

colonies is the lure of the desert island; the lure of an uninhabited
world where status is not measured according to achievement.
As long as the natives are firmly controlled, or it suits them for
reasons of their own to make a show of obeisance, the colonial
may live in a daydream peopled by fantasies, his life stable owing
to his confidence that his daydream will not be interrupted. Such
dreaming is a form of paralysis. It is also an alternative to life.
An explanation that verges perilously close on Viennese quackery
is made more acceptable by the remembrance of its echo of
Disraeli's description of the duke of St. James. Having stayed in
bed all day dreaming of the woman with whom he has fallen in
love, St. James breaks off his dream upon realising that, when
they next meet, her behaviour will show that she has not been
dreaming in the meantime of him. Choosing life over fantasy, he
therefore decides to get up next day to hunt.[4]

The colonial will prefer to go on dreaming. He will have no
choice about this – he is required to daydream – nor may he
choose what to dream about. Why daydreaming is compulsory
and what dreams are appropriate is shown most clearly in the
Code of the Pukka Sahib; and to find out how the code itself
worked one must turn to fiction. Literary sources have gone out
of fashion among 'new' social historians, armed with computers,
the jargon of demography, and pride in their ability to count.
Nobody need be taken in. Their figures are all made up: choosing
to be convinced by them rather than by an analysis of texts is a
matter of taste, in relation to British India, bad taste. 'No other
portrait of British India half as accurate [as Kipling's] was ever
produced.'[5]

Although the history of British India is littered with useful awful
novels, it is likely to be remembered, as it ought to be, for its four
most distinguished creations: Kipling's Simla, E.M. Forster's
Chandrapore, George Orwell's Kyauktada, and Paul Scott's
Pankot.[6] The effects of the Code of the Pukka Sahib upon the
behaviour of the inhabitants of these four towns ought therefore
to reveal why, in the late 19th and early 20th centuries, the
stability of British India, if not of Great Britain as a great power,
depended upon the ability of Pukka Sahibs to feign the exploits
of Henty Heroes.

The pictures of British India painted by Kipling, Forster, and
Orwell are much alike. Forster had no more wish than the Indian
National Congress to destroy the *Raj* Kipling heartily admired.

Congress wanted to take it over; Forster to hand it over to them. Orwell, whose loathing of British imperialism was as intense as Kipling's admiration of it, nevertheless preferred it to Bolshevism and Fascism, and despised – as who would not – the bearded, sandal-wearing, dimple-kneed eaters of lettuce who thronged the Labour Party more than he despised Colonel Blimp.[7] Kipling won Orwell's respect for facing up to the disagreeable truth most Bloomsburies, hiding behind their private incomes, were fond of overlooking: that the civilised are kept by the sweat of slaves. The easiest way to raise the standard of living of the English working man was by forcing coolies in India and Africa to work harder on plantations and down mines.[8] Such conflicting views of the *Raj* as an institution can, and must, be separated, however, from accounts of the plight of the Anglo-Indian official, which was portrayed by all three writers as the same.

   Although the life of officials in the Simla of *Plain Tales from the Hills*, *Wee Willie Winkie*, and *Under the Deodars*, in the Chandrapore of *A Passage to India*, and in the Kyauktada of *Burmese Days*, was constrained by the Code of the Pukka Sahib, neither the code, nor the pukka sahibs who must live by it, are what they seem. Thoughts of peppery old colonels and district commissioners, who have never read anything but *Blackwell's* and *Punch* and whose fat bottoms, pink cheeks, and white whiskers could supposedly be seen in the corner of any club in Tunbridge Wells or Cheltenham Spa, boring fellow members with tales of frontier victories long forgotten, need to be banished from the mind. When Orwell's hero, John Flory, is permitted to list the rules of the code he ostensibly despises – stiff upper lip, iron fist without velvet glove, no fraternising – he is being ironic. The code of the Pukka Sahib did not emulate the Public School tradition of trying to turn out a certain style of man: it merely trained all men to live as if nobody were around. Everybody was asked to follow a strict, all-encompassing routine, and his success in following it was measured by an ability to stand still. The ideal Pukka Sahib never moved.

*   *   *

The Whig historians were once diagnosed by Arnold Toynbee as suffering from the lunatic hallucination that history had reached its apotheosis in an upper middle class paradise in St. John's Wood. This spell was broken for Englishmen sooner than for Anglo-Indians, who remained frozen in mock-heroic posture until the twentieth century; said that they alone could provide India with vigorous and capable rulers; and acted as if the time when Indians would be able to govern themselves would never come. The paralysis was the result of treating India as if it were uninhabited. India was, for example, ideally to be defended by drawing frontiers around near-eastern states on maps, just as Africa was to be partitioned by drawing lines along rivers or lines of longitude. Complications arose when other states produced their own maps on which they had drawn the wrong lines: witness the irritation of the foreign secretary during the Ochakov Affair in 1791 at having to learn the political geography of Turkey, and Beaconsfield and Gorchakov bargaining so spiritedly at the congress of Berlin over towns in the Caucasus of which neither knew the whereabouts. They were wise not to try to find out. Whereas ignorance gave confidence, knowledge sapped the will. From the passing of Pitt's India Act in 1784 or, if not then, from the moment in 1798 when the Marquess Wellesley set out to turn himself into a Mogul Emperor with an Anglo-Irish face, the British had to make certain that the stability of the Empire was not compromised by local incidents. Empires have to have an existence independent of the lives, often the needs, of their inhabitants.

To say that India was ruled as if uninhabited does not always mean that nobody was thought to be living there; only that the British, on having to take notice of anyone, saw themselves. In the 18th century, Edmund Burke and Earl Cornwallis, classic whigs who believed the preservation of rank to be a necessary restraint on the power of the state, treated zamindars in Bengal as landed gentry, Indian independent country gentlemen able to resist the allure of patronage at court. By the 1830s, after the first phase of the industrial revolution, evangelicals and utilitarians represented by George Macaulay and Charles Trevelyan, believing that rank must give way to equality of opportunity, saw Indians wearing the clothes of the industrial poor and in need of stimulant or security for the just rewards of labour.[9]

When, after the First Afghan War, the Utopian dream of the Poor Law Amendment Act and Macaulay's minute on the education of Indians faded in the 1840s into the Condition of England Question, both Britain and British India entered the period of Tennysonian doubt. While loss of faith was accompanied by emphasis upon the rules of behaviour faith had traditionally prescribed, the reform of India had turned into rule by example. As either the task of reform was more difficult, or Indians less amenable than had been supposed, India offered a field for the dissolution – ideally by sublimation rather than over-indulgence – of excess sexual energy.[10] The separation between Anglo-Indians and Indians, implicit both in the Whigs' anxiety to preserve native customs, while making Englishmen in India behave as they would at home, and in the utilitarians' offer of higher European values, was made explicit in the Code of the Pukka Sahib. The code was first exemplified in the biographies written by Sir John Kaye, where heroes of the East India Company's civil service, such as Sir John Malcolm and Lord Metcalfe, were turned into guides in whose footsteps their young successors were exhorted to follow.[11]

Although the formalisation of the code would await the Indian Mutiny in 1857, and would depend for success upon the increasing number of wives and hill stations to be found in India, its origins can be traced back to 1800. When Arthur Wellesley's fellow officers refused in the 1790s to pay sums owed to Indian merchants for fodder,[12] they were copying what they mistook for either aristocratic self-confidence or the usual behaviour of Indians to one another. Such actions were increasingly deplored: shortly after copying Indian behaviour had been forbidden by Burke, proper English behaviour had been changed by the evangelicals. The purest strain of Victorian high seriousness had been bred in the colonies. In 1800 Lord Wellesley complained to the authorities at London about 'the idle practice of acting, dancing, singing, and playing in public (indulged in at the Cape of Good Hope) *under the immmediate eye and sanction of the government*'. Anyone calling at the Cape on his way out to India or sent there to recuperate 'may be infected by the contagion of this dissipated example'.[13]

Although social acceptability in England has therefore been denoted by correct behaviour since the beginning of the 19th century, setting out the rules of behaviour was not thought to be the responsibility of the state, nor was public duty carried into private life: the earl of Carlyon expected magistrates to smuggle.[14] No Englishman at home would have tolerated the intrusion demanded by Wellesley. In India, on the other hand, Englishmen were to behave as Englishmen. The government was able to set the example which was to be, indeed had to be, followed, and any distinction between private and official life was to be given up. This disappearance of privacy in Anglo-India can be dated precisely to 16 February 1824, to a letter written by the president of the board of control to the governor of Bombay. In 1823 William Erskine, the eminent orientalist who worked for the recorder's court in Bombay, was dismissed by the chief justice. Erskine had also, however, been secretary to the Bombay literary society and at his departure, the governor, as president of the society, had moved an address of thanks. The chief justice, on learning of it, protested to the board of control. The president of the board responded to the governor in ominous words that athough 'quite aware that this was done in your individual capacity as a member of the literary society . . . It cannot consider its effect as less prejudicial to the public interest since it distinctly marked a dissension' between two British officials. British officials must not quarrel; certainly not be seen to quarrel. 'At so great a distance from the mother country . . . authority can only be maintained by that mutual support which functionaries . . . may afford each other.'[15]

By the time the East India Company was abolished, following the Indian Mutiny in 1857, these assumptions that private life could not be separated from official life and that everybody must stand or fall together, had transformed the British code of conduct in India from one appropriate to an agent of higher civilisation into one appropriate to a symbol of greater power. The transformation was itself the cause of a widening gap between appearance and reality, and the wider the gap became, the greater the stress suffered by Pukka Sahibs who were asked to bridge it. To cite one of the most often quoted exchanges in all Forster, when Ronnie Heaslop tells his mother that India likes Gods and she replies that Englishmen like posing as Gods, both are referring to an Almighty all-powerful rather than all-wise. The Pukka Sahib must symbolise the might and determination of an empire ruled by force, while seeming to bear the White Man's Burden by dragging the reluctant resentfully towards Light. At Chandrapore Heaslop could seem – but only seem – to be administering British justice. At Kyauktada, the assistant commissioner and the superintendent of police as well as the local businessmen know, but may not admit, that they keep the peace solely to permit the more efficient extraction of timber.

Time as well as occupation widened the gap. Kipling's heroes, Strickland, Tarrion, and Cusack-Bremmil, have no reason to doubt the permanence of the *Raj*. Forster's, created partly before and partly after the Great War, cannot be so confident: Orwell's have no confidence at all. Beset by Congress on the one hand, Paget MPs on the other, the best they can hope for is that nothing will happen. Events will lead to self-government; to rebellion, accompanied, Mrs Lackersteen assumes, by rape; to a return to England and shabby-genteel poverty in middle age. Even if Whitehall and Westminster showed no signs of pessimism after the First World War about the future of the empire, and treated bargains with the Wafd and the Montagu-Chelmsford reforms as nothing more than new routes to traditional goals, Pukka Sahibs recognised that the empire's early demise was bound to be taken for granted, as soon as they gave any sign that its permanence was in doubt.[16]

The wider the gap and the greater the stress, the odder and more extravagant the behaviour of Pukka Sahibs appeared, and the greater its underlying uniformity. The code of the Pukka Sahib made extraordinary demands for submission. The new arrival not only had to fit in quickly; to do so he had to perceive straightway that whereas Anglo-India might look like an English suburb transplanted to the tropics, nothing there is what it seems. Debts of honour need not be paid; one may flirt outrageously but not fall in love nor marry; one must join in everything, ask no questions, give nothing away nor hide anything: in short, cut the cord with England and give up hope of privacy. Life will be lived in public; everything in life determined by one's rank. Kipling's stories are littered with failures; men and women who have broken rules and who, even if they survive, are to warn others not to follow their rash ways – Otis Yeere, who falls in love with Mrs Hawksbee; Kitty Beighton who will not marry Barr-Saggott; Henry Faizanne, who writes home too often; and the 'Boy' whose suicide must be covered up, lest anyone in England should guess what Anglo-India is really like.

The code of the Pukka Sahib is as constraining, the demand for obedience as severe, as in a prison; perhaps as in the concentration camp made famous by Stanley M. Elkins. Elkins described his concentration camp in such a way as to provide an image of the experience of the North American slave. Even though a southern plantation before the Civil War could not be compared, even metaphorically, with a concentration camp, they possessed common features to the extent that both functioned as perverted patriarchies. In both, the sanctions of authority were effective and pervasive enough to create a recognisable personality type. As social behaviour is regulated, if only partly, by adjustment to symbols of authority, Elkins assumed that the more diverse the symbols, the more varied the permissible responses to them. What happened, he asked, in both the plantation and the concentration camp – and, maybe, in Anglo-India – when the symbols were few and identical?[17]

Three aspects of the life of inmates of Elkins's concentration camp bear comparison with Anglo-India. To survive, inmates had to detach themselves quickly and thoroughly from all former ties and values; they had to disappear without trace into their group by conforming to a routine that gave them only one part to play and only one way in which to play it; and they had to adopt a new time scheme. The present, for inmates, did not lead towards the future. The camp became the world and the world was. As Thornton says of Anglo-Indians, inmates 'could not see far and did not know much. They knew that beyond the lighted circle . . . lay an area of darkness'.[18] Naturally, they stayed in the light. To stray into the darkness was to court death.

The image of the concentration camp as a perverted patriarchy has drawn heavy fire. For Terrence Des Pres, Elkins's camp is too comfortable. Far from being a closed system in which survival is possible by instinctive adaptation, it ought to be described as a machine designed – and bound – to kill one unless a way can be found to outwit it. Survival depends upon beating the system, not conforming to it.[19] Even if Des Pres is right, however, and even if Elkins's image of the concentration camp is misleading, it provides a useful image of British India, full of Kipling's 'gilded convicts', who must detach themselves from their backgrounds completely and at once. They must conform to the new demands made on them as wholeheartedly as Elkins's prisoner and must obey as readily the commands of their two guards: their seniors who provide their example, and the natives they must seem to control who will see that they follow it.

The result of conforming is also similar for the Pukka Sahib as for Elkins's prisoner and slave. The ostensibly powerful and the obviously powerless end up in the same condition: both revert to childhood. This claim, too, has been challenged by Elkins's critics. Sambo has gone out of style.[20] Maybe rightly, but visit an intelligent and sensible, if elderly and sick, aunt after she has been in a nursing home for two months and one will be surprised and appalled by the change in her behaviour. Mrs Moore twice tells her son Ronnie, at times when he is conforming most closely to the code of the Pukka Sahib, that he sounds like a schoolboy. Similarly, the relationship permitted between junior officials on leave at Simla and Mrs Hawksbee is adolescent infatuation, regarded as a useful aid to adaptation. Such relationships are neither personal, sexual, nor passionate. The code will not permit them to be. Mrs Hawksbee's rival, Mrs Reiver, who encourages sexual passion, acquires the nickname 'Regula Baddun' in recognition of her menace to society.

In an attempt to sidestep what is perceived to be a Freudian obstacle to this theory, that personality once settled in childhood is unlikely to change dramatically later on, Elkins turns to the interpersonal theory of Harry Stack Sullivan, in which one's personality shifts in response to relationships with one's significant others. Mannoni sidesteps the same obstacle more neatly. Although the adapted colonial, like the adapted prisoner, is assumed to be adolescent, Mannoni confines himself to explaining who will adapt to the colonies most easily and live there afterwards with least stress. For Mannoni, the Pukka Sahib's favourite play ought to be *Peter Pan*.

The British *Raj* was a closed society if one chose to stay, but unlike the concentration camp where death offered the only escape, if one chose to pay the price, one might leave. The fortunate rash who do not conform, like Pluffles, are permitted to return home to England, often to live lives as successful as they would have been failures in India. Ronnie Heaslop sees at once that nothing he has done or known in England has prepared him for Chandrapore. He quickly adapts, qualifying to be 'one of us' by his deference to his superiors. Not much good at games or languages, without much notion of the law he administers every day, he is nevertheless 'the type we want'. His fiancee, Adela Quested, on the other hand, on arriving to visit him, can no longer understand him any better than she can fathom her new surroundings. At the party given in her honour, to which the district commissioner invites the local Indian notables in response to her request to meet Indians, she gives great pleasure by accepting an invitation to visit an Indian family; then causes consternation by assuming that the visit will take place. Miss Quested will be forced to return home to England as a result of her failure to grasp that all events in Anglo-India are merely rituals. They cannot be permitted to have consequences, because the consequences will not be the ones expected. Nor will they be manageable.

To treat ritual as event and to break with routine is to flirt with death. Insistent on seeing more of India and despite the attempts made to dissuade them, Miss Quested and her prospective mother-in-law, Mrs Moore, go on a picnic to Chandrapore's only object of curiosity, the Marabar Caves. The caves are all alike: nothing is in them, and whatever one does inside, the effect is always the same – 'boum'. Go into the caves with an open or enquiring mind and one will come out distraught. Mrs Moore, who has been questioning the values she has lived by throughout her life, abandons them and dies. Miss Quested accuses her host, Dr Aziz, of trying to rape her. Even Fielding, the apparently independent schoolmaster, who goes into the caves only to look for Miss Quested, pays a price. A few days later, standing looking at the hills from the verandah of the British club, Fielding suddenly senses that his life has been wasted. Only Dr Aziz comes out of the caves untouched. As a Muslim dreaming of the Moguls, he knows no more about India and has no more interest in it than the most hidebound Pukka Sahib.

The caves are, of course, India, or the nearest any Anglo-Indian will get to it; a denial of his rationalism that will prove beyond the comprehension of the ordinarily dull people who are needed to run an empire and are least likely to feel constrained by the code of the Pukka Sahib.[21] The code therefore protects those whom it constrains. Follow its rules and one will come to no harm. Both Forster and Orwell echo Kipling in warning the Anglo-Indian that he cannot hope to understand India or to make friends with Indians. Although all relationships with Indians are meant to be kept official, this is not the reason for the warning. India is – or must be accepted as being – impenetrable. What Forster describes as an echo beyond the most distant echo, an arch beyond the furthest arch, Orwell translates into a conspiracy behind a conspiracy, a plot within a plot. Meddle in a quarrel between two Indians, warns Kipling in 'The House of Suddhoo', and one is bound to end up breaking the law, maybe abetting an attempt at murder. At Kyauktada, John Flory is driven to suicide by the consequences of his decision to take sides in the struggle between U Po Kyin and Dr Veraswami for membership of the club.

If India is impenetrable, the British must stick to themselves and closely together. The most celebrated Anglo-Indian institution was the club, the last sanctum to be thrown open to Indians. The code demanded that everbody go to the club after work. At the end of 'A Wayside Comedy', the five Pukka Sahibs at Kashima meet each evening for a drink despite the fact that four of them hate or despise one another. The fifth, however, insists that they must all be friendly. Why? To relax at the end of a tiring, probably tiresome, day? Hardly. The club offered only modest amusement. They attend to remind themselves who they are, and where they are. Club society, being the only society available, was needed to sustain the self. For both Kipling and Warburton in Somerset Maugham's 'The Outstation', keeping up appearances was the only barrier to despair and chaos.[22]

The code protects the natives as well as the Pukka Sahibs who must appear to rule over them. The so-called 'imperial factor' in the European colonies of the late 19th and early 20th centuries was much less prominent than one might suppose from glancing at brightly coloured political maps. Colonies were annexed on maps only, not on the ground. The symbols of annexation were kept as few and as cheap as possible; their role, given the fondness – indeed the necessity – for indirect rule, similarly restricted. The arrangement suited the natives, who were able to go on leading their lives according to their usual habits, making sure that their European overlords acted as Pukka Sahibs. Flory's manservant is most upset by his unwillingness to shave and change his shirt in the afternoon in order to put in the obligatory appearance at the club. No more than the government can the natives permit Englishmen in India to feel at home. Home is England, more often Scotland.

In Anglo-India, therefore, telling who are the prisoners, who the guards, is not easy. One well-known example of the success of the natives at controlling their overlords is given in Orwell's autobiographical story of the young official at Moulmein in Burma who is summoned to deal with a reportedly rampaging elephant.²³ In case he should have to shoot the elephant, he sends for an elephant gun, an action interpreted by the natives as a decision that the elephant is to be shot. An action intended to provide a choice therefore turns out to have taken the choice away: the elephant is shot lest the official make a fool of himself. Had he been an excellent shot, he could have risked disappointing the natives by going close enough to the elephant to find out whether, as he suspected, it had calmed down. Not being one, he must shoot from too far away to tell. He keeps order and appears to be in control of the natives only by doing as they demand.

How different from the conduct of such a typical Pukka Sahib is that of the Henty Hero, to whom life offers a series of opportunities to show the qualities necessary to surmount crises by action, and as a reward, to take his place in a stable society where both foreigners and the working class will be kept in their place. Follow, for example, the career of Angus Campbell in *To Herat and Kabul*, whose challenges on the road to manhood are introduced into Sir John Kaye's account of the First Afghan War, itself a sermon preached to an earlier generation.

Left an orphan at Tabriz at the age of sixteen owing to the death of his parents of plague, Campbell is employed by the British ambassador as a secret agent, because during his four years in Persia he has become fluent in Arabic and Persian and can 'get on in' Armenian and Kurdish. He is sent to encourage the ruler of Herat to stand firm against a besieging Persian army, meets the legendary Eldred Pottinger, and quickly picks up Afghani. There is nothing impenetrable in the East of Henty. Nor any challenge to one's view of the world. Even if the ruler of Herat is a tyrant, he must be helped, because in helping to hold back the Persians, he serves the British Empire.

On leaving Herat and Pottinger, Campbell is taken up by a second hero, Alexander Burnes, and sent with the Indian army to invade Afghanistan. When he is kidnapped outside Ghazni and imprisoned, providence provides a spar, with which he bars himself in his prison cell until the timely arrival of the British. When he is sent to spy beyond the Hindu Kush, providence next supplies a wounded Afghan chief, who never dreams for a moment that Campbell is not the Persian he claims to be. Campbell knows nothing of anatomy or medicine. Yet he sets a splint, extracts a bullet, later saves more lives by quick thinking in a snow storm, and earns the undying gratitude of enemies who reflect his own code of honour. They repay their debt by kidnapping him before the disastrous retreat from Kabul.

The Henty Hero has, in fact, never left England. The foreign lands he travels in, the vile climate he endures, the natives he manages: all of them exist in a daydream exactly opposite to Alice's. In Wonderland nothing is predictable; in Henty's world the hero is never taken by surprise. He is always in control of his surroundings, favoured by providence, which provides opportunities merely to illustrate his capacity for self-improvement. Therefore, whereas Alice staggers in Wonderland from surprise, to astonishment, to crisis, as one by one everything – space, time, meaning, causation – she has taken for granted is denied her, the Henty Hero reinforces the values and habits of the world he has supposedly left but to which he will assuredly return. She, in desperation, destroys her dream world: he, in his, suffers not one moment of stress.[24]

Orwell, who knew what Henty was up to, permits one of Henty's heroes to visit Kyauktada, the policeman Verrall. My students dislike Verrall intensely. They dislike his self-assurance, his rudeness, his seduction of Elizabeth Lackersteen, his hasty departure to avoid a scene at the station. They find him arrogant and selfish, and dismiss him as the representative of a class-ridden society they are thankful not to live in. Verrall is all they say. Orwell, however, means us to admire him. Verrall has great strength of character. He knows what he values – clothes, horses, physical fitness – and what he despises – creature comforts, alcohol, and womanizing. He has advantages, of course. The younger son of a peer is as rare as a dodo in Upper Burma. But his strength of character, not his social position, enables him to behave in the same way everywhere, towards everyone. Verrall makes no concessions to the tropics, remaining firmly in control of his own life. He is the only inhabitant of Kyauktada who lives rather than daydreams.

Maybe this claim is unfair to everybody else. Verrall's social position as well as his strength of character accounts for his mobility. Should Burma prove unendurable, he can go home to England or arrange a transfer back to India. The others are stuck. What happens to them is presented obliquely. If Verrall is a head struck on one side of a coin, John Flory's head is struck on the other side. Flory's admirable traits of character are more obvious than Verrall's, but we are not meant to admire him, merely to sympathize with him in his dilemma as a Pukka Sahib.

U Po Kyin, his Burmese antagonist, accuses him of cowardice, but such emphasis on Flory's individuality would disguise Orwell's point: all Pukka Sahibs are in the same state. Flory's life is stable as long as he merely seems to act. Although he seems to be a friend of Dr Veraswami, both men understand that for Flory the relationship is merely comforting routine. He cannot be expected to put up Veraswami for the club. Nor does Veraswami ask him to. The routine suits them both, because association with any Pukka Sahib will enhance Veraswami's social position.

The routine suits Flory because he lives in a dream, a dream of a life of books and intelligent conversation to be shared with a wife in an otherwise uninhabited world. To daydream in the colonies is necessary for survival, but Flory's is the wrong dream. Its fault lies in its need of one other person. Flory heads for destruction shortly after the arrival of Elizabeth Lackersteen, because in his determination to fit her to his imaginary model, he also tries to act according to his daydream of himself. The incidents marking their relationship illustrate Flory's success or failure at resembling a Henty Hero; rewarded for rescuing Elizabeth from a peaceable water buffalo, punished for falling off a horse owing to a loose girth. Flory cannot expect to catch Elizabeth while Verrall is around; nor has he the self-confidence to wait, knowing that he is bound to catch her quickly enough as soon as Verrall has gone. In struggling to measure up to Verrall, he brings about his own destruction. If Pukka Sahibs are to play their parts as symbols of the Empire, they must seem to be – not try to be – Henty Heroes.

To nominate Veraswami for the club is to take an action whose consequences will demand a self-assurance Flory does not, and cannot be expected to, possess. Having decided to undermine Veraswami by disgracing Flory, U Po Kyin sends Flory's former mistress to make a scene in church. Verrall would have kicked her out, to applause from Elizabeth. Flory, who cannot show the same determination, flees; whereupon Elizabeth abandons him, he commits suicide, and she marries the assistant commissioner. Only in death does Flory overcome the disfigurement of the birthmark down one side of his face that becomes more colourful the more he is ill at ease, and is used by Orwell to signify his difficulty in dealing with other people.

That Flory's troubles arise not only out of his attempt to act out rather than merely dream his daydreams, but also from dreaming the wrong dream, cannot have surprised E.M. Forster. At Chandrapore both Adela Quested and Fielding have made the same mistake. Miss Quested, one thinks of her always as *Miss Quested*, the informality of Adela jars, is everything she seems not to be. The English at Chandrapore think she will never fit in. She thinks so too. Aziz, however, knows better. To him she seems to be the typical Pukka Sahib she in fact is. The India she is so determined to see is a tourist landscape: nobody lives there, or nobody she wants to meet. Neither Fielding's tea party nor the picnic at the Marabar Caves is a success, because neither offers sights to see. Miss Quested lives in plans. She dreams of improving race relations with the speed and self-confidence of a Utilitarian and upon an identical assumption: that everybody is at heart like her or wishes to be, particularly the Indian couple who ask her to tea but do not mean her to come, and whose name she cannot remember.

Miss Quested is not given her name for nothing: hers is a story of self-discovery. The Turtons, Burtons, Callendars, whom at first meeting one dislikes and assumes one is meant to dislike, turn out to be right. India is too perilous a place to wander about in; nor as inviting as it seems (and here Orwell again explicitly mimics Forster) when looked at from the safety of the compound and the club. Miss Quested's insistence upon venturing outside leads to so nasty a surprise that she is compelled, like Alice, to give up daydreaming and make do with life. Accordingly, she goes home to England. Life in India would be too demanding, the constraints of life in Anglo-India no longer bearable. Intimacy without intimacy: to see people every day without getting to know them any better. Perhaps, if one *is* to see them every day, forever, one had better not try.

Whereas Miss Quested chooses life, Fielding, the most sympathetically portrayed inhabitant of Chandrapore, chooses dreams. Fielding stands somewhere between Flory and Verrall, possessing both advantages and attractive traits of character. Neither help him much. He is mobile to the extent that he has arrived in India in middle age, has friends in England with enough influence to get him the job of headmaster of the local government college, and has no doubt that he could find another job if he needed to. At the end, he does. His greatest advantage, however, is that, like Verrall, he has so far, as he puts it, travelled light. At Chandrapore he tries to take on baggage. The crisis that develops at Chandrapore, changing the lives of all of the people caught up in it and ruining many of them, arises out of Fielding's attempt to make friends with Dr Aziz. Fielding is disliked at Chandrapore. He is perceived, accurately, to be a troublemaker. His fault, however, lies in the wish to make friends, not in the choice of an Indian. Of course Pukka Sahibs are supposed to stay away from the natives. More important, they are supposed to stay away from one another. As everybody has to get along, everybody *must* get along: nobody may disparage the bad play put on by the local drama society, whatever he may have thought of it in England; everybody must turn up at polo and the club, even if, as at Kyauktada, one of the seven members is a drunken lecher, another a foul-mouthed lout, a third a Bolshie and two others a nostalgic bore and a pompous ass. Nothing follows from their extraordinary behaviour. When the book opens they are at tea with the Mad Hatter and the clock has stopped. Frozen in time, symbols of the empire have no need to make choices. As long as they are also forbidden to make them, friendship, indeed all forms of intimacy, must give way before routine.

Fielding knows this. He returns from Chandrapore to England, where he marries. Unlike Miss Quested, however, he comes back to India, the lure of dreaming stronger than the call of life. When his new job takes him on a visit to one of the Hindu princely states, he meets his erstwhile friend, Dr Aziz. They enjoy a touching reconciliation before going their separate ways, attributing their inability to keep up their friendship to the stultifying officialism of the *Raj*. True enough, in general. In this instance, however, one senses a personal relief. Aziz, dreaming of his Moguls, is no more at home among Hindus than he was in British India; Fielding has always known that the welcome he received from Aziz's friends and the parents of his pupils was an unconscious method of propitiating the British regime. When asked to choose, as he must after the crisis of Dr Aziz's trial, between individuality and privilege, he picks privilege without difficulty. For Fielding, status is desirable, whereas routine is not a constraint.

For Pukka Sahibs it never is. Their one wish in life is to avoid surprises. Typically, according to Orwell, the sons and daughters of the lower upper middle class, without land or money behind them, are drawn to the state, to the services, the church, and the colonies, in their determination to escape the contamination of trade, and in the hope that they may move closer to a style of life they know all about in theory but have had no opportunity to practice.[25] They know how to shoot, but have no guns; how to ride, but have no horses; how to order dinner in the best restaurants, which they will never enter; the amount to tip every grade of servant at the country houses at which they dream of spending weekends, while mortified by the knowledge that should they go, they may be discovered to have shabby underwear. Their life is an unending struggle to keep up the appearances of gentility upon inadequate incomes; their nightmare, the day each quarter when the bills must be paid. A. J. P. Taylor suggests that in Germany they might have been lured by the Nazis.[26] In the British Empire of Paul Scott, they earn an equivalent reward. They know their place, they are members of a community, but they pay a high price: they bury their emotions so deep that they turn into statues.[27]

Remember this and one will sympathise with Elizabeth Lackersteen. Her childhood has been spent in shifts; her youth wasted away in poverty in Paris as a governess to a French family. She works too hard, for too little, and is pinched by her employer. What lies ahead? On Sundays she dreams. In the library, in the glossy magazines, she occasionally sees the faces of girls with whom she once, during a moment of parental prosperity and extravagance, went to school. That moment had set her values: what is not Lovely is Beastly. Her own life is Beastly; her former friends' lives all too Lovely. Rescue comes in the form of an invitation from her uncle and aunt to join them in Burma. She loves the voyage out, when everybody lives as if he were rich, and dreams of a future of bronzed horsemen playing polo, wafted punkahs, and cool drinks handed on wide verandahs by silent servants in starched white liveries. New Delhi? Dalhousie? Simla? Instead she arrives at Kyauktada, an up-country timber station, where everybody suffers from prickly heat, nobody rides, and even walking is unendurable. There is nowhere to go to, nobody to visit, and nobody will call.

Is she upset? Not at all. Kyauktada boasts five single Englishmen, one of whom she will marry. Marry one she must, to escape from an uncle whose intentions are soon made plain; also to escape from having to return Home – to black beetles, as her aunt puts it. Sensibly enough, it seems, she chooses Flory: he, after all, had seemed to rescue her from a buffalo and he does take her shooting. That he is not as she wishes to dream of him does not matter, or

would not have, had not her aunt tempted her to make a bid for
Verrall. And how could she refuse? Verrall *is* what she had dreamed
of; what she tries to persuade herself Flory will turn out to be: his
status is also transferable to England or New Delhi. As marriage to
Verrall will bring mobility as well as status, Elizabeth cannot be
faulted for throwing everything she has, even her sexuality, onto
the scales. Naturally it is not enough, and equally naturally, when
Verrall escapes her, she turns back to Flory, and when Flory
embarrasses her in church, marries the assistant commissioner. At
least, she will one day be transferred to Rangoon.

Elizabeth does all this without a qualm, without any sign of
disappointment. She has no reason to be disappointed: she needs a
husband, not a man. If she can catch one, Kyauktada will provide
an escape from Paris into the world inhabited by her old friends,
who are envied not for their riches but for being able to sit still. No
surprises for them. Routine, even more than status, is the stuff of
Elizabeth's dreams. On the voyage out from England she had
enjoyed playing at being rich; she enjoyed still more the feeling of
detachment. When she posed for the ship's photographer she posed
as an aristocrat, a pose she was happy to keep up for the rest of her
life. To be well dressed; her food cooked; her house cleaned; to have
her rank and know her rank in society: she asks nothing more. The
Empire asks nothing more of her. Her response to nationalism and
demands for self-rule will be hysteria.[28] They represent everything
Beastly. As long, however, as Elizabeth Lackersteen sits unmoving
on the verandah of the club at Kyauktada, the British *Raj* will
stand.

NOTES

1.   A. P. Thornton, *For the File on Empire: Essays and Reviews* (London, 1968)
     p. 18.
2.   Noel Annan, 'Kipling's Place in the History of Ideas', *Victorian Studies*, iii
     (1959–60) 323–48.
3.   O. Mannoni, *Prospero and Caliban: the Psychology of Colonization* (New York,
     1956) Part II; Thornton, *File on Empire*, pp. 328–43.
4.   Benjamin Disraeli, *The Young Duke*, Ch. X.
5.   A. P. Thornton, *Imperialism in the Twentieth Century* (Minneapolis, 1977)
     p. 97.
6.   Pankot will have to be left out here. I prefer Paul Scott's novels of Anglo-
     India to any others, but am not yet sufficiently master of them. Tiresomely,
     they are too long to teach.

7.   George Orwell, *The Road to Wigan Pier* (London: Penguin, 1974) p. 152.
8.   *Ibid.*, pp. 139–40; see also his 'Rudyard Kipling', in *Collected Essays* (London: Mercury, 1961) pp. 179–94.
9.   See F. G. Hutchins, *The Illusion of Permanence: British Rule in India* (Princeton, 1967); and G. D. Bearce, *British Attitudes towards India, 1783–1858* (London, 1961).
10.   Ronald Hyam, *Britains's Imperial Century, 1815–1914* (New York, 1976) pp. 135–47.
11.   Sir J. W. Kaye, *The Life of Major-General Sir John Malcolm* (2 vols, London, 1856); and *The Life and Correspondence of Charles, Lord Metcalfe* (2 vols, London, 1858). Certain aspects of Metcalfe's life, notably his children by an Indian wife, had to be forgotten.
12.   Elizabeth Longford, *Wellington: the Years of the Sword* (New York, 1969) pp. 82–3.
13.   Wellesley to Dundas, secret and confidential, 7 October 1800, *Two Views of British India: the Private Correspondence of Mr. Dundas and Lord Wellesley, 1798–1801*, ed. Edward Ingram (Bath, 1970) p. 304.
14.   See Georgette Heyer, *The Reluctant Widow* (London, 1952).
15.   R. D. Choksey, *Mountstuart Elphinstone: the Indian Years, 1796–1821* (Bombay, 1971) pp. 402–6.
16.   Sir Algernon Rumbold, *Watershed in India, 1914–1922* (London, 1979) pp. 315, 321; John Darwin, *Britain, Egypt, and the Middle East: Imperial Policy in the Aftemath of War, 1918–1923* (London, 1978) p. 275.
17.   Stanley M. Elkins, *Slavery: a Problem in American Institutional and Intellectual Life* (3rd ed, Chicago, 1976) ch. iii.
18.   Thornton, *Imperialism in the Twentieth Century*, p. 97.
19.   Terrence Des Pres, *The Survivor: an Anatomy of Life in the Death Camps* (New York, 1976).
20.   See, for example, Willie Lee Rose, *Slavery and Freedom*, ed. William W. Freehling (New York, 1982) ch. 12.
21.   See Stanley F. Cooperman, 'The Imperial Posture and the Shrine of Darkness: Kipling's 'Naulahka' and E. M. Forster's "A Passage to India"', *English Literature in Transition*, i (1963) 9–13.
22.   Alan Sandison, *The Wheel of Empire: a Study of the Imperial Idea in Some Late Nineteenth and Early Twentieth-Century Fiction* (London, 1967) pp. 77–8.
23.   George Orwell, 'On Shooting an Elephant', *Collected Essays*, pp. 15–23; see also Bernard Crick, *George Orwell: A Life* (London, 1980) p. 96.
24.   See Donald Rackin, 'Alice's Journey to the End of Night', in *Aspects of Alice: Lewis Carroll's Dreamchild as Seen Through the Critics' Looking-Glasses, 1865-1971*, ed. Robert Phillips (London: Penguin, 1974) pp. 452-80.
25.   Orwell, *Wigan Pier*, ch. 8.
26.   A. J. P. Taylor, *The Course of German History* (London, 1945) pp. 206–7.
27.   Paul Scott, *The Birds of Paradise*, ii. i.
28.   See Philip Mason, *Patterns of Dominance* (London, 1970) p. 161.

5   Shadow and Substance: Mackenzie King's Perceptions of British Intentions at the 1923 Imperial Conference

JOHN M. CARLAND

In the summer of 1969, while browsing in a bookshop in Nairobi, Kenya, I picked up a copy of A. P. Thornton's *The Imperial Idea and Its Enemies*. By the time I returned to New York, I had not only read the book, but was a firm friend of the imperial idea. I was also determined to go to Toronto to study with Professor Thornton. At that time, for an American male, crossing into Canada usually meant putting distance between oneself and the United States Selective Service. However, a minor hearing loss made me undraftable so I was perhaps unique among Americans in that I viewed the border crossing as a way of getting closer to the Empire and into the Commonwealth. I entered graduate school at the University of Toronto in 1970, studying and working with Professor Thornton, until I completed my degree.

Recently, while reading the diary of William Lyon Mackenzie King and his description of the Imperial Conference of 1923, I was reminded of a point Thornton often makes in his graduate seminar – namely that 'At any time in history it is not what is true but what is thought to be true that is significant.'[1] It is this idea, more Thorntonian than imperial, which has suggested the approach taken in this article.

Generally speaking historians have accepted Mackenzie King's belief that the Imperial Conference of 1923 was called to persuade the Dominions to support the principle of a common foreign policy for the British Empire, i.e. to continue the system worked out in 1917 and 1918. I would like to argue, using King's diary as the key to his perceptions, (1) that Mackenzie King believed Canada faced a more serious challenge than just the establishment of a common foreign policy, and (2) that his actions and behaviour at the Conference were based on this belief. The serious challenge King perceived was a plot which he believed had been hatched by imperialists (he also called them centralisers) in the British Government to transform the Imperial Conference into an Imperial Cabinet or Council or Parliament whose authority would exceed that of the Dominions.

It is true that something called an Imperial War Cabinet had come out of the 1914–18 War, and it is also true that the 1921 Imperial Conference had been seen in the same light as the Imperial War Cabinet. But what the Imperial War Cabinet had been and what Mackenzie thought of as an Imperial Cabinet were two different things. King filled his definition with an emotional content and sinister intent that made it more dangerous than its Canadian proponents, Sir Robert Borden and Arthur Meighen, ever allowed it to be. Neither Borden nor Meighen in their decade of leadership (1911–21) permitted their desire to achieve unity compromise Canada's national autonomy.[2] However, in context it is clear that when King spoke of an 'Imperial Cabinet' or 'Imperial Council' he meant an institution which would violate Canadian autonomy: an institution which would be the executive of a united empire in which Canada would be subordinate to Great Britain. Therefore, it was his duty to prevent this from happening in 1923 by defeating the centraliser's scheme to perpetuate the idea of a common foreign policy for the British Empire. As it turned out, once the Conference got under way, none of the other Dominion leaders with whom he shared his fears seemed unduly concerned. His realisation that he alone perceived the plot not only strengthened his resolve but added to his sense of having a decisive role at the Conference.

This article chronicles Mackenzie King's activities at the 1923 Imperial Conference *vis-à-vis* that Conference's discussion on imperial foreign policy. King's biographer, Robert MacGregor Dawson, accepted King's view and claimed that Britain planned the 're-establishment of the unity of the Empire'.[3] But it should be made clear here that there was really no plot to achieve such

a goal. Believing something does not make it so. Along these lines
C. P. Stacey, who has reflected deeply on the nature of King's
character and on his relationship with Britain, wrote that 'there
were probably no plots' against King and Canada in 1923 nor
in any other year. In fact, Canada was a 'very small object' on
the British horizon:

> the vast majority of British politicians were not sufficiently
> interested in Canada, or even in the Dominions as a whole, to
> bother plotting about them. Ignorance and apathy were the
> real problems.[4]

The last thing King would have been willing to accept was the
idea that Canada simply wasn't that important. His obsession
with his own and Canada's impact on imperial affairs made him
overestimate Britain's program for the future. King's peculiar
and incorrect notion of British intentions animated all his
contributions to the Conference. In consequence, King's perception had a significant impact not only on the Conference, but on
the process by which the Empire was transformed into the
Commonwealth. His performance provided an interesting illustration of Thornton's view that it is the perception of the real, rather
than the real itself, that makes history.

CANADA AND THE BRITISH EMPIRE AND COMMONWEALTH FROM MACDONALD TO MEIGHEN

In 1887 during the celebration of Queen Victoria's fiftieth year
on the throne various officials and representatives of the self-
governing colonies, Crown Colonies, and India met and
exchanged views at the first Colonial Conference. Ten years later,
Victoria's sixtieth anniversary celebration was the occasion of a
second, and similar, conference. A third Colonial Conference was
held at the time of King Edward's coronation. It was then decided
that holding these useful meetings should not be left to the
vagaries of monarchical celebrations and ceremonies, and it was
agreed to convene them on a regular basis. The self-governing
colonies and Great Britain would be represented as a matter of
right; other British possessions would send representatives only

by invitation. At the 1907 Conference it was decided that the terms 'Colonial' and 'colonies' would no longer be used to describe the Conferences or their participants. Thus the first Imperial Conference attended by Dominions was held in 1911. World War I changed the system. In 1917 and 1918 Imperial War Conferences were held. Concurrent with these meetings the British Government invited the Dominion Prime Ministers to be members of the British War Cabinet, thereby transforming it into the Imperial War Cabinet. Sir Robert Borden, then Canadian Prime Minister, had no reservations about committing his country to the policies arrived at by the Imperial War Cabinet. Through it he achieved his goal of the past six years – an 'adequate voice' for Canada in the formation of high imperial policy. In 1921, at a special conference which was an Imperial Conference in all but name, the principle of meeting to form common policies was re-affirmed. Arthur Meighen, Borden's Conservative successor, was especially enthusiastic about this concept but not undiscriminatingly so. undiscriminatingly so.

In the years after Confederation Canada's attitude toward the Empire, and in particular toward the Anglo-Canadian relationship, had swung from Sir John A. Macdonald's vision of an active alliance to Sir Wilfrid Laurier's preference for passive participation and then back to Sir Robert Borden's and Arthur Meighen's interest and involvement in the formation of imperial policy. C. P. Stacey in his survey of Canadian external policies notes that the election of Borden in 1911 was 'a turning point' in Canadian history. From 1911 on Borden attempted to change the nature of the imperial relationship. He wished to see Canada more actively engaged in world affairs, and felt this could be achieved through more vigorous participation in the British Empire. Stacey further notes that Borden, unlike Laurier, was

> happy to contemplate the Dominion making a contribution to 'imperial defence,' but only on condition of its being conceded a 'voice' in the formation of imperial policy.[5]

Borden met with little success until 1917. During the early years of the war he observed Asquith's incompetence but was helpless himself to influence events. All of this changed when David Lloyd George became Prime Minister in December 1916. Lloyd George felt that the Dominions ought to be more formally consulted as to the progress and course of the war, as to the steps that ought to be taken to secure victory, and as to the best methods of garnering in the fruits of their efforts as well as of our own.[6]

In implementing the above Lloyd George ushered in an age of imperial unity and cooperation that was brief, but significant. It was one of the more important periods of imperial history. At his direction Imperial War Conferences were held in 1917 and 1918; and under his leadership the Imperial War Cabinet came into being in 1917. When the Imperial War Cabinet met in 1917 and 1918 it seemed that Borden had found a workable way to give Canada its 'adequate voice' in the formation of imperial policy. Borden hoped that the principle behind the Imperial War Cabinet could be continued and built upon after the war. However, through all this, Borden remained a Canadian nationalist even while he acted as an imperialist. One would not be far off the mark to call him, rather awkwardly, an imperialist nationalist. In London to attend the Imperial War Conference and Cabinet in 1918, Borden addressed the Empire Parliamentary Association and made clear his firm belief that the Imperial War Cabinet was useful and not at all dangerous to Canadian autonomy. This institution, he said,

> is a Cabinet of Governments. Every Prime Minister who sits around that board is responsible to his own Parliament and to his own people; the conclusion of the War Cabinet [i.e. the policy decision] can only be carried out by the Parliaments of the different nations of our Imperial Commonwealth. Thus, each Dominion, each nation, retains its perfect autonomy.[7]

This phrase 'Cabinet of Governments' should be emphasised because of the contrast it makes with one of Mackenzie King's own favourites – 'Conference of Governments'. As Prime Minister Meighen reinforced the concept of the Dominion role. Regarding the Imperial Cabinet idea he wrote that

> the term 'Imperial Cabinet' is really open to no objections. None but a crank or a demagogue with an anti-British slant could take exception to it.[8]

No one should doubt their nationalist credentials. Both Meighen and Borden clearly indicated that any action taken as a result of Conference resolutions and the like would have to be ratified by the Canadian Parliament before it was carried out.

BEFORE THE CONFERENCE: MACKENZIE KING, O. D. SKELTON, AND THE BRITISH EMPIRE

William Lyon Mackenzie King, as everyone knows by now, was a very curious person. By 1923, at the age of 49, he had been a civil servant in Ottawa, a member of Parliament, a member of Laurier's last government, a consultant for – and close friend to – the Rockefeller family, leader of the Canadian Liberal Party after 1919, and Prime Minister since 1921. All this despite a peculiar, but at the time secret, propensity to talk to dogs and dead people in his dreams, and to seek approval from them. There is no doubt of Mackenzie King's real affection toward Britain. However his Britain was an idealised country, ruled by Liberal politicians and statesmen. The villains in King's Britain were Conservatives who were also imperialists of the worst sort. Indeed, King

> thought of a British Conservative as a man who believed in centralising the Empire, and who spent a good deal of time plotting to that end.[9]

In 1923 the British Government was Conservative. This no doubt contributed to the confrontational relationship that Mackenzie King at times seems to have established between himself and the British Government during the Imperial Conference of 1923.

King believed in the British Empire, but (again) his belief was founded on his particular version of that entity. He told the South African Premier, Jan Smuts, that he saw the Empire 'as a league of *nations*, as a community of free nations'.[10]This notion of 'free nations' within a community is worth emphasising. As long as he could see the Empire in this light he would continue to wish that he and Canada would remain part of it, associated with and protected by it. Perhaps some found this hard to believe. At one point during the Conference King – rather plaintively – asked the participants to keep in mind that those of us who differed from the centralising point of view should not be regarded as less the friends of a permanent imperial relationship than those who were using high sounding phrases.[11]

In this same context the previous Liberal Prime Minister, Sir Wilfrid Laurier, also an admirer of British Liberals and Liberalism, was very unenthusiastic about the idea of common imperial policies. Laurier had been King's mentor in political life, and in some ways his model in private life: the origins of some of King's views and suspicions can be found in his respect for Laurier's opinions. In a more general sense one can say that Mackenzie King has a Whiggish approach to imperial history. The history of the British Empire was and should be that of increasing autonomy, equality, and freedom for the Dominions within the Empire. Therefore King believed the actions taken by Borden and Meighen in the decade 1911–21 represented a perversion of imperial and Canadian history and should be reversed. In the final analysis King was what might be called a nationalist with isolationist tendencies. He was willing to go to an Imperial Conference and talk but adamantly refused to commit Canada to any action or even to suppose that he as Prime Minister had the authority to commit Canada. However, he was very much at one with the Canadian tradition of supporting Great Britain if Britain's survival was at stake. He made this point rather obscurely when he addressed the Conference on 8 October 1923 and said "If a great and clear call of duty comes, Canada will respond...".[12] In short, a world crisis would find Canada at Britain's side; a police action in Turkey would not.

The Canadian delegation to the Imperial Conference of 1923 consisted of King, two ministerial colleagues, and numerous advisers. It was, however, King's adviser, O. D. Skelton, who most encouraged and supported King in the fight against the imperialists. He provided King with advice on a day to day basis, prepared memoranda, and helped draft King's speeches. A professor at Queen's University, Skelton had first come to King's attention with his biography of Sir Wilfrid Laurier. King very much approved of Skelton's nationalist interpretation of Laurier's career. In 1922, when Skelton, in a speech to the Canadian Club, attacked the idea of a common foreign policy, Mackenzie King was so impressed that he later persuaded Skelton to attend the Imperial Conference as his adviser.

A memorandum prepared for King prior to the Conference is of relevance here. Entitled 'Canada and the Control of Foreign Policy' it stated that 'the fundamental question before the Imperial Conference will be the control of foreign policy'. The memorandum proposed that Canada should challenge the Imperial view, which he maintained was

> a theory of control of foreign policy of a revolutionary character . . . , namely: that the British Empire can only have one foreign policy . . .

In this memorandum Skelton went on to suggest that if not effectively countered this approach could spell disaster for Canada and the other Dominions. Such an approach offered

> a maximum of responsibility and a minimum of control. It commits a Dominion in advance to an endorsement of courses of action of which it knows little and of which it may not approve, or in which it may have little direct concern.[13]

Skelton argued that those who supported the idea of a common foreign policy were trying to implement a revolutionary policy which went against the grain of fifty years of Canadian history. This argument was strong on rhetoric but weak on history because it totally ignored the new orthodoxy that Borden and Meighen had been developing while in office. It began in 1911 with Borden's election and continued with his strenuous efforts during the war. His obvious desire to gain an 'adequate voice' in imperial policy could be seen in the abortive offer to provide ships to the Royal Navy in return for a say in policy formation. He was also the prime mover behind the drafting and acceptance by the 1917 Imperial War Conference of Resolution IX which claimed, among other things, 'the right of the Dominions . . . to an adequate voice in foreign policy and in foreign relations' and went on to say that policies and concerted action should be based on 'continuous consultation in all important matters of common Imperial concern'.[14] Borden also took an active role in the deliberations of the Imperial War Cabinet in 1917 and 1918 and then did the same as a member of the British Empire delegation at the

Versailles Conference in 1919. It is worth emphasising that Borden's theory of action can be traced back, as a Canadian tradition, to the days of Macdonald. Donald Grant Creighton, in his vigorous narrative of *Canada's First Century*, states that in 1878 the nature of Anglo-Canadian relations was coming into clearer focus. 'Henceforth', Creighton wrote,

> the conduct of the Empire's foreign affairs must become a collective enterprise, in which Canada and the other great British colonies must play the part and exert the influence which their new importance required.[15]

This point of view of course makes Laurier appear as the man breaking with tradition. But Skelton and King both ignored the history of Canadian external policy. It is, for example, extraordinary that Skelton in his memorandum did not so much as mention Resolution IX. But, understandably, Skelton and King probably felt that if they attacked first with the epithet of 'revolutionary' they would discredit the idea of an Empire foreign policy.

BEFORE THE CONFERENCE: THE REALITY OF THE BRITISH POSITION ON IMPERIAL FOREIGN POLICY AND A UNITED EMPIRE

The most important British leaders at the Conference were: Lord Curzon, the Foreign Secretary; Leopold Amery, First Lord of the Admiralty; Lord Salisbury, Lord President of the Council; and Stanley Baldwin, Prime Minister. Curzon had a strong and long-standing belief in the British Empire, and Amery had long been an advocate of imperial unity. (Of Amery King said 'he is all for a single imperial organisation'.[16]) But by 1923 they were no longer convinced that an imperial foreign policy, or indeed imperial unity, was a workable proposition. Lord Salisbury, son of the great Prime Minister and Foreign Secretary of the late 19th and early 20th centuries, occasionally pressed for more signs of unity at the Conference, but King frequently warned Salisbury that the Conference should not regard itself 'in any sense as a Cabinet . . .' because to do so would be to take 'a wholly erroneous view' of what should be.[17] Salisbury eventually agreed with King on the impossibility of a common foreign policy. Describing Prime

Minister Baldwin's contribution to the Conference, Curzon wrote that "Nothing can exceed the cheerfulness, good temper and courtesies of Baldwin, except for his impotence."[18]

Whatever Curzon's and Amery's imperialist aims may have been in the immediate post-war years, they soon realised that they might have to lower their sights and expectations. Mackenzie King first began to obscure their vision of imperial unity in September 1922, during the Chanak crisis. The British Government suggested that imperial interests were affected by Britain's quarrel with Mustapha Kemal and the Turkish nationalists. When they asked the Dominions for a commitment on the issue, King responded that no assistance could be offered or given without the sanction of the Canadian Parliament, and he, as Prime Minister, saw no compelling reason to summon Parliament to discuss it.[19] Mackenzie King felt, and rightly, that British leaders were willing to risk involving the Empire in war with Turkey for domestic political reasons. This appalled him. Indeed the poor performance of the British Government did a good deal to shape King's approach to the 1923 Conference. In addition to bad judgement and political irresponsibility, this episode revealed to King the lack of machinery necessary too keep the Dominions informed, and such machinery had to be the basis of any meaningful consultation especially in time of crisis.

When the Lausanne Conference was convened later in 1922 to regularise relations with Turkey, the British Colonial Office suggested that the Dominions be represented as part of a British Empire delegation. At the Foreign Office, Curzon, remembering Mackenzie King's reluctance to be involved, and reluctant himself to bother with the Dominions while conducting intricate negotiations, decided not to invite the Dominions to the Conference.[20] This did not displease Mackenzie King.

The following year King gave supporters of imperial diplomatic unity a real shock. When the United States and Canada agreed to establish a means of conserving halibut in the Northwest Pacific, King insisted that only a Canadian representative should sign the treaty. The British objected to this as being contrary to past practice. However, Mackenzie King continued to insist, and the British ultimately had no choice but to accept his argument that this was a Canadian matter, and not an issue of imperial concern. And so there was no British signature on the Halibut Treaty. The British Foreign Office began to modify its view on imperial diplomatic unity. More importantly, officials there began to wonder if maintaining a common policy was worth the effort. In Philip Wigley's words, the British position right before the 1923 Imperial Conference was that

> If Canada – and, after her, other dominions – were now going to be taking diplomatic initiatives . . ., then rather than accept an overriding responsibility for . . . policies they could not control, they preferred to see the overseas governments go their own way in these matters on their own responsibility.[21]

Despite these growing concerns, the British Government had made no decision, before the Conference began, to end imperial unity. Indeed the British would make no move in that direction except in response to a Dominion's initiative. Seemingly, at this stage British inertia controlled the situation, and so the shift in British thinking was not communicated to any Dominion government. Action based on this shift later on in the Conference therefore came as a pleasant surprise to King, e.g. when the British draft resolution on treaty making accepted the Canadian position without a murmur no one could have been happier than King. Indeed because of the earlier British reaction to the Halibut Treaty signing procedure he had anticipated a fight. In his diary he recorded 'Had I drafted the memorandum on treaty making I could not have better expressed the views which were in my mind.'[22]

It is ironic that Curzon and Mackenzie King, though they never realised it, were occupying the same ground. They both believed that each unit of the Empire, Great Britain included, should have the right to an independent foreign policy. Neither wished to bear the burden or pay the price of having to consult in any meaningful way with others in the Empire regarding foreign policy.[23] Freedom to maneuver was far more valuable to the British Foreign Office, and indeed to the British Government, than imperial unity. This was the reality of British policy before the Conference began.

MACKENZIE KING'S PERCEPTION OF BRITISH INTENTIONS: THE BASIS OF HIS ACTIONS

Mackenzie King's preconceived ideas about the purpose of the Conference and the intentions of the British delegation were the basis of his actions in London. Unaware of the change which had taken place in British priorities as he prepared for the Conference, King looked forward with dread and delight to a hard fought battle, convinced that the British Government was scheming to control the Dominions and that he alone could outwit Whitehall. Always inclined to see his actions in an heroic light, King saw himself continuing the struggles of his grandfather, William Lyon Mackenzie, and of his mentor, Sir Wilfrid Laurier. He believed he would have to be constantly on guard and ever vigilant in defending Canada's right to a separate external, or foreign, policy. It would not be an easy task. King recorded in his diary 'I am filled with terror at the thought of having to speak many times and at my inability to work out themes.'[24] Entries such as this one indicate his alternating fear and fascination with his self-appointed role of challenger to the centralisers and defender of autonomy and self-government. Determined to play David to Britain's Goliath, he would not only defend Canada's rights but also save the Empire from itself.

The consequences of his coming struggle, King felt, would be of immense importance to the future. He firmly believed that the imperialists were plotting to impose a single foreign policy on the Empire which would centralise authority in an Imperial Council. King would later tell the Conference

that the time had come . . . to make very plain that as far as Canada was concerned, we were not prepared to regard the present Conference as in any shape a Council or Cabinet with power to decide on a single policy; I stated our position very plainly in this particular.[25]

King believed that he had no authority from the Canadian electorate to help shape imperial policy: to arrogate such authority to himself would be unconstitutional. This constitutional aspect 'could not be too carefully viewed'.[26] King made several references in his diary to his fear of and opposition to an Imperial Cabinet/Council[27], and discussed this question frequently with other Dominion premiers and with sympathetic, and some not so sympathetic, British politicians. This fear may well have been, in fact it was, something he was imagining, but – and this is the point to emphasise – he felt the danger to be a real and present one. For example, the Prime Minister of Australia, Stanley Bruce, was a keen supporter of the common foreign policy idea, provided that policy was arrived at through real consultation. When Bruce tried to gain King's support, King told him

> I could never consent to the Conference assuming the role of an Imperial Council, laying down policies for the Empire as a whole, and . . . to attempt to commit us by resolution in any way was simply to make impossible any subsequent approval by Parliament [in Canada] of anything that the Conference has done in this direction . . . .[28]

King was certain that the result of an attempt to create formal imperial unity would be disastrous. In a conversation with King George V about empires in history, Mackenzie King told him that 'the old empires had not endured because of the effort to centralise in matters of government'. He was pleased to discover that the King 'agreed entirely' with him.[29] (Mackenzie King never considered the possibility that King George was simply being tactful.) If forced to choose between remaining in the Empire as a subordinate or going its own way, King hinted that Canada might be forced to do the latter. However, neither alternative was attractive or inevitable.[30] He insisted that a middle way could be found with self-government as the bedrock principle of the imperial structure.[31] Along these lines he argued that

> occasions may arise in which co-operation between the several parts of the Empire may be advisable and necessary, but the extent and manner of co-operation are all kept within the control of the several Parliaments concerned.[32]

On the eve of the Conference then Mackenzie King was determined to turn the Conference away from the single foreign policy idea and, in doing so, to reject the imposition of an Imperial Cabinet or Council. Even though his perception of British intentions was wrong he acted on it. In doing so he would exercise substantial influence on the 1923 Conference and ultimately on the shape of the future Commonwealth itself.

MACKENZIE KINGS'S CONFERENCE PERFORMANCE: 1 OCTOBER–8 NOVEMBER 1923

King arrived in London before the Conference opened, and met with Sir Maurice Hankey, Secretary to the Conference, who admitted that no one would be surprised if King questioned the concept of a single foreign policy for the Empire.[33] He noted in his diary the next day that he had 'shocked' Leopold Amery

> by declaring openly against the idea of one foreign policy, pointing out that it was absurd to expect us to interest the people [of Canada] in matters which were far beyond their concern.[34]

The Conference opened on 1 October. After the first session King met privately with Stanley Baldwin. Perhaps trying to anticipate and defuse King's suspicions, he suggested that the Foreign Office wanted to have the Dominions' views on foreign policy so as to prevent British action from creating a serious situation for the Dominions. True this would mean Canadian involvement in consultation, but it would mean a knowledgeable involvement of the sort Sir Robert Borden had supported when he was Prime Minister. Mackenzie King totally rejected this view. He did not want a better form of consultation: he wanted no consultation at all. No consultation meant no responsibility. He told Baldwin

> that what . . . people in Canada were afraid of was that the desire [on the part of the Foreign Office for us] to take part in foreign policy was largely that of drawing us into European and world politics from which we should be free.

King also made clear to Baldwin his general views on a single foreign policy. They are worth quoting at length.

> I . . . spoke . . . about foreign affairs, and that the view that there should be one foreign policy in the Empire; more particularly of the absolute impossibility of our taking part in the shaping of foreign policy other than with respect to matters with which we had an immediate and almost direct concern. I pointed out that we were not desirous of shaping foreign

policy; we did wish to have brought to our attention matters
which were likely to be of concern to us. Matters affecting the
people of Great Britain should be settled by the people of Great
Britain themselves.[35]

He did not preclude the possibility of Britain and Canada arriving
at the same foreign policy, but he insisted on Canada's right to
reach that point independently and after an assessment of
Canada's direct and immediate interest.

Later the same day, during a discussion of the Chanak
Crisis with Lord Salisbury, Salisbury agreed that the British
Government's attempt to commit the Dominions to British policy
'was an example of how a thing should not be done'. This was
more sympathy than King usually received and he quickly went
on to point out, as he later recorded,

> wherein I felt the Dominions would hesitate to accept responsi-
> bility for foreign policy generally; that I could not but think
> that each part of the Empire should manage its own foreign
> policy in which there was an immediate and direct interest by
> that part; but that the outlying dominions would have to be
> relied upon to do their part where a just cause arose; that
> certainly in participation in war Canada would agree to
> nothing other than by consent of her Parliament.

But Salisbury suggested that the British Government might want
to know, in advance, the views of the Dominions on foreign policy
to avoid taking a course which the Dominions would not support.
But King only insisted once again that 'where we [the Dominions]
were not affected, there was no need for consultation . . .'.[36]

Mackenzie King's momentous (for him) confrontation with the
imperialists took place in two phases. The first began on 3 October
when the Imperial Conference went into its second meeting.
Curzon, in his opening remarks to the meeting, referred to the
Imperial Conference as a 'Cabinet'. King pounced: ever vigilant
he quickly pointed out that although the Conference might be
similar in its proceedings to a Cabinet it was NOT a Cabinet.
King said it was 'a conference of Governments'. As head of the
Canadian delegation he had no mandate to act on issues before
the Conference.[37] This might be contrasted with Borden's notion

of a "Cabinet of Governments". In any case Curzon responded soothingly,

> I only mean what you mean, Mr. Mackenzie King. I am the strongest possible advocate of your conception of the nature of the work of this body. When I spoke of a Cabinet I only meant that we should treat each other with the same confidence that Cabinet Ministers do . . . .[38]

Far from being the chief spider in an imperial web of deception designed to deceive and trap Canada, Curzon was simply stating the truth. He was willing to agree with King. Mackenzie King however saw this exchange as a preliminary probe by the imperialists and felt he had foiled the effort. 'The imperialist group', he noted in his diary, "never seems satisfied unless in some visible public way they can appear to be effecting control from London.'[39] King believed that his actions indicated to the British his awareness of their imperialist strategy.

Lord Curzon addressed the Conference again on 5 October. King felt that in Curzon he was up against a splendid adversary. After being enraptured by Curzon's two and one-half hour survey of foreign affairs, King confided to his diary:

> Lord Curzon's manner throughout was one of quiet strength and dignity; he is an impressive figure; a real emperor in appearance and manner with a dominating intellectual force which must constantly influence those who are in his immediate environment.

He noted, whith admiration and horror, that one could be swept off one's feet by 'the power and majesty of the language which Lord Curzon uses with such facility . . .' and commit one's country to almost anything![40] Mackenzie King seemed to relish the temptations of such seductive oratory. No doubt he felt that an impressive adversary would only add to the victor's consequence. And King planned to beat Curzon in this battle.

A few days later (8 October) King took the initiative in a major address to the Conference. He spoke for over an hour, discussing the European situation and Canadian relations with the United States, Japan, France, and of course Great Britain. Then he addressed the crucial question of a common foreign policy for the Empire. "I made it quite clear', he recorded in his diary

> that we could not subscribe to the one foreign policy doctrine; so clear, in fact, that I think it was evident to all present that . . . no one could have taken exception to the reasonableness of the position as stated. I feel that by getting on record what I did and in the manner in which I did I have helped to lay the foundations, in a way that it will be difficult to alter, of subsequent development in our inter-imperial relations.[41]

Prime Minister Bruce spoke after King. Bruce was the one who in reality played the role King had cast Curzon for. Arguing that a united policy 'on important questions and on the broadest lines' was essential, Bruce offered a reinterpretation of King's statement. King promptly objected.[42] In his diary King wrote that Bruce 'had no alternative but to take back what was evident misrepresentation of my attitude'.[43] A few days later, when the discussion on foreign policy seemed to have been completed, King was extremely pleased with the results of the deliberations and with his role. He had held his own and steadfastly refused to cooperate with the centralisers' strategy. He was sure that he had succeeded in his purpose and that the most difficult part of the Conference was over.[44]

One of the ironies of the developing situation was that when Curzon or Amery told King they had no desire to create an Imperial Cabinet or Council to centralise the Empire, or when Lord Salisbury told King of his sympathy for King's position, King would not believe them. He had come to the Conference with such strong notions of British intentions that the facts could not impress him or distract him from his highly personal view.

The second phase came as the Conference drew to a close in early November. King's preconceptions about British Conservatives, the fact that a Tory Government was in power, and the advice he was receiving from O. D. Skelton, drew him inexorably to the conclusion that he had found more evidence of a plot in the foreign policy section of the Conference communique. Centralisers obviously never rested. The communique was discussed on 5, 6, and 7 November. The basis of the discussion was a draft statement written and presented by Curzon on 5 November. King was very much disturbed: the statement was clearly 'an attempt to commit the Conference to a common foreign policy' regarding Turkey and Egypt. He felt threatened because he had an understandable concern that Canada might become disadvantageously involved in a dangerous international incident, and also because surely this was part of a scheme to corral Canada into a united empire.[45]

The statement was examined and debated paragraph by paragraph by the Conference. King would only go so far as to admit that the Dominions could give advice on foreign policy. Nonetheless he was careful to restrict this to matters where a Dominion was interested, informed, and prepared to accept responsibility. He quickly protested against the Conference's assuming, through this draft statement, 'the rights of a cabinet in the determination of foreign policy'. Although the Foreign Office's telegraphic despatches on foreign affairs that Canada received were informative, they were hardly a serious basis for policy formulation. Indeed he doubted that the Foreign Office could ever develop a method of consultation which would make it possible for the Dominions to contribute to policy formulation. King announced that if the British Government's purpose in inviting the Dominions to Imperial Conferences was to commit them to policies over which their own Parliaments had no control, the Canadian Government just might refuse to come to future conferences. To refuse to attend in the future implied withdrawal from the Empire. King's diary indicates that he might have pulled back from this drastic step. Nevertheless, for King to threaten this action reveals his absolute conviction that this contest was of tremendous significance for Canada and the Empire. In making his stand, Mackenzie King felt very much alone. He noted later that he had 'had a most difficult and unpleasant hour or two opposing many paragraphs . . .'. Not only were Smuts, Bruce, and Massey (of New Zealand) eager to help shape imperial foreign policy, they also believed that the information they received from the Foreign Office was equal to that which the British Government itself had.[46] That they appeared satisfied with current arrangements made opposition more difficult for King. Paradoxically, this difficulty seems to have been an incentive to continue. He must have consoled himself with the notion that he was very brave.

The heart of King's argument was that the Imperial Conference was not an Imperial Cabinet or Council. It had no executive authority, and had no right to determine imperial foreign policy. Although at this point the final draft of the foreign policy section had still to be written King believed that by the simple expedient of absolutely refusing to cooperate he had succeeded again. His assessment of his day's work showed great satisfaction.

> I was very outspoken, and perhaps too much so, but I know I have saved a very serious situation from developing so far as Canada is concerned.[47]

However, as mentioned above, the final form of the foreign policy draft was not yet set, although Mackenzie King certainly felt that agreement in principle had been reached. Curzon however maintained that there should be general policies; the Dominions could then decide the degree to which they would adhere to them. In particular he wanted the Conference to support policies of economic assistance to Turkey and also the establishment of a new Turkish Government along lines satisfactory to Great Britain. In the case of Egypt, Curzon wished to gather support for Empire wide adherence to continued British control of the Suez Canal. King in response adamantly maintained that if Curzon insisted on these points he (King) would insist that a Canadian reservation be inserted in the communique. this reservation would state that

> nothing in the report could bind Canada without the express endorsation in the first instance by her Government of what it contained, and secondly approval by her Parliament . . .[48]

This would be unsatisfactory to everyone. Such a reservation would draw unwanted attention to dissent among the Dominions, thereby spoiling the effect Curzon wished to create.

On 6 November King saw Hankey to discuss the differences between himself and Curzon, and to see where a middle ground could be found. Hankey, running back and forth between the two, eventually reported to King that Curzon still wanted the final report to include policy statements on Turkey and Egypt. King remained steadfastly against any reference to Empire-wide policies, and again threatened a public reservation.

I held out in the strongest possible fashion against committing our Parliament to any obligation of the kind, and told Hankey that if Lord Curzon held to the position he did I must add a reservation so far as Canada was concerned . . .

The idea behind King's reservation was one he never tired of reiterating: Canada could only be committed in matters of direct and immediate concern to Canada. Once again he felt the necessity of insisting that 'from our point of view . . . the proceedings of the Conference were to be regarded merely as those of a conference and not of a cabinet'. Seeing King and Curzon at a stand-off, Hankey tried a different approach. He brought Smuts, who was on good terms with both men, into the process. After considerable discussion, Smuts persuaded King to accept a compromise. King agreed to confine himself to a brief statement (in the communique) indicating that the proceedings of the Conference were all subject to the approval of individual Parliaments *if* the specific proposals regarding Turkey and Egypt were dropped. Smuts then convinced Curzon to agree, and this compromise was reflected in the Conference's report on foreign affairs.[49] All references to Turkey and Egypt were rendered innocuous, and the concluding paragraph of the foreign policy statement, i.e. King's reservation made general, read

This Conference is a conference of representatives of the several Governments of the Empire; its views and conclusions on Foreign Policy . . . are necessarily subject to the action of the Governments and Parliaments of the various portions of the Empire, and it trusts will meet with their approval.[50]

King felt victorious. He had bearded the lion in his den, and had frustrated the centralisers in their attempt to achieve a common foreign policy. More importantly, so he thought, he had prevented the establishment of a formal imperial organisation in which Canada was a subordinate, not an equal. Much of the strength to take on this arduous task had come from his stubbornness, and that had come from a firm, almost fanatical, belief in a single doctrine, best enunciated in a conversation he had had with Lord Salisbury on the very first day of the Conference: 'I told him that maintenance of the principle of responsible Government in all relations of the British Empire is the cornerstone of the entire structure . . .'.[51] As the Conference ended King was certain he had done a great thing by foiling a scheme to transform the Imperial Conference into an Imperial Cabinet or Council. Even though the scheme, or plot, was non-existent, he thought he had emulated his mentor Laurier, who had scuttled a series of imperial unity proposals at Colonial and Imperial Conferences from 1897 to 1911. Had he failed, King was sure that Canada would have had to leave the Empire to preserve its integrity, and the consequence of this ultimately would have been the dissolution of the Empire itself.

CONCLUSION

It would be difficult to find a better illustration of Thornton's notion about the perception of truth in history than the story of Mackenzie King at the 1923 Conference. Although King's misperceptions had totally obscured for him Britain's real intentions, the consequence of his actions for the future development of the Empire was significant. 'Obstinate, tiresome, and stupid'[52] though he may have seemed to be, he nonetheless compelled the British and others in the Empire to reassess their expectations of the Dominions and to consider what form the Empire would eventually take. More to the point he convinced British leaders at the Conference that a common policy was not a prerequisite for cooperation within the Empire. King, more than anyone else, dispelled the notion that the Empire must unite or disintegrate. He helped to initiate a process of replacing the discarded doctrine of unity. What King wanted was an Empire in which Canada could remain with its sovereignty intact. With his ideal of a community of free nations, he provided a middle way which manifested itself at the 1926 Imperial Conference when the principles of autonomy, equality of status, free association, and common allegiance to the Crown became the defining characteristics of the British Commonwealth of Nations.

Curiously enough, King's suspicions about imperialists and their plots were never laid to rest. He was to fight this illusory battle many times more. In 1948, during his last trip to London, heart trouble prevented him from attending the sessions of the Commonwealth Prime Ministers Meeting (successor to the Imperial Conference). However, his replacement, Louis St.

Laurent, conferred with him regularly. One day St. Laurent suggested that something should be done to 'make the Commonwealth a unit'. This could hardly have done King's heart any good, but he responded like an old charger to a bugle call. King said, 'in reality [a quaint expression for him] there was no such thing as a Commonwealth – as an entity – with policies of its own'. And more importantly, he continued, even though there was no such thing as a Commonwealth entity, 'the whole plan here was to bring that to pass'. He warned St. Laurent that 'this had to be guarded against'.[53] Mackenzie King remained vigilant, and wrong, to the end. If his assessment of reality had been more accurate, his actions might not have been as significant for the history of Canada and the Empire. In fact, King's misreading of British intentions at the Imperial Conference of 1923 substantially influenced the evolution of the British Empire into the Commonwealth of Nations.

NOTES 5

1. A. P. Thornton, *Imperialism in the Twentieth Century* (Minneapolis and London, 1977) p.15.
2. C. P. Stacey, *Canada and the Age of Conflict: a History of Canadian External Policies: Volume I: 1867–1921* (Toronto 1977) pp.209.
3. Ibid., p.333.
4. C. P. Stacey, *Mackenzie King and the Atlantic Triangle* (Toronto, 1976) p.66.
5. Stacey, *Canadian External Policies*, I, 151.
6. *Ibid.*, 204, citing *Documents on Canadian External Relations*, I, 302–3.
7. *Ibid.*, citing *The War Cabinet: Report for the Year 1918*, British Parliamentary Papers, Cmd 325, 1918.
8. *Ibid.*, 332.
9. Stacey, *Mackenzie King and the Atlantic Triangle*, 15.
10. Mackenzie King Diary (hereafter MKD), 3 October 1923. Public Archives of Canada.
11. MKD, 17 October 1923.
12. C. P. Stacey, ed., *Historical Documents of Canada*, vol. V: *The Arts of War and Peace, 1914–45* (New York, 1972) p.437.
13. *Ibid.*, pp 432–4.
14. *Ibid.*, pp 368–9. The story of Borden's role is best told by R. Craig Brown and Robert Bothwell in 'The "Canadian Resolution" ' in Michael Cross and Robert Bothwell, eds., *Policy by Other Means* (Toronto, 1972).
15. Donald Creighton, *Canada's First Century* (Toronto, 1970), p.44.
16. MKD, 30 September 1923.
17. MKD, 1 October 1923.

18.   R. MacGregor Dawson, *William Lyon Mackenzie King: a Political Biography, 1874–1923* (Toronto, 1958) p.460, citing Marchioness Curzon of Keddleston, *Reminiscences* (London, 1955) p.183.

19.   See Philip Wigley's precis of the Chanak Crisis in his *Canada and the Transition to Commonwealth: British-Canadian Relations, 1917–26* (Cambridge, 1977) pp.160–6.

20.   *Ibid.*, p. 168.

21.   *Ibid.*, p. 174.

22.   MKD, 25 October 1923.

23.   Wigley, *British-Canadian Relations*, p. 193.

24.   MKD, 2 September 1923.

25.   *Ibid.*, 17 October 1923.

26.   *Ibid.*, 1 October 1923.

27.   See, for example, entries in King's diary for 1, 3, 9, 17 and 31 October, and 5 and 7 November 1923.

28.   MKD, 31 October 1923.

29.   *Ibid.*, 9 October 1923.

30.   *Ibid.*, 5 November 1923.

31.   *Ibid.*, 1 October 1923.

32.   *Ibid.*, 3 November 1923.

33.   *Ibid.*, 29 September 1923.

34.   *Ibid.*, 30 September 1923.

35.   *Ibid.*, 1 October 1923.

36.   *Ibid.*, 1 October 1923.

37.   *Ibid.*, 3 October 1923.

38.   Stacey, ed., *Arts of War and Peace*, p. 435.

39.   MKD, 8 November 1923.

40.   *Ibid.*, 5 October 1923.

41.   *Ibid.*, 8 October 1923.

42.   See Dawson's *King*, p. 466.

43.   MKD, 8 October 1923.

44.   *Ibid.*, 13 October 1923.

45.   *Ibid.*, 5 November 1923.

46.   *Ibid.*, 5 November 1923.

47.   *Ibid.*, 5 November 1923.

48.   *Ibid.*, 7 November 1923.

49.   *Ibid.*, 7 November 1923.

50.   Arthur Berriedale Keith, ed., *Speeches and Documents on the British Dominions, 1918–31* (repr. of 1932 ed; London, 1966) p.318.

51.   MKD, 1 October 1923.

52.   Dawson, *King*, p. 477, citing Marchioness Curzon, *Reminiscences*, pp. 181–2.

53.   MKD, 15 October 1948.

6 Emergencies and Elections in India*

D. A. LOW

The secular Western institutions that the retreating empires left
behind them are still on trial . . . the concept [of democracy]
is essentially alien, and was brought to these continents as part
of their mental baggage by imperialists who supposed that
power and responsibility were mutually interchangeable terms.
A. P. Thornton, *Doctrines of Imperialism* (1965) p. 226

When I was on a visit to India in the mid-1970s, I flew one
morning from Delhi to Jaipur. After we had all settled back into
our seats a short, dapper, moustached man in an ordinary western
suit, climbed into one of the front seats. At Jaipur he was the first
off the plane, and was met at the foot of the steps by several army
officers, with much saluting and clicking of heels. It happened
that when I flew back the next day he was on the same plane
once again; and at Delhi airport I eventually realised who he
was. He was met there by several members of his well-dressed
family, and was shown to his huge car by his seemingly even
larger, magnificently turbaned, driver. He was, I realised, Sam
Maneckshaw, the Indian Army's only Field Marshal since
Independence, the hero of its spectacular victory in the Bangladesh
war, now, very evidently, living in enviable, luxurious, much
honoured retirement.

What a contrast to those political generals, the house-bound
ex-Presidents of the day, Ayub Khan and Yahya Khan, in
Pakistan next door! What a contrast too to Generals Ne Win,

* This chapter was presented as the Kingsley Martin Memorial Lecture,
University of Cambridge, 1980.

Suharto, Zia and others of their ilk still wrestling with the intractable problems of their countries.

That day, what I saw of Sam Maneckshaw neatly symbolised the remarkable abstention of the Indian Army from any direct control over India's politics in all the thirty years and more since Independence.

For some time now various scholars have been making a range of new enquiries into India's political history in the late 19th and 20th centuries. From these studies it is now beginning to be possible to make some suggestions about how the Indian body politic actually operates. The purpose of this chapter is to canvass one feature of this – one which links the maintenance of parliamentary government in India, based on periodic democratic elections, to its handling of political emergencies. The fact that, unlike so many of its Asian neighbours, India has not seen a military takeover is related to these circumstances; so is its astonishingly persistent adherence to universal suffrage, open elections and governments based upon majority electoral support; so too, it will be suggested, were Mrs Gandhi's remarkable decisions in the years 1975–7, not merely to impose a national state of emergency in mid-1975, but her even more remarkable decision to hold national elections early in 1977. It is beginning to be possible to see how all these exemplify the distinctive ways in which the Indian body politic functions. Ultimately the issues relate to the relationship in India between the holding of elections and the management of what those at the apex of its political system see as political emergencies.

There are, however, four preliminaries to be considered first.

To begin with, there is the fundamental fact of the relative depth in India of the acceptance of the legitimacy of superordinate political authority. There are many ways in which this can be illustrated. Perhaps the most striking is by reference to the persistence in India, over two millennia and more, of the notion of the *chakravartin*, the supreme ruler. Supreme rulership in India has by no means always been actually in operation, and its writ has only rarely been comprehensive. But from the dynasty of the Mauryas, through the Guptas, to the Moguls, the British, and the Congress, the dominance of a supreme, overall, political authority has periodically come close to being operational in India, and that has served to keep the notion of its legitimacy healthily alive. The system has readily allowed, moreover, for several layers of rulership underneath: in its heyday – beneath the Emperors – Nawabs and Nizams, Maharajas and Rajas, Viceroys and Governors. And the prevalence of the idea of rulership all the way down to the lowest levels of the political structure is well exemplified by the common address of 'Maharaj" to any superior even at village level. The legitimacy indeed of political authority all the way up to and down from Delhi is, as Max Weber would have put it, deeply traditional in India. Though the particulars are significantly different one could say the same of China. But one could not say the same – if the contrast may be emphasised – of Africa whose countries, and capitals, are so often entirely new, and, by the same token, unsupported by such traditions; nor even, to the same extent at least, of Islamabad, Dacca or Rangoon.

That is the first point to bear in mind. In India the authority of superordinate political power is not much in question, and this has major implications for the way the body politic actually operates.

The second point to note is that we should be in no doubt that, whatever may be a commentator's interest in elections at state and national levels in India, and the emergencies which have punctuated their history, these only quite marginally affect what happens at village level. There, in the half million and more villages in which the overwhelming majority of Indians live, the body politic has its own distinctive ways of working. There (if one may generalise over a vast array of particular variations) one witnesses, in so many cases, what the anthropologists have called the dominance of the dominant castes. At the apex of Indian village society, that is, there are numbers of more prosperous peasants who have economic, ritual and social preeminence and who possess a position of political primary which, if periodically challenged, is only very rarely undermined. In many areas these dominant peasants come from only one caste. Their ownership of land per head of household is well above the village average; and they tend to live in the brick-built rather than the mud-built houses in the village. Though their leaders frequently quarrel amongst themselves, and factionalism is indeed a feature of their interaction with each other, the prevalence of village factionalism chiefly reflects the very dominance which the richer peasants hold within it. For if this dominance were not secure, these dominant peasants would – and do – soon close ranks.

Contrary to the general belief, the middle echelons of village social structures are, moreover, highly variegated, and thus fluid. Accordingly they provide ready recruiting grounds for prosperous peasant faction leaders who are looking for subordinate supporters. Underneath all of these are the agricultural labourers, often of untouchable caste, and generally fixed in their misery. Only very rarely can they influence village politics, and, even then, very often only as the paid hirelings of their superiors.

This is a situation at village level across the length and breadth of India which now seems for the most part fixed hard. From above decrees may go out for land reform; but they do not succeed in lowering the ceilings upon any single individual's ownership of land below 20–30 acres – for at that point they encounter the impermeable resistance of the richer peasants. From below there may, from time to time, be attempted eruptions. But the richer peasants can afford guns, and can also afford to employ one group of impoverished labourers to suppress another group of impoverished labourers, and do so. The 1970s showed in particular – especially in the experience of the violent, revolutionary, Naxalite parties – that those who have sought to organise rural revolutions against this system can make little headway. Only in Kerala, where different circumstances apply (for example, because settlement, as the geographers would say, is not nucleated but dispersed) has this situation been somewhat ameliorated under the impact of a succession of Marxist influences on the State government. In the years after 1977 a Marxist government has ruled in Bengal. It was exceedingly careful, however, particularly after the unhappy experiences of two United Front Governments in the 1960s, not to upset the prevailing order in the villages of Bengal too abruptly, lest it ran its head prematurely against the brick wall of rural rich peasant dominance there too.

Most Indian political parties, of whatever formal designation, have reflected this rural situation in their make-up since at least the 1930s. In 1979 the hold of rich peasant dominance upon the Indian political system was neatly symbolised at national level in the persons of two Prime Ministers and the Leader of the Opposition. For all the differences between them, Morarji Desai – an Anavil Brahmin from south Gujarat – Charan Singh – the ideologue of the north Indian Jats for over thirty years – and Y. B. Chavan – a quintessential dominant caste Maratha from

Maharashtra – all had strong rich peasant backgrounds, and their actions reflected this.

So, while the first point to underline is the depth of the acceptance in India of the legitimacy of political authority all the way up to and down from Delhi itself, the second is the persistence of the dominance of the dominant rich peasant communities both at the village level where so many Indians live, and all the way through several political layers up to the national Parliament itself. Elections in India may come and emergencies may go, but both operate in an arena which is bounded by these two parameters, is dependent upon both of them, and has little or no effect upon either.

Into this arena the Indian Army has never so far marched. This is not to say that the Army has had no political involvement in India. On the contrary, their role has in certain respects been critical. Some of the specifics will explain the case.

Perhaps the starting point lies in the profundity of the shock for the British when in 1857 their Sepoy army mutinied. The British repressed that mutiny, and its accompanying rebellions, with great ferocity; and from that moment onwards they paid very careful attention to the role which the army should play in the structure of the Indian state. Under the British for long afterwards Indian troops were not allowed to man fieldguns, and for most of the remaining years of their rule the British maintained in India large numbers of British troops to buttress their position.

In the course of the army reforms they instituted in India in the first decade of the 20th century (at a time when Lord Kitchener was British Commander-in-Chief), the Army in India – as the combination of British and Indian troops came to be called – was quite explicitly (and for our present purposes very significantly) divided into three categories: the field army, for service beyond the frontiers of India; the covering troops, for service in the frontier regions; and the internal security forces. By the 1920s the internal security forces were composed of fifty battalions of British and Indian troops. These were carefully positioned, moreover, at strategic points about India, particularly near railway junctions, from where they could be swiftly despatched to overawe, more especially the towns and cities of India, whenever these turned turbulent.

It needs to be emphasised that in the British period there were numerous occasions when the Army was called out, as the classic phrase had it, 'in aid of the civil power'. This was frequently done in order to suppress communal disturbances. The Army was massively employed, moreover, by the British against Gandhi's last, and greatest, civil disobedience campaign (the so-called Quit India campaign of August 1942) when the British used well over fifty battalions of troops against it.

It is not therefore that the Indian Army has had no tradition of employment for political ends. It has been frequently used indeed for these purposes, both before and after Independence. It has been calculated, for example, that the Indian Army was called out in aid of the civil power between 1961 and 1970 no less than 476 times. It has often seemed, moreover, as if in Bihar and Bengal significant parts of the Indian Army have been openly stationed so as to provide a perpetual reminder, and on occasion an actual expression, of the fact that the existing social and political order in India is only to be challenged by its critics at their direst peril.

Its role in such matters has long been supplemented, moreover, by para-military forces of armed policemen. These have their origins in three quarters. It may be recalled that for centuries there have been 'social bandits' in India; armed groups, on the fringes of settled societies – the famous (or infamous, according to one's choosing) *dakaits*. Against them most provincial and later state police forces have for a century and more despatched remarkably intrepid, specially trained, armed police. To the extent that *dakaits* in particular situations have periodically merged with the more deliberately revolutionary groups, the role and size of special police forces has been enlarged as well. In certain areas special police forces were explicitly formed as such. The violent uprisings of the Muslim Moplah community in what used to be Madras Presidency under the British (and is now part of Kerala) led the British, back in the 1920s, to create the Malabar Special Force. We have noted already that the British also mobilised special forces to guard India's borderlands.

In independent India these various elements were in due course developed into such well known para-military forces as the Central Reserve Police and the Border Security Force. These have generally been commanded by army officers, and amounted at one count to 800 000 men, or the equivalent of two-thirds of the size of the regular Army. After the metal-tipped-stave-armed police they became indeed the Government of India's prime line of attack against disruptive forces; and against these there has been very little hesitation in using them.

Coercive force, that is, has been at once a latent and an actual element in the workings of the Indian body politic, to a degree that has sometimes been underestimated.

But the earlier point remains. Thus far at least, the Indian Army has never sought to be the arbiter, let alone the controller, of the country's political affairs (nor the Central Reserve Police either).

There is one further preliminary to mention too. This concerns the Indian bureaucracy. Since independence the seniormost Indian administration – represented quintessentially by the Indian Administrative Service – has been at once very unBritish and very British. In the first place it really has, of course, no counterpart in Britain itself; nor in the White Dominions either. For there is nothing there to resemble the centrally appointed generalist official/magistrate with large responsibilities over one of the many districts into which the country has long since been divided, who remains the key agent in exercising the power that the Indian Government possesses. But in the second place the Indian administration has at the same time been in many ways very British indeed, since the highly elitist Indian Administrative Service, which dominates its central and local bureaucracies, is in every sense the direct descendant of the premier Indian Civil Service that the British created. Its members are trained, moreover, as their predecessors had been, to rule, and when called upon – for example during political emergencies – very readily proceed to do so.

Nevertheless, for all that has been said so far, the fundamental fact remains that at the core of India's changing politics there have since Independence been rulers who have made the key day-to-day political decisions, who have been politicians who have regularly competed with each other at contested elections at the head of political parties at which they have won electoral majorities. This is a sufficiently rare phenomenon in any country, let alone in one which is as large, and which has been as economically impoverished, as India, to call for some substantial explanation; and to this we shall now turn rather more directly.

Let it be emphasised straight away that elections to legislatures in India have been very frequent, and that they are accordingly a remarkably well-established part of its regular political routine.

There are several reasons for this. To begin with, the system of electoral politics was not introduced into India at, or shortly before, Independence, as in so many other newly independent countries. It has a very much longer history than that. Nowadays studies are frequently made of contemporary Indian elections. There are also detailed studies, however, of provincial elections in India back in 1912 and even earlier. Those early elections were fought, moreover, with all the energy to which the studies of more recent elections have now accustomed us. Such evidence points to the fact that open parliamentary-style elections have been part of the political life of large areas of India for most of this century.

This consideration is reinforced by a further consideration which is all too frequently overlooked. The popular version of the history of India's national movement in the first half of this century is primarily associated with the person of Gandhi and his successive civil disobedience movements. His and their importance is not to be gainsaid. Without them the Indian national movement would have been much less vigorous than it was, whereas, compared with its counterparts elsewhere in Asia, it was for thirty years quite extraordinarily substantial. It has, nevertheless, to be said that none of the three great Gandhi-led phases of nationalist agitation – between 1919 and 1922; 1929 and 1934; 1940 and 1943 – ever succeeded in overthrowing the British. These agitations certainly made the British very uncomfortable, and their position periodically precarious. They succeeded too in advancing the cause of Indian nationalism amongst Indians themselves. But they did not succeed in wresting political control over India from the British. That only came when the Indian National Congress started to win elections.

Congress, to begin with, had a strong tendency to boycott elections. It did so in 1920 at the onset of Gandhi's first non-cooperation campaign (there are signs that this was because it was not confident at that time that it would win them). When in 1923, and more particularly in 1926, many members of the Congress contested the legislative elections after all, they were not as successful as one might well have expected the leaders of a vigorous nationalist movement would have been.

The turning point here came in 1937 when, after the collapse of the civil disobedience campaigns of the early 1930s, Congress decided it would, once again, contest the upcoming elections, and, to everyone's surprise, proceeded to win a majority position in seven of the eleven provincial legislatures of India. Shortly afterwards, in accordance with the provisions of the new Government of India Act of 1935, and despite Congress' own initial hesitations, it took control of the provincial governments in all of these Provinces.

That outcome had a major effect. For when, after a further – again initially abortive – agitation against the British during the Second World War, the Congress leaders came out of prison once again, they promptly set about organising, not a nationalist revolt, nor a further vehement agitation, but rather a major campaign for the state and national elections which were called in 1946. When in the non-Muslim majority areas, they won these overwhelmingly, their course became firmly set in the direction of the transfer of power from the British which occurred in August 1947.

As a consequence of these experiences – which had few parallels elsewhere in Asia – the Indian nationalist leadership was in no doubt that its success in parliamentary elections had played a vital role in India's attainment of independence; and, as a result, their commitment to parliamentary-style elections was strongly reinforced.

It happened that the franchise for the 1937 and the 1946 elections was based on property qualifications and was limited to something between 11 per cent and 14 per cent of the population, or in other words, in the rural areas, to the dominant peasants mentioned earlier. These comprised the bulk of those who could afford to give their time and their money to electoral politics. When, after independence, universal suffrage was introduced, the already established patterns of electoral activity were not, it seemed, greatly changed. Accordingly, the political élite, with the powerful dominant castes at their core, remained happily staunch in their commitments to them.

Since independence there has as a consequence been a continuous succession of elections in the Indian States. There were, for example, twelve in 1978; six more in 1979.

At national level there has also been an all but systematic succession of parliamentary elections too. Following upon the first general elections in 1952, general elections occurred with an orderliness which puts those of us who have lived in Australia, with four general elections between 1972 and 1977 in five years, to shame. With two slight, but self-adjusting exceptions, these

regularly took place every five years. In 1971, in the aftermath
of the Congress split in 1969, and following her triumphs in the
Bangladesh war, Mrs Gandhi called the election a year early.
Because of the way she handled the national emergency in 1975,
she did not then call the next general election until nearly a year
late; but she did then hold it early in 1977. And with that the
succession of Indian parliamentary elections appeared to move
back on its orderly quinquennial course. It did not, of course,
turn out that way. Half way through its ensuing term the new
Janata Government, which was elected in 1977, broke apart, in
circumstances which in most other new democracies would surely
have put paid to parliamentary government. In India, however,
in 1979 there was the astonishing spectacle of a considerable
political crisis being handled by a calm decision to mount new
general elections four months later. All in all it has been, by any
standards, an extraordinary record.

It is buttressed by the further fact that, for a century or so,
there have in many places in India been growing traditions of
remarkably open elections at city, town, district, and even at
village level. One might be tempted to wonder indeed whether
India has not lumbered itself with more than its fair share of
elections, particularly if one is sceptical, as many observers
would be, as to whether they really make any difference at
all to the lot of most ordinary people. But India is a large
country, and it can be persuasively argued that such a plethora
of elections serves to relieve some of the strains in an otherwise
aching social and economic system. Such elections certainly
reinforce the commitment of the Indian body politic to the
regular testing of the electoral support of those holding
superordinate political power at its various levels; and their
succession continues.

The central point to be made here is, however, that such a
commitment to electoral politics might nevertheless not have
sufficed to hold India to its continuing systems of parliamentary
government, had India not also had its own special methods for
dealing with political emergencies – or at all events with what
the powers-that-be conceive to be political emergencies. For these
have certainly occurred, and on a scale which, had this been
Africa, would – I venture to suggest – long ago have wrecked the
institution of parliamentary government in India, for all that can
be said about the attachment of so many there to it.

The expedients which have been employed in India to deal with such circumstances would seem to be all but unique; and it is upon these that we may now dwell.

They are more easily understood as they operate at the State level of politics. Here the method employed is known as 'President's Rule'. The general form of its application is written into the Indian Constitution, and stems, as so much of that Constitution does, from the British Government of India Act of 1935. Section 93 of that Act was designed to deal with a situation in which the British Government had come to believe that a locally elected provincial government was not fulfilling its functions in accord with the declared law of the land. In such circumstances it allowed for a Governor appointed by the British to take over charge of the government of his Province, notwithstanding that a transfer of power to an elected government had previously taken place. Section 93 of the 1935 Act was in fact used in several of the Provinces of British India during much of the Second World War, mainly because the Congress Governments previously elected to power in them had resigned in protest against Britain's wartime policy towards India.

After a good deal of anxious debate in the Indian Constituent Assembly after Independence, much of the essence of Section 93 of the British Government of India Act of 1935 was translated into Sections 356 and 357 of the Indian Independence Constitution. Section 356 of this Constitution has since then provided that:

> If the President, on receipt of a report from the Governor . . . of a State or otherwise, is satisfied that a situation has arisen in which the Government of the State cannot be carried on in accordance with the provisions of this Constitution, the President may by proclamation . . . assume to himself all or any of the functions of the Governor of the State . . .

Because these powers are formally assumed upon such occasions by the President himself, their operation is now generally known as President's Rule. The President does, as it happens, come into the business personally, since he is required to be the recipient of the formal report which needs to be submitted before President's Rule can be brought into operation; and he then has to sign the necessary proclamation. But in practice the President acts, of course, upon the advice of the Government of India, and it is thus the central government of India which assumes authority over the government of a State when President's Rule is instituted there. Under President's Rule the governance of a State is, however, to a greater or lesser extent, actually conducted by the Governor of the State, who ceases *pro tem* to be the 'constitutional monarch' he is otherwise expected to be. To say here 'to a greater or lesser extent' is deliberate; because, according to whether or not a particular Governor has himself had significant administrative experience, there has been an increasing tendency to provide him with experienced Administrative Advisers who, in one way or another, perform the tasks previously undertaken by State Ministers. Such Advisers have usually been drawn from the senior ranks of the Indian Administrative Service. Their capacity and their readiness to take charge on such occasions, as has been earlier indicated, is not in doubt, so that under President's rule orderly government has been readily maintained, where indeed it has not actually been restored.

While, almost by definition, the proclamation of President's Rule entails the dismissal of the State executive, it does not necessarily involve the immediate dismissal of the State legislature – even though this often occurs. However, under the provisions for President's Rule the functions of the State legislature nevertheless fall to be exercised by the national Parliament. This provision has had a somewhat chequered history; but increasingly such functions have come to be delegated by the national Parliament to a consultative committee presided over by the central Minister for Home Affairs. That committee has generally been composed of national parliamentary members from the State in question, broadly in proportion to their party representation in the national parliament. The detailed operation of President's Rule has thus become extensively elaborated.

All manner of arguments have, of course, surrounded every imposition of President's Rule. But its operation has long since become a quite familiar feature of the Indian political system. In the ten years after 1967 there was never, for example, a moment when one or other Indian State was not under President's Rule. Up to 1977, when an authoritative count was done, all but five of the Indian States had been subjected to President's Rule on at least one occasion since the Constitution was first promulgated in 1952. Between 1952 and 1977 President's Rule was imposed around forty times. On five occasions it persisted for up to six months; on ten occasions for between six months and a year; on eight occasions for over a year.

The intriguing point then is that upon every occasion, once political heels had cooled – and the time necessary for this varied of course a good deal – new elections to the State legislature were invariably called; a new government was formed; President's Rule was brought to an end; and parliamentary-style government was then restored.

It cannot be said that the emergencies which led to the proclamation of President's Rule were all deep-seated. There have been occasions when it was simply introduced to meet the convenience of the government in New Delhi, either because its own party in the State was in some kind of disarray, or because the government in New Delhi was anxious to bring down the government of an opposing party whose control of a State it wished to end. Three kinds of crisis can be more generally discerned from the multiplicity which have led to President's Rule. It has been proclaimed when a State Government has been defeated, in a situation where there seemed to be no early prospect of a successor government being installed. It has been proclaimed where there has been such extensive floor-crossing in the State legislature that stable government has become an unlikely prospect. It has been proclaimed when grave allegations of corruption have been advanced.

When one looks through any list of the occasions and the causes of President's Rule, one soon has good reason to believe that, but for its existence, parliamentary government in many Indian States would long since have broken down irredeemably. One has the impression too – if the earlier point may be underlined – that had the President of the Organisation of African Unity had anything like the powers possessed by the President of India, the breakdown in Africa of parliamentary government would not have been anywhere near so widespread.

One also has the impression that the existence and the use of President's Rule has been as vital – perhaps even more vital – to the maintenance of electoral politics in India as the relatively strong tradition in India of electoral politics itself.

There is at first sight no similar system for dealing with comparable political emergencies at the national level. The main point to be made here, therefore, is that in the light of the events of 1975–7, one may now suggest that there exists a great deal more of a system for dealing with what the powers-that-be see to be a great crisis at the national level than the Constitution or common understanding have hitherto suggested.

To explain this proposition it is necessary to retrace one's steps once again back to the British period, and consider first the history in modern India of the expedient of 'Preventive Detention', since the present provisions for this stretch back in a fairly direct line to the famous Regulation III of 1818 of the British administration in Bengal. This was used by the British throughout the nineteenth century to lock up those they wanted out of the way, but against whom they could not readily bring criminal charges.

Then, as nationalist forces gathered momentum in the two opening decades of the 20th century, and some few terrorist groups came to be formed, the British Government of India began to feel that Regulation III was an altogether too ineffectual weapon for their needs. They required, they believed, some much more substantial methods for dealing with what they soon came to term 'Revolutionary Crime'; and in due course they decided to establish Special Tribunals before whom existing rules of evidence, advocacy and appeal were not to obtain. These arrangements were then embodied in the so-called Rowlatt Bills of 1919 – named after the British judge who presided over their formulation; and it was against the British Government of India's promulgation of these that Gandhi led his first great nationalist campaign, the so-called Rowlatt Satyagraha of 1919. That, combined with various other upheavals in the Punjab, pre-cipitated the great Punjab disturbances of April that year. Confronted by these, both the British Government of India and the British Government of the Punjab made the critical decision to call in the Army, and in a spine-chilling communiqué issued in April 1919, the British Government of India emphatically expressed the view that:

> It remains for the Governor-General in Council to assert in the clearest manner the intention of Government to . . . employ the ample military resources at his disposal to suppress organized outrages, rioting, or concerted opposition to the maintenance of law and order.

Martial Law was thereupon declared in the Punjab, and in full accord with the Government's declared doctrines as here set out, there immediately followed the notorious massacre at the hands of General Dyer of a large political meeting in the Jallianwallah Bagh at Amritsar in the Punjab.

The shock of that outrage put the British regime back on the defensive; and they reconsidered furiously. Against the next Gandhi-led agitational wave, the so-called Non-Cooperation movement of 1921–2, they were not only very careful not to use the Army; they deliberately refrained for as long as they possibly could from taking action against the leaders of the movement, until the leaders themselves, with Gandhi at their head, became so concerned at the way the movement was slipping into violence, that they themselves brought it to an end.

For the purpose of the present argument the crucial developments came ten years later. In opposing the next great Gandhi-led agitation, the British began once again by taking the line of least resistance that had served them so well in 1921–2. But this time, such was the strength of the agitation against them, that they very soon began to feel that their authority in India was in real danger of being seriously undermined. With memories of the massacre in the Jallianwallah Bagh in 1919 still hanging over them, they were very reluctant, however, to call in the Army. What they needed was a quite new approach; and this they proceeded to create.

The new policy which the British fashioned, and which it is here suggested Mrs Gandhi followed, almost to the letter, in 1975, was first unveiled on 4 January 1932 – when the British put into widespread operation against the Indian National Congress what one British offical engagingly called '*civil* martial law'. Its essentials can be readingly specified. There were to be no deliberate political killings; no dramatic political trials; no suspension of the Constitution; no dismissal of the legislatures; no employment of the Army. Rather, there was an immediate declaration of a state of emergency and the assumption of substantial emergency powers by the Government, which was promptly accompanied by widespread, unannounced, arrests by police of a carefully pre-pared list of political opponents, who were then imprisoned without trial for quite indeterminate periods. It is significant that some care was taken to see that the conditions of imprisonment for some of the leading figures were a good deal better than for ordinary prisoners. Care was taken, that is, to reduce the danger of creating political martyrs.

In the upshot, however, all of this was only the half of it, and in due course the other half unfolded. For as the air cleared a series of unannounced releases of lesser figures then occurred spasmodically over a period of several months. In due course even the leading figures themselves were released from detention. And then new legislative elections were called, so that the country's politics could be put back once again on what the Government believed to be its proper rails. This system, it will be noted, while different from President's Rule, has several important similarities with it.

During the 1930s, 'civil martial law', as it may be termed, served Britain's immediate political purposes in India remarkably well. Not only was Gandhi's great civil disobedience campaign effectively halted; but first in 1934 and then more particularly in 1937, Congress, instead of boycotting, set about contesting the legislative elections which the British then called.

At the same time details of the new system were being committed to printed handbooks in case they should be needed again. The new policy was in fact employed by the British ten years or so later, first in 1940 and then in 1942, against Gandhi's last two great agitational campaigns; and with similar results – though given the widespread rural revolt in north-eastern India in 1942 it had to be supplemented on the latter occasion, as has been mentioned earlier, by massive army intervention.

During the first twenty-five years or so after Independence, because of the persistent one-party dominance of the Nehru-Gandhi Congress, no similar crisis seemed to threaten India's polity at its apex. The expedient of 'civil martial law' was, however, employed against the Indian Communists in the 1960s, and then, in a notable instance in 1974, against a national strike of railway workers.

This is not the place to rehearse the details of the onset of the grave emergency which Mrs Gandhi believed she saw overtaking her in 1975, nor the ensuing Emergency itself. There is already a large literature upon it, beginning with the proceedings of the Shah Commission and typified in such understandably polemical books as David Selbourne's *An Eye to India. The Unmasking of a Tyranny* or Michael Henderson's *Experiment with Untruth*. The point to be made here is that when – like the British rulers of India early in the 1930s and again in the 1940s before her – Mrs Gandhi believed she saw in June 1975 a threat to the very stability of the supreme political authority which she exercised over India, she set to work to act precisely as they had done. She did not turn to the Army; nor did she dismiss Parliament. Rather, she sent the police to arrest her political opponents, and put them into preventive detention for indeterminate periods. None of them was shot. None of them – with the rather particular exception of Mr George Fernandez – was put on trial. And just as in 1942 the British incarcerated Gandhi in the Aga Khan's not uncomfortable home in Poona, so in 1975 Morarji Desai and some of the other opposition leaders were sent to the really rather pleasant Haryana State Tourist Centre just above the hot springs at Sohna southwards of Delhi. Though the press was seriously curbed, rioters were suppressed, an emergency was declared, and in a good many prisons quite appalling brutalities were inflicted, there was neither martial law nor military intervention.

This suggests that, like it or not (and most of it no one does), the Indian body politic seems to have at its disposal a well-tried method for dealing with perceived crises at the political centre which is scarcely less potent and patent than is provided by President's Rule for the States. This system has been openly used during this century upon four successive occasions: in 1932, 1940, 1942, and 1975. It has its own distinctive characteristics. It turns upon action, not by the Army, nor by firing squads, nor by special tribunals, but by the Police and then the prison services.

There is confirmation for the view that what was witnessed in 1975–7 is on the way to becoming an established method by which crises at the political centre in India may be handled in the future in the similarities between the developments that occurred subsequent to the onset of the Emergency. For precisely in four stages, as the British had before her, Mrs Gandhi began to set free her lesser opponents from prison. In due course she authorised the release of their leaders too. About the same time she decided that the only way by which the national political system could be placed back on its rails was to hold an election. And she then wholly miscalculated – as the British had done before her – the strength of the hostile reaction her Emergency had evoked. As a consequence, just as in the aftermath of the first imposition of 'civil martial law' in 1932–4, supporters of the British lost heavily in the ensuing 1934 and 1937 elections, so in the 1977 elections supporters of Mrs Gandhi lost heavily as well.

It was not merely therefore that the emergency measures she employed were those fashioned by the British; her way out of them followed very precisely the pattern which they had set as well.

Perhaps some of the threads here can now be brought together. What all this is suggesting is that the 1975–7 Emergency in India, placed in a longer and wider context, served to indicate that the Government of India – whoever may be in control of it – now has at its disposal an established means of managing a perceived crisis at the political centre, which is now as notable a feature of the way in which the Indian body politic actually operates as President's Rule itself. Let it be reiterated that this does not call for intervention by the army; nor for political killings; nor for political trials. It calls in the first place for a now well-tested police operation against carefully listed political opponents.

But, as with President's Rule, there seems to be as well a propensity within the operation of 'civil martial law' towards bringing it to a conclusion by then holding elections. This is no doubt a tribute to the widespread commitment to the electoral process which exists in India: it may indeed be said that this would now seem to be strong enough to make new elections appear in India to be the best way out of the impasse into which authoritarian rule almost inevitably finds itself drawn. All of which then implies that while over the longer run the existence of emergency procedures actually assists in maintaining the commitment to elections in India, so the relatively very strong sense there that only those willing to submit themselves to an election within a reasonable time span have a legitimate right to hold governmental office, serves to check the prolongation of such an emergency once this has been declared. In quasi-technical language there is a two-way functional association, that is, in India between emergencies and elections.

There remains the irony of the evidence that the longer such elections are delayed, and the more stringent the conduct of the Emergency, the greater the chance that the electorate will vote against the supporters of those who declared the Emergency. This could lead to one of two conclusions. Either the next employers of 'civil martial law' will call an election sooner than Mrs Gandhi did in 1977, so as to avoid her defeat upon that occasion; or, fearing a like defeat, they will brazen out their position for very much longer as at one stage some observers thought that she would do. Should any future declarers of an emergency really take the latter course, the Indian body politic will have abandoned its moorings (as it has not, it is here suggested, done so far) and would then enter some quite new seas. The 1980 election may have made this even less likely than before. For it may be suggested that it showed that in India a leader who loses badly in one election, and is severely hounded for his pains in the aftermath, can in fact be back in an even stronger position just three years later. Here one has only to contrast the return of Mrs Gandhi to power with the execution of Mr Bhutto to obtain some appreciation of the distinctive characteristics which the Indian body politic seems to display.

It would of course be foolhardy to suggest that the system of 'civil martial law' could never be discarded. But the essential point remains, and it brings us back to the issue with which this chapter opened. A major reason why the Army has not up to this point moved in to take control of India's political system – as its counterparts have in so many other countries in Asia and elsewhere – is, it may be suggested, because, very unusually, India has evolved systems both at state and national levels for handling what the powers-that-be see to be crises in the working of parliamentary government. These systems have many harsh, brutal, and worse features. But, as they have operated so far, they have always ended with a new start in the holding of new elections.

Parliamentary government has persisted in India, that is, not merely because it has been an important part of the country's political life for quite a while now, but because at its apex India has developed methods for the management of political emergencies that have the special features that they allow for the reintroduction of parliamentary government once the immediate emergency has apparently receded. Emergency President's Rule is now all but routine for the States. Emergency Prime Ministerial rule, or 'civil martial law', or whatever one may term it, seems to be a no less readily available expedient at the centre as well.

SELECT BIBLIOGRAPHY

Austin, Granville, *The Indian Constitution: Cornerstone of a Nation* (Oxford, 1966).
Cohen, Stephen P., *The Indian Army* (California, 1971).
Griffiths, Percival, *To Guard My People: the History of the Indian Police* (London, 1971).

Hart, Harry C., ed., *Indira Gandhi's India: a Political System Reappraised* (Boulder, 1976).

Henderson, Michael, *Experiment with Untruth* (Delhi, 1977).

Low, D. A., 'The Government of India and the First Non-Cooperation Movement 1920–1922', *Journal of Asian Studies*, xxv, 2 February 1966 pp. 241–59.

Low, D. A., ed., *Congress and the Raj: Facets of the Indian Struggle 1917–1947* (Delhi, 1977).

Maheswari, S. R., *President's Rule in India* (Delhi, 1977).

Mason, Philip, *A Matter of Honour* (London, 1974).

Selbourne, David, *An Eye to India: the Unmasking of a Tyranny* (Harmondsworth, 1977).

Woodruff, Philip, *The Men Who Ruled India*, 2 vols (London 1974).

The Works of A. P. Thornton

GEORGE URBANIAK

1950

'A Donsman Counters'. *Isis* (February 1950).

1952

'Agents of Empire: the Buccaneers', *The Aberdeen University Review*, 34 (1952).
'The Argument about South Africa', *Corona* 4 (1952) 427–9.
'The Modyfords and Morgan: Letters from Sir James Modyford on the Affairs of Jamaica, 1667–1672, in the Muniments of Westminster Abbey', *Jamaica Historical Review*, 2 (1952) 36–60.

1953

'The Argument about Africa', *Fortnightly Review*, 1033 (1953) 134–5.
'Colonial Policy and Colonial Politics', *Fortnightly Review*, 1034 (1953) 376–81.
'Afghanistan in Anglo-Russian Diplomacy, 1869–73', *Cambridge Historical Journal*, 11 (1953) 204–18. See also *For the File on Empire*, 151–69.
'Merchants in Company', *Fortnightly Review*, 1034 (1953) 22–6.

1954

'G. A. Henty's British Empire', *Fortnightly Review*, 175 (1954) 97–101. Also in *For the File*, 16–22.
'Some Statistics on West Indian Produce, Shipping and Revenue, 1660–1685', *Caribbean Historical Review*, 3–4 (1954) 251–80.
'British Policy in Persia, 1858–90', *English Historical Review*, 69 (1954) 554–79; and 70 (1955) 55–71. Also in *For the File*, 171–218.
'An Imperial Twilight', *The Historical Journal*, 11 (1954). Also in *For the File*, 125–29.

1955

'Experts and Islanders', *Corona* (October 1955).

'Gladstone', *Aberdeen University Review*, 26 (1955) 185–9.

'Realms of the Commonwealth, 1955', *Encyclopedia Britannica Yearbook* (1955).

'The Organization of the Slave Trade in the West Indies, 1660–85', *William and Mary Quarterly* 12 (1955) 399–455.

'Wide Open Spaces', *Ideas*, ed. Geoffrey Grigson (London: Grosvenor Press, 1955). Also in *For the File*, 344–8.

'My Country, Right or Wrong', *Ideas*, ed. Geoffrey Grigson (London: Grosvenor Press, 1955). Also in *For the File*, 283–6. 'The Century of the Common Man'.

'Spanish Slave-Ships in the English West Indies', *The Hispanic American Historical Review*, 35 (1935) 374–85. Also in *For the File*, 100–12.

1956

'Charles II's American Policy', *History Today*, 6 (1956). Also in *For the File*, 65–77.

'The American Saga', *History Today*, 4 (1956) 497–9.

'The Commonwealth: the Major Nations, 1956', *Encyclopedia Britannica Yearbook (1956)*.

West-India Policy under the Restoration (Oxford: Clarendon Press, 1956).

'The G.R.G. Conway MS. collection in the Library of the University of Aberdeen', *Hispanic American Historical Review*, 36 (1956) 345–7.

'The Reopening of the 'Central Asian Question" '. *History*, 41 (1956) 122–36. Also in *For the File*, 134–49.

1957

'The Partition of Africa', *History Today*, 7 (1957) 345–7.

'The British in Manila, 1762–64', *History Today*, 7 (1957) 44–53.

1959

The Imperial Idea and Its Enemies (London: Macmillan, 1959, 1963, 1980; New York: St. Martin's Press, 1966; Doubleday, 1968; 2nd edn, with new Introduction, Macmillan and St Martin's Press in the press).

'The Rights of Men.' (Kingston, Jamaica: University College of the West Indies, 1959). Also in *For the File*, 381–94.

'The Idea of a University' (Kingston, Jamaica: University College of the West Indies, 1959). Also in *For the File*, 395–409.

1960

'John Strachey, *The End of Empire*', *The Nation*, 190 (1960). Also in *For the File*, 300–4.

1961

'Colonialism', *International Journal*, 7 (1961–2) 335–57.
'Bernard Semmel, *Imperialism and Social Reform*'. *Victorian Studies*, 4 (1961). Also in *For the File*, 31–4.

1962

'Bomber Command in the Dark', *Canadian Forum*, 42 (1962) 16–63. 'West Indian Attitudes', *International Journal*, 15 (1962). Also in *For the File*, 317–27.
'Ronald Robinson and John Gallagher, *Africa and the Victorians*, *International Journal*, 17 (1962). Also in *For the File*, 152–7.
'Rivalries in the Mediterranean, the Middle East and Egypt', in *The New Cambridge Modern History*, vol. XI, *Material Progress and World-Wide Problems, 1870–98*. (Cambridge University Press, 1962) pp. 567–92. Also in *For the File*, 220–51.

1963

'Decolonization', *International Journal*, 19 (1963–4) 7–29. Also in *For the File*, 349–74.
'Imperialists at Noon', *International Journal*, 18 (1963). Also in *For the File*, 9–15.
'*Imperialism* by Richard Koebner', *English Historical Review*, 78 (1963) 546–52. Also in *For the File*, 287–99.

1964

'Mid-Day with the Imperialists', *International Journal*, 18 (1964–5) 536–53.
'James Eayrs: *The Commonwealth and Suez*'. *Commentator*, 8 (1964). Also in *For the File*, 258–62.
'Jekyll and Hyde in the Colonies', *International Journal* 20 (1964–5) 221–9. Also in *For the File*, 328–43.
'J. S. Galbraith, *Reluctant Empire*', *Journal of Modern History*, 36 (1964) 344–5. Also in *For the File*, 130–2.
'V. B. Kulkarni, *British Statesmen in India*', *International Affairs*, 19 (1964). Also in *For the File*, 305–7.

'Stewart C. Easton, *The Rise and Fall of Western Colonialism*', *International Journal*, 19 (1964). Also in *For the File*, 308–10.

1965

'Interview with A. P. Thornton', *Colloquium*, no. 3 (New York: John Wiley, April 1965) 26–31.
'The World of Prester John', *International Journal*, 21 (1965–6).
Doctrines of Imperialism, (New York: John Wiley, 1965).
'*Lord Salisbury and Foreign Policy: the Close of the Nineteenth Century*, J. A. S. Grenville' *Canadian Historical Review*, 46 (1965) 262. Also in *For the File*, 23–7.
'A. M. Gollin, *Proconsul in Politics*', *Journal of Modern History*, 37 (1965) 394–5. Also in *For the File*, 28–30.

1966

The Habit of Authority: Paternalism in British History (London: Allen & Unwin, 1966).
'*Empire*, by Richard Koebner and Dan Schmidt', *English Historical Review*, 81 (1966) 127–32.
'*Lion Rampant* by D. A. Low; *England's Mission* by C. C. Eldridge; *British Economic Policy* by I. Drummond'. *American Historical Review*, 71 (1966) 140–1.
'Smuts: a Journey with Maps', *International Journal*, 22 (1966–7). Also in *For the File*, 35–50.
'*The Founding of New Societies* by Louis Hartz et al.', *Canadian Historical Review*, 47 (1966) 59. Also in *For the File*, 311–16.

1968

'Small-Island Men', *International Journal*, 24 (1968–9) 590–600.
For the File on Empire: Essays and Reviews (London: Macmillan, 1968).

1969

'Ulysses in Ithaca', *International Journal*, 24 (1969) 816–21.

1970

'A Context for the Civilized', *The Round Table*, 237 (January 1970) 103–12.

'Overseas Empires: the Century of European World Power', in *The Nineteenth Century: the Contradictions of Progress*, ed. Asa Briggs (London: Thames and Hudson, 1970) 229–39.
'Your World, and Welcome to It', in *Visions 2020*, ed. Stephen Clarkson (Edmonton: Mel Hurtig, 1970) 66–72.

1971

'The Kings of the Sunset', *International Journal*, 26 (1971) 303–24.
'V. G. Kiernan, *The Lords of Human Kind*', *The Historical Journal*, 26 (1971) 303–24.
'Imperialism', in *Perspectives on the European Past: Conversations with Historians*, ed. Norman Cantor (London: Collier-Macmillan, 1971) vol.II, 143–63.

1972

'D. Dilks, *Curzon in India*', *Journal of Modern History*, 44 (1972) 285–6. 'K. O. Morgan, *Keir Hardie*', *Canadian Forum*, 54 (1972) 32–3. 'Garnet Joseph Wolseley', *Encyclopaedia Britannica*, 23:620–1.

1973

'Another Day's Work', *New Statesman*, 86 (1973) 18–20.
'Imperialism in the Twentieth Century', *Journal of Imperial and Commonwealth History*, 2 (1973) 38–55.
'The Sound of Running History', *International Journal*, 28 (1973) 591–611.

1974

'A Reserved Occupation', *International Journal*, 30 (1974–5) 1–14.

1975

'With Wavell on to Simla and Beyond', *International Journal*, 31 (1975–6).

1977

Imperialism in the Twentieth Century, (University of Minnesota Press, 1977, 1980; London: Macmillan, 1978, 1980).

1978

'The Memory Bank', *Gargoyle*, University College, Toronto.
'The Trouble with Cousins', *International Journal*, 34 (1978–9) 181–8.

1979

'W. Roger, Jones, *Imperialism at Bay*', *American Historical Review*, 84 (1979) 712.
'With Wavell on to Simla and Beyond', in 'Essays in Honour of Nicholas Mansergh', *Journal of Imperial and Commonwealth History*, 8 (1979) 175–85.
'Edward Ingram, The Beginning of the Great Game in Asia 1828–1834', *International History Review*, 1 (1979) 582–5.

1980

Me-Time, or, The Department: An Operetta in Three Acts, Copyright, Ottawa, 1980.

1982

'Riding off in all Directions', *International History Review*, 4 (1982) 160–5.

1983

'Britain and Zion', *Queen's Quarterly*, 90 (1983) 590–3.

1984

'Scotland, 1789–1832: Problems of a Political Satellite', *Queen's Quarterly*, 91 (1984) 100–13. 'The Change in the Wind', *International Journal*, 39 (1984) 456–65.

Index